# WITTGENSTEIN
# STUDIES

THOEMMES

Printed and bound by
Antony Rowe Ltd., Chippenham, Wiltshire

WITTGENSTEIN STUDIES

# Ludwig Wittgenstein
## *Philosophy and Language*

**EDITED BY**
**ALICE AMBROSE &**
**MORRIS LAZEROWITZ**

THOEMMES PRESS

This edition published by Thoemmes Press, 1996

**Thoemmes Press**
11 Great George Street
Bristol BS1 5RR, England

*US office: Distribution and Marketing*
22883 Quicksilver Drive
Dulles, Virginia 20166, USA

*Wittgenstein Studies*
6 volume hardback set : ISBN 1 85506 494 4

Paperback : ISBN 1 85506 488 X

Publisher's Note

The publisher has gone to great lengths to ensure the
quality of this reprint but points out that some
imperfections in the original book may be apparent.

# PREFACE

Technical, academic philosophy is a discipline with a long and distinguished history. Many great minds have enriched it with original ideas which they have supported with subtle and complex arguments, but no philosopher has brought to it an understanding of the nature of the subject. F. H. Bradley has said that 'when twilight has no charm – then metaphysics will be worthless'; and it can no longer be doubted that philosophers practise their art in a dusk into which understanding is not permitted to enter. Ludwig Wittgenstein may be truly described as the Prometheus of philosophy : he has brought a special light to the subject that makes visible the semantic mechanisms by which it produces its remarkable effects. And he has given us a lens for bringing into clear view the peculiar way in which a philosophical theory and its verbal expression are bound up with each other.

The studies in the present volume are on a variety of topics Wittgenstein was concerned with, particularly in his later work : such topics as the philosophy of mathematics, abstract entities, logical necessity, the privacy of experience, private language, psychoanalysis, ethics. All of the papers are serious attempts to elucidate Wittgenstein's thought, and the editors wish to express their appreciation to the contributors.

Wittgenstein was not only a vastly important philosopher; he was also an arresting and compelling personality who, though he never sought, and even avoided, the limelight, has come into its full glare. Alice Ambrose's portrait gives us a picture of the person behind the legends that have grown up around him.

MORRIS LAZEROWITZ

*Northampton, Massachusetts*
*March 1971.*

# CONTENTS

|  |  | page |
|---|---|---|
|  | Preface | 9 |
| 1 | Ludwig Wittgenstein: A Portrait<br>ALICE AMBROSE | 13 |
| 2 | Wittgenstein on 'Private Language'<br>JOHN WISDOM | 26 |
| 3 | Solipsism and Language<br>JOHN W. COOK | 37 |
| 4 | Wittgenstein on Psychoanalysis<br>CHARLES HANLY | 73 |
| 5 | Wittgenstein and Ethics<br>THEODORE REDPATH | 95 |
| 6 | About the Same<br>GEORGE PITCHER | 120 |
| 7 | Philosophy as Grammar and the Reality of Universals<br>W. E. KENNICK | 140 |
| 8 | Saying and Meaning<br>FRANK EBERSOLE | 186 |
| 9 | The Notion of Erklärung<br>TAKASHI FUJIMOTO | 222 |
| 10 | Necessity and Language<br>MORRIS LAZEROWITZ | 233 |
| 11 | Wittgenstein's Philosophy of Mathematics<br>R. L. GOODSTEIN | 271 |
| 12 | Mathematical Generality<br>ALICE AMBROSE | 287 |
|  | Appendix: Bibliography | 319 |
|  | Index | 323 |

# LUDWIG WITTGENSTEIN: A PORTRAIT

## ALICE AMBROSE

When a person who is intensely alive also has great originality of mind the impact on those who work with him is a blend in which intellectual substance and spell of personality are difficult to disentagle. It has been said that students of Wittgenstein are unable to distinguish between what they gained from him philosophically and what the impress of his compelling personality made them feel they had gained. At the distance of thirty-five years it is easier to separate the two components which reinforced each other in Wittgenstein's lectures, dictations, and discussions. The written word is a screen between the ideas and the personal presence, so that although the form of expression in which his ideas were clothed is entirely familiar to me, since I was among those to whom the *Blue and Brown Books* were dictated, I think I can now keep the memories it gives rise to at a distance, as I perhaps could not the impact of the person himself. With this detachment from the past, one is in a better position to recognize that his ideas on the fundamental question as to the nature of philosophy were important insights. Perhaps none of us during the period 1932–5, when I was a student at Cambridge, realized how revolutionary some of his thoughts were, especially those given expression in the *Blue Book*. My journal for that period records that during the first term I felt that I was hearing a lecture in which there were gaps, such as intermittent deafness might produce. Yet only Moore could match Wittgenstein's simplicity of expression and freedom from technical terminology, so that a failure of understanding could not be laid to anything abstruse in his presentation. Moore, who as a special guest was provided with a deck chair for the year of lectures he attended in 1932–3, evidently felt that Wittgenstein had something out of the

13

ordinary to say; and Wittgenstein used Moore as a touchstone to test his own clarity of thought and exposition. Wittgenstein told me that he thought that he had a method of going about doing philosophy which Moore lacked; but he respected Moore greatly and had discussions with him at 86 Chesterton Road once a week during term, on a day Moore specially set aside for him.

In this introduction to the studies on Wittgenstein's later thought I should like to record the radical break with his intellectual past to which I was a naïve witness, and to indicate from memory pieced together with and borne out by the works published since his death the departure he made not only from most of the *Tractatus* but, more important, from the centuries-long conception of philosophical investigation. Since his death a number of studies have been made of the *Tractatus*. When I first came to Cambridge as a research student, with Wittgenstein as supervisor (soon to be replaced by Moore, who was better able to cope with a student of my preparation and needs), I went to my first meeting with him in his rooms in Whewell's Court with the *Tractatus* in hand, expecting that we might work on some of its doctrines, in particular on some ideas about the nature of logical necessity. Although this concept was central in his later thinking, he had no interest in pursuing what he had done there, and refused to use it even as a starting point. It is possible that he felt about his truth-table representation of a tautology the thing which found expression in the *Investigations*: '[Philosophy] . . . leaves mathematics as it is. . . . A "leading problem of mathematical logic" is for us a problem of mathematics like any other.'[1] It is also possible that he did not wish to be pulled back into philosophical doctrines he had developed in the *Tractatus* – into philosophy in a traditional sense. These he reconsidered, according to G. H. von Wright, perhaps no earlier than 1935, the resultant criticisms appearing in the course of the first 136 paragraphs of the *Investigations*.

Cambridge in the years 1932–5 was indeed on the philosophical heights. By the end of my first term I, as well as other Moral

[1] p. 49.

Science students who attended both Moore's and Wittgenstein's lectures regularly, found it cause for regret that the eight-week term cut short the lectures. Moore, in the lectures listed in the *Reporter* as 'Metaphysics', had been discussing analysis and definition. Wittgenstein had two sets of lectures, one entitled 'Philosophy for Mathematicians', in which he discussed critically various of Russell's views, e.g. of logic as the foundation of mathematics, of number as definable by reference to the notion of $1 - 1$ correlation, of identity between $x$ and $y$ as meaning the possession by $x$ and $y$ of all their properties in common. During this term I was attending both sets of lectures, as well as Moore's and going to Moore once a week to discuss certain tenets of the finitist position on mathematics. I had thought to attend lectures by Prof. Littlewood, I believe on theory of functions, and went to one lecture after which we agreed that the topic was not particularly relevant to my concerns. But an entry in my journal reports my being charmed by the way he took the class into his confidence. Not so Wittgenstein, who was formidable in his impatience if he found a student question not to his liking. In consequence few questions were raised, though he tried desperately to grasp their point, sometimes by the disconcerting procedure of threading his way through the chairs brought into his rooms from Trinity Chapel, to confront his questioner at close quarters. Moore's patience with students was extraordinary, though, to me at least, his mastery and tremendous clarity set up a discouraging ideal.

Wittgenstein worked very hard in lectures, sometimes with perspiration streaming down his face, despite the fact that his small stove, in which for one term he burnt quite ineffective coke, gave off an imperceptible heat. There is no saying whether this was because of the difficulty of articulating ideas which he still had not thought his way through, but this is possible. As compared with the language of the *Tractatus* in which he used words in an unusual sense, e.g. 'objects', or 'pictures', or introduced new expressions such as 'elementary proposition' and 'atomic fact', the language of his lectures presented no puzzle. He used the language of everyday speech. And there was no hint of mysticism, no reference to the unsayable. What was puzzling was his use of picturesque examples, which in themselves were easily comprehensible, but of which the *point* they were intended to make escaped one. It was like hearing a parable without being able to draw the moral. In the intervals between dictation of the *Blue Book* in the year 1933–4 (to a group of five,[2] which was later augmented to seven) he sometimes gave 'hints' or 'pointers' in the course of the informal discussion he then engaged in, and of which Mrs Braithwaite (Margaret Masterman) and I took down as full notes as possible.[3] To the question of what he meant by giving hints his answer as recorded in these notes was: 'Such a remark as "This is one of the most typical problems of philosophy" would be a hint. This remark may set you on the right track in solving a problem. But I could leave out all the hints and just treat special problems. It is only a psychological fact that people only understand what I am driving at when they begin to understand my general remarks, my hints, and cannot imagine what I am talking about when they hear me dealing with some special difficulty. . . . All you need do is to observe what we do, which will be the same sort of thing each time. . . . Suppose someone said "My craving is to get a general comprehensive picture of the universe. Can you satisfy this craving?" I would say "No". . . . Let us see whether doing such and such, or thinking such and such a way will, not satisfy the craving, but make you cease to have it.' This general hint about his treatment of a specific philosophical problem is, looking back, an indication of his preoccupation with, and developing conception of, the nature of philosophical problems.

In the growing literature on Wittgenstein's work some writers have taken the stand that it is a more or less continuous development of a central problem of the *Tractatus*: what the limits of language are, or as it has sometimes been put, the limits of the sayable. Wittgenstein's concerns, earlier and later, are conceived as being the same. In effect it is denied that there is a later Witt-

[2] H. M. S. Coxeter, R. L. Goodstein, Margaret Masterman, Francis Skinner, and myself.
[3] This compilation we called *The Yellow Book*.

genstein. Other writers find in the *Blue Book* a discontinuity between the *Tractatus* and the *Investigations*. It appears to me that both of these interpretations ignore the iconoclastic ideas which came out in lectures, dictation, and discussions during the Olympian years 1932–5. The one interpretation gives them no recognition at all, the other recognizes them in a way that mutes them. On the second interpretation the *Blue Book* is a stranger which does not belong in Wittgenstein's thought, on the first it does not exist. The effect is to push out of sight the work he did in those three years. Regardless of the nature of his concerns in the years following, and regardless of the amount of more conventional treatment of philosophical problems during those years, a quite new conception of philosophical statements was being formulated, and was illustrated in the treatment of certain problems. Although it often expressed itself in 'hints' and 'pointers' in which it did not find explicit formulation and development, it is there nonetheless. The fact that it was not everywhere predominant in his work from 1932 onwards does not mean it was not of first importance to him in the three years when the *Blue and Brown Books* were done. My own impression, which has remained with me, is that it was central to his thinking.

Wittgenstein's presence, which was always attended by an atmosphere that was in some way charged, together with his intense concentration on the immediate problem, was somewhat of a deterrent to diverting him. And although he was in no way pompous, there was something oracular about him. A comment in my journal gives a sense of the group feeling during dictation : 'We sat quietly and waited for dictation to begin.' We hesitated to interrupt him and only rarely did we press him to elaborate on those general remarks which, as indicated above, he himself recognized as giving people some idea of 'what he was driving at'. John Wisdom, who went to the lectures of 1934–5 (and who, like Moore, was provided a deck chair, but with the added comfort of a hot-water bottle), wrote about him : '. . . when people listened to Wittgenstein they often found it difficult to get a steady light giving an ordered view of what they wished to see and . . .

when they now read him they still have this difficulty.'[4] I have wondered whether what made it so difficult was the disturbing idea that philosophical statements are not either true, or false, or nonsense, and the corollary of this, which most philosophers find unacceptable, that conventional philosophy is not the pursuit of truth. This idea was not made entirely clear, but it was implied by things he said, for example, that philosophers draw new linguistic boundaries while supposing themselves to be rejecting a position as false.

During the year 1933–4 when Wittgenstein was dictating the *Blue Book* and also giving lectures to a larger group (people attending both dictation and lectures were with him as much as six hours per week), he was much occupied with various solipsistic theses, such as 'Only my pain is real' and 'I cannot know that he has toothache'. What has appeared in published form on these theses speaks for itself. But what informed his treatment of them, a certain view of their nature which oriented his approach to them, comes out more clearly in his lectures and informal discussions. I shall try to summarize some of the things he said on solipsism and connected topics, to indicate the view which was forming in his mind. I shall draw from lecture and discussion notes of Margaret Masterman and myself, leaving it to the reader who knows Wittgenstein's style of expression to select what was most likely to be his own words.

For some time he was preoccupied with the view expressed by the words 'I alone have real toothache', and for purposes of the point he wished to make he imagined his own nerves being connected with someone else's tooth. To the question, 'Who has pain in the tooth, he or I?', he said he could make either of two replies, one, 'I don't know whether he's got pain, but I know I have', the other, 'All that I feel is pain in this tooth. I can't say who has it'. These two responses to the question draw two different linguistic boundaries, one in which the contrast between the pronouns 'I', 'he', etc. is preserved, as in 'I have toothache, he has toothache, etc.', the other which mentions no proprietor at all but confines itself, in effect, to 'There is toothache

[4] Preface to Morris Lazerowitz, *The Structure of Metaphysics*, p. x.

in one tooth'. The latter permits an owner of the tooth, but not of the pain. It is the notation the solipsist *should* use, one in which it is logically impossible to assert that someone else has toothache and hence logically impossible to say *I* have. The point of the example of having a toothache in someone else's tooth was to show that under certain circumstances one might be tempted to do away with the simple use of 'I'. Such examples make one feel less at home in the normal notation, so that we see that the 'I' notation is not the only notation that can be used. Not that this familiar notation is shown to be wrong, in as much as everything that can be said in the one can also be said in the other. But if certain facts were different – if one often had pains located in other people's teeth – one might simply report 'There is tooth-ache' and give its locality and description. When 'I' is no longer opposed to 'he' and 'they' it vanishes from the language. Or if 'I have pain' were kept as another way of saying 'There is pain', its contrast with 'He has pain' would be a contrast between talk about pain and talk about behaviour. But Wittgenstein insisted that this does not mean that I have real toothache and the other persons does not. I quote from my notes the reply he makes to the solipsist who says this :

If only you can have real toothache, there is no sense in say-ing 'Only I can have real toothache'. Either you don't need 'I' or you don't need 'real'. Your notation makes too many specifications. You had much better say 'There is toothache', and give the locality and the description. This is what you are trying to say. . . . 'Only I have real toothache' either has a commonsense meaning, or, if it is a grammatical [philosophical] proposition, it is meant to be a statement of a rule; it wishes to say 'I should like to put, instead of the notation "I have real toothache", "There is real toothache".' Thus the rule does not allow 'Only I have real toothache' to be said. But the philosopher is apt to say the thing which his own rule has just forbidden him to say. . . . What the solipsist wants is not a notation in which the ego has a monopoly, but one in which the ego vanishes.

Wittgenstein often talked about the philosophical illusion, fostered by ordinary language, that new existents were being discovered or new facts about the nature of phenomena were being brought to light. For example, on noting that the word 'I' does not mean 'my body' we are tempted to suppose we have discovered a new entity, an ego, in addition to the body. If someone were to appear at our door informing us that he had had an overnight change of bodies, we might use as criteria for his being the same person as our acquaintance A that he could report the same details of his life as A could have. But this fact, said Wittgenstein, 'does not show that besides A's body there is something else, another object, which is A. We must refrain from looking for a substance when we see a substantive, but not from thoroughly examining the use of a word'. On this example Wittgenstein then made an important remark : 'But nothing compels me to use these criteria. I might perfectly well say that the man who reported a change of bodies, even if he satisfied my tests, was not A but someone else who had the same memories.' Nor would this justify a claim to having discovered that A and A's body were identical. To do this would be analogous, he said, to the mathematician's saying there is no such entity as a number and then going on to say that numbers are scratches on paper.

There is no doubt that an alternative notation can have the appearance of expressing a new fact. Wittgenstein used the following analogy to combat this appearance in a philosopher's language. Of parallel lines *A*, *B*, *C* cutting two nearly parallel lines one would ordinarily say that whereas *A* and *B* seem to be the same length, and likewise *B* and *C* (though they are not), *C* seems to be no longer than *A*. About this description he made the following remark : 'But I can say "In visual space *A* and *B* are the same length and likewise *B* and *C*, and *C* is longer than *A*". I have not made a discovery. I have only translated from one kind of language to another.' From this, to quote from notes, he went on to make the following point :

In philosophy, when people talk of sense data, they are really only making this kind of translation, but they talk as though they had made some important discovery, and found some new entities. The two languages could be characterized roughly in this way, that one would talk about chairs, etc. [physical objects] and the other about 'perceptual objects'. [Philosophers often call this second language 'phenomenalistic language'.] But these terms are misleading, for they make it appear as though only a further analysis of the known facts could lead us to use such a language, whereas the truth is that there is nothing in the one language which cannot also be said in the other, only it will be said differently. We are talking about the same things in each case.

The idea that in presenting and arguing for a position a philosopher is introducing an academic[5] linguistic innovation, not a discovery, has had a profound influence on some of his followers. One of John Wisdom's papers, 'Philosophical Perplexity', is a particularly clear expression of this influence, as is also G. A. Paul's paper, 'Is There a Problem About Sense Data?'. Both of these appeared in the *Proceedings of the Aristotelian Society* in 1936, a year after Wisdom and Paul attended Wittgenstein's lectures. Several years later, after his return from Cambridge, Norman Malcolm gave further concrete expression to this influence in his paper in *Mind* (1940), 'The Nature of Entailment'. Morris Lazerowitz, to whom I lent the *Blue Book* when I came from Cambridge to the University of Michigan during C. H. Langford's sabbatical leave, went on to elaborate certain of Wittgenstein's ideas into what he later called the three-layer structure of a philosophical theory. This theory he used to explain the mystifying irresolvability of philosophical disagreements. In Wisdom's opinion, bringing out how close philosophical theories are to verbal innovations 'makes vastly plainer the character of these old and mysterious disputes'.

Claim and counterclaim in philosophy have traditionally been put forward as truths. Wittgenstein's break with tradition was expressed quite clearly, not in the form of 'hints' or 'pointers', in Easter term lectures of the year the *Blue Book* was dictated.

[5] Academic because here 'language is like an engine idling'.

What he said, as recorded in my notes, highlights the difference between his way of doing philosophy and Moore's: 'The fallacy we want to avoid is this: when we reject some form of symbolism we're inclined to look at it as though we had rejected a proposition as false. . . . This confusion pervades all of philosophy. It's the same confusion that considers a philosophical problem as though it concerned a fact of the world instead of a matter of expression.' It seems to me that in the writings of most people who have been exposed to this outlook, the intellectual breakthrough which it represents has been muted or ignored or even denied outright. But the fact that many hotels do not list a thirteenth floor does not remove it from existence. It is more than possible that it was the approach he was taking which was responsible for the qualms Wittgenstein expressed in the *Investigations*: 'Where does our investigation get its importance from, since it seems only to destroy everything interesting, that is, all that is great and important?' If he had qualms in the years 1932–5 it was not evident, although the *Brown Book* which was dictated in 1934–5 to me and to Francis Skinner, a research student who had taken his degree in mathematics with a B-star seems less explicitly iconoclastic than the *Blue Book*.

At the beginning of the Michaelmas term lectures of 1934–5 Wittgenstein, with Skinner, came to me to propose a class with the two of us, the plan being to set down thoughts which might be definitive of what he had to say. At one time he remarked that with age there comes a deterioration of subtlety, at which point one should give up doing philosophy. At this time he was 45 years old. He always looked preternaturally young. (My landlady who served us dinner mistook him for an undergraduate.) That year was a period of most intensive work. Dictation of what came to be known as the *Brown Book* occupied four days a week and took a minimum of two hours per day, most usually three or four. On days when he also lectured we were with him as much as seven hours, and each day was exhausting to the three of us. We often had lunch together, in Skinner's rooms, or in Lyons in Petty Cury, or in my flat in the Braithwaites' house, at nearly four in the afternoon. The morning, which began at 9:30, was interrupted only by coffee; on alternate days when the cream was new and heavy we had *Kaffee mit Schlag* in the Viennese manner. I sometimes brought fudge which I had made, and before Christmas and on his birthday I made chocolate pie and there was an exchange of gifts. These were the small pleasures of an intimate circle, and after the day's work we sometimes took a walk, fed the birds in the Fellows' Garden, or, now and then, to 'wash off his mind', went to a western film (which he viewed with complete absorption). The relationship was an easy one; nevertheless it was not a relaxation to be with him. He drove himself mercilessly, and I believe worked after we parted for the day in preparation for the next day. Dictation during the Michaelmas term continued beyond the term's end. In consequence, by the second term of each of the years when he dictated the *Blue Book* and the *Brown Book* he reached exhaustion point and looked unwell.

The progress of the dictation accordingly suffered, proceeding slowly and painfully; and sometimes there was a complete blockage. The hours of dictation were very demanding on Skinner and me as well, our work consisting in interpolating questions or considerations we thought would be useful. Wittgenstein's perfectionism drove him to redictating previous material. At one low point of mental fatigue dictation covering the same ground was done three times. This was a worry to Wittgenstein, not only because his serious purpose was failing of accomplishment, but because of his feeling of responsibility to us. Meanwhile I had my own nagging worry, work on my doctoral dissertation which perforce was shifted to the vacations between terms and was moving ahead too slowly. I had come to Cambridge at the base of the depression, the prospects for a teaching post were still meagre, and I was returning to America at the end of the academic year. Wittgenstein was aware of this, and offered to help me get on with the thesis. Moore had accepted both parts of a paper which constituted part of the dissertation and had already published Part I in *Mind*. This paper drew heavily on what I thought I had learned from Wittgenstein. But on seeing it Wittgenstein considered it not to represent his views properly and not yet in a shape acceptable for publication. He advised withdrawal of Part II. There was disagreement over this, although I did not question that Wittgenstein was in the best position to know whether his views had been properly represented. But I thought at the time that the paper was nevertheless publishable, as did Moore, who advised me to proceed with it. Both Moore and I may have been wrong on this, but at the time I did not think so. In the end, there was a break between Wittgenstein and me, and dictation of the *Brown Book* ceased.

This was a grief to me, as there was never the slightest doubt in my mind that what Wittgenstein had to say was very important. It was therefore a burden to feel responsible for the cessation of a piece of work. For it was evident throughout the year that a dependency existed involving Skinner and me. I saw him once more, for lunch at my flat on the day I left Cambridge in August, and parted with his blessing. But the magic circle was broken.

Accounts of Wittgenstein sometimes leave the predominant impression that he was a difficult person. This he was, but this was not all that he was. The intensity of his inner life and the compelling force of his own values communicated themselves to others and made demands for adjustment to him. But whoever has not experienced the directness of his gaze and the warmth of his reaction to small attentions is likely to underestimate this other side of his personality. A small gift, a visit when he was ill in bed, seeing him off on the train, all elicited unreserved and sensitive response. Wittgenstein certainly was not English in his manner; but neither was he markedly continental. Perhaps the master–disciple relationship which we naturally fell into reflected something of another educational tradition. But there was no hint ever of expectations of conventional marks of respect for his status. Only now and then did he betray his background : I was surprised during my first year to have a note prior to his coming to dinner in my rooms, making the point that he had no evening dress. Wittgenstein not only gave affection to his students; he exercised himself in a practical way in their behalf. In one case he became concerned about a promising student who lacked funds to stay on in Cambridge and made every effort to help him, both from his own Fellowship income and by involving a number of us in seeking out funds. As for himself, money and the amenities it buys were of no importance. But what was important to him was philosophy, and the proper way of doing it; and his demand that others share his attitude and his standards was uncompromising. Doing philosophy was a moral matter for him. To do it in order to score in a game of wits was quite beyond his horizon. Accordingly, Moore's integrity and single-mindedness could merit nothing but his unwavering respect. One had the feeling that he was intolerant in matters of both morals and taste. But in the years from 1932 to 1935 he did not discuss moral or aesthetic judgments which constitute the focus of traditional ethical and aesthetic theories. If he thought such judgments were neither true nor false, or concerned matters about which one could not meaningfully dispute, he did not say so. But about philosophical theories to which he did give his attention he enunciated a view, albeit somewhat falteringly, which traditional philosophers are loath to look at: '[Philosophical problems] are, of course, not empirical problems; they are solved, rather, by looking into the workings of our language, and that in such a way as to make us recognize those workings: *in despite of* an urge to misunderstand them.'[6] It would have helped us all had he given some explanation of why there should be such an urge in philosophers. But he drew the line at this point. In the *Investigations* he made the arresting remark that 'the problems arising through a misinterpretation of our forms of language have the character of *depth*. They are deep disquietudes'.[7] But he did not to my knowledge elaborate on what these disquietudes are, nor did he make a similar comment to Skinner and me. The new and revolutionary idea he gave students to think about was that what philosophers want who make claim to having a true solution to a problem is a new notation. Few philosophers have followed Wittgenstein in this direction.

[6] *Philosophical Investigations*, p. 47.
[7] ibid.

25

# 2

# WITTGENSTEIN ON 'PRIVATE LANGUAGE'

### JOHN WISDOM

1. Is what Wittgenstein says about one's knowledge of the sensations of another and of one's own sensations relevant to what he says about private language?

My reply is 'Yes'. But I would not say that what Wittgenstein says about one's knowledge of sensations is relevant to Wittgenstein's argument about private language. I would not say this because I would not say that he presents an argument for a conclusion or even that he presents a conclusion. He presents or 'quotes' things which in certain circumstances one may feel inclined to say – such things as 'When I say "How blue the sky is" I know what I mean but no one else knows what I mean, no one else can know what I mean'. He reminds us of things we normally say which seem to conflict with the things which we feel inclined to say occasionally in philosophical moments. He asks questions calculated to lead a person who has made one of these extraordinary or philosophical remarks to ask himself such questions as 'Do I mean what people naturally take me to mean when I utter these words?' 'What do I mean when I utter these words?' 'Have I any coherent idea of what it would be for that sort of thing to happen which I say never does happen?' He writes like one who avoids presenting an argument for a conclusion or even a conclusion. Is this not part of what is sometimes referred to as the evasiveness of what Wittgenstein writes?

2. If a person writes in this way in what sense can one part of what he writes be relevant to another?

One way of meeting this question is to imagine a conversation between a person, P, who does not speak evasively and a person, Q, who speaks extremely evasively. He confines himself to 'quoting' P and asking questions.

P. 'When you say "How blue the sky is" you know what you mean but I don't know and can't know what you mean and nor can anyone else. When you say "I see a green after-image" or "I see a red after-image" then you know what you mean by "red" and "green" but I don't know and can't know what you mean. Even if I know that what you mean by "red" is different from what you mean by "green" I don't know what you mean by these words. The assumption that what you mean by "green" is what I mean by "green" and that what you mean by "red" is what I mean by "red" may be true but it's unverifiable. The assumption that what you mean by "green" is what I mean by "red" and that what you mean by "red" is what I mean by "green" is also unverifiable but it may be true.'

Q. '*Don't* you know what I mean by "green", "red", "blue"? What reason have you for saying that you don't know what I mean? What do you mean when you say you don't know what I mean? What would it be for you to know what I mean? Are you saying that each of us uses a language which no one else *could* understand? If so, what do you mean? What would it be for this to be so?'

P. 'When you say "How blue the sky is" or "I see a green after-image" or "This is sweeter than that" or "I am in pain", I never really know what your experience is. I observe your behaviour, I hear what you say, but I never really know what your experience is, I never could know what your experience is. When you say "The after-image I now see is green" or "How blue the sky is" you know what you mean but I can't know what you mean and nor can anyone else.'

Q. '*Don't* you know what my experience is? What reason have you for saying you don't? What do you mean when you say that neither you nor anyone else could know what my experience is? What would it be for you to do so? Do the words "I, P, know what Q's experience is" present to you a coherent possibility or an idea as inconsistent as that of squaring the circle? What would it be for me to know what my experience is though no one else could?'

3. Although I am ready to say at once that the questions Q asks in his second 'challenge' are relevant to the questions he asks in his first challenge and relevant to what P says in reply to Q's first challenge and to what P says to begin with, I would still like to ask 'In what sense is what Q says in his second challenge relevant to what he says in his first, and in what sense is it relevant to what P says?'

Is Q in his second challenge denying a premiss presented by P in justification of what he, P, first said? No. Q in his second challenge no more denies something P has said than he does in his first challenge. Q does not make the mistake which Wittgenstein referred to when, after I had reported my failure to reach agreement with someone in a philosophical 'argument' he (Wittgenstein) said to me 'Perhaps you made the mistake of denying what he said'.

Is Q in his second challenge *asking questions* which *suggest* the falsehood of a premiss presented by P in justification of what he said to begin with? Certainly Q's question *'Don't* you know what my experience is?' is likely to put into P's head, and the head of anyone else who hears it, the suggestion that what P has said is false. Q's second question is likely to put into one's head the idea that what P has said is unfounded. On the other hand Q's third question, 'What do you mean when you say that neither you nor anyone else can know what my experience is?', while it carries a suggestion that Q does not know what P means, does it not also carry the suggestion that P does not know what he, P, means? It carries or seems to carry the innuendo that P came out with the shocking pronouncement 'You know what your experience is but nobody else could' without giving a meaning to his words. And this suggestion conflicts with the suggestion that what P said, what P meant, was false or unfounded. Q's question 'Do the words "I know what your experience is" present for you a concept as inconsistent as that of squaring the circle?' may readily put into one's head the idea 'So when P says "I can never know your experience" he says what, in the sense he gives to his words, *could* not but be true'. Q's last question 'What would it be for me to know what my experience is though no one else

28

could?' suggests that when P said 'You know what your experience is but neither I nor anyone else could' he used those
words for an inconsistent idea. Q's last question suggests that what
P said could not be true.

4.   I think it is clear that in trying to describe what Q does one
may find oneself offering descriptions which are not merely different but different in ways which make it difficult to extract from
them a description of what he does which is consistent and helpful. However, one may try. One may try to give a description of
what he does which is a better guide than many others though it
is still not to be trusted completely. One may say : Q in his second
challenge asks questions which suggest that P's words, though
neither P nor Q have a fully formed idea of what they mean,
may incline P and others to think what is false; and may, on the
other hand, help P and others to see more clearly a necessary
feature of one's knowledge of the experience of another and of
one's own experience. Q's words carry the suggestion that P's
words need further consideration, if P and Q are to avoid the
confusion and illusion that may be associated with them and
reach the enlightenment they may bring. Q's words are an
attempt to begin that further consideration.

   Q's first challenge carried similar suggestions in connexion with
P's words about a person who understands words or certain
words although no one other than he could know what the words
mean to that person. Q's first challenge is an attempt to begin the
consideration which he thinks P's words call for. His questions
encourage a reply from P. His second challenge begins with a
consideration of P's reply and also carries further the consideration of P's first words. The questions Q asks in his second challenge are in this sense relevant to those he asks in his first
challenge.

5.   Nevertheless there is a sense in which Q's questions in his
first challenge are independent of his questions in his second
challenge. There is a sense in which 'what Q says about a person
who knows what he means by certain words although no one

else could' is independent of 'what Q says about a person who knows his own experience although no one else could'. There is a sense in which 'what Q says about a private language' is independent of 'what Q says about one's knowledge of one's own experience and one's knowledge, or lack of knowledge, of the experience of another'.

This appears if we think of someone, T, who says: 'When Q says "How blue the sky is" or "The after-image I see is green", then he knows what his experience is but P doesn't and couldn't know what Q's experience is and nor could anyone else. In my jargon, Q's experience is private. But that doesn't imply that when Q says "How blue the sky is" or "The after-image I see is green" then he knows what he means although neither P nor anyone else could know what he, Q, means. In my jargon: experience is private; but that doesn't imply that language is private. Put it this way. What is expressed by the words "When Q says 'How blue the sky is' or 'The after-image I see is green' then he knows what his experience is but P doesn't and couldn't know what Q's experience is and nor could anyone else" does not imply what is expressed by the words "When Q says 'How blue the sky is' or 'The after-image I see is green' then he knows what he means although neither P nor anyone else could know what he, Q, means". The proposition expressed by the second form of words isn't true; when Q or anyone else says "How blue the sky is" or "The after-image I see is green" P and plenty of other people know very well what he means. The first proposition doesn't imply that the second is true nor even that it could be true. Anyone who infers the second proposition from the first makes a mistake, and anyone who having said or in some way suggested that the second isn't true then thinks it necessary to show or suggest that the first isn't true is making a mistake. And anyone who having said or suggested that the second proposition couldn't be true thinks it necessary to show or suggest that the first proposition couldn't be true is making a mistake.'

6. Now P in his reply to Q's first challenge says to Q 'When you say "How blue the sky is" or "The after-image I see is green"

you know what your experience is but I don't know what it is, I couldn't know what it is and nor could anyone else. And so when you say "How blue the sky is" or "The after-image I see is green" then you know what you mean but I don't, I couldn't know what you mean and nor could anyone else.' And Q in his first challenge asks, among other questions, the question 'What would it be for me to know what I mean when I say "How blue the sky is" or "The after-image I see is green" although no one else could know what I mean?' which carries a suggestion that what P expresses when he says 'When Q says "How blue the sky is" or "The after-image I see is green" then Q knows what he means though no one else could' could not be true. And in his second challenge he seems to think it necessary to suggest that what P expresses when he says 'When you say "How blue the sky is" or "The after-image I see is green" then you know what your experience is, but I don't, I couldn't, know what your experience is and nor could anyone else' is something which couldn't be true.

Is Q mistaken and P also? Or is T mistaken? And if neither of them is mistaken how can this be so?

Such expressions as: 'the proposition expressed by the first form of words namely, "when Q says 'How blue the sky is' or 'The after-image I now see is green' then he knows what his experience is but no one else could know what his, Q's, experience is" '; and 'the proposition expressed by the second form of words "When Q says 'How blue the sky is' or 'The after-image I see is green' then he knows what he means but no one else could" '; and such expressions as: 'what is said by one who uses the first form of words'; and 'what is said by one who uses the second form of words'; hinder us from considering the possibility that the proposition expressed by one person who uses the first form of words is not always the same as the proposition expressed by another person who uses that form of words, and the possibility that what is being expressed by one person who uses the second form of words may be different from what is expressed by another person who uses that same second form of words.

When T says: 'When Q says "How blue the sky is" or "The

after-image I now see is green" Q knows what his experience is
but neither P nor anyone else could know what Q's experience
is' he, T, is like P at least in this respect that he is talking like
P and talking in a way disturbing to common sense.[1] When he
says 'When Q says "How blue the sky is" or "The after-image
I see is green" then he knows what he means and so does P and
many other people too of course' he is not talking in a way disturbing to common sense and not talking like P, who says the
opposite, and on this point also talks in a way disturbing to common sense. I suggest that what P means by the words 'Q knows
what he means but other people do not and could not' is not
what they mean to T.

7.   A further way in which what is expressed by the first form
of words 'When Q says . . . then he knows what his experience
is though no one else could' is detached from what is expressed
by 'When Q says . . . then he knows what he means though no
one else could' appears if we now think of someone, F, who says :
'When Q says "How blue the sky is" or "The after-image I see
is green" he knows what he means but P doesn't and couldn't
know what Q means and nor could anyone else. In jargon, Q's
language is private. But that doesn't imply that when Q says
"How blue the sky is" or "The after-image I see is green" then he
knows what his experience is but P doesn't and couldn't and nor
could anyone else. In jargon, Q's language is private; but that
doesn't imply that his experience is. And, in general, language is private; but that doesn't imply that experience is
private.'
   This person F, when he says 'When Q says . . . he knows what
he means but P doesn't and couldn't know what Q means and
nor could anyone else' talks like P and talks in a way disturbing
to common sense. When he says 'When Q says "How blue the sky
is . . ." then he knows what his experience is and so does P and
so do or could many other people too of course' he is not talking

---

[1] I am not here saying that T and P, who both use the first form of words
'When Q says "How blue the sky is" or "The after-image I see is green"
then Q knows what his experience is but no one else could', mean the same
by those words. That is a point which calls for further consideration.

in a way disturbing to common sense and he is not talking like P who says the opposite. I suggest that what P means by the words 'knows what his experience is but other people couldn't' is not what they mean to F.

I am suggesting that what F means by 'When Q says . . . he knows what he means but no one else could' does not imply what F means by 'When Q says . . . then he knows what his experience is but no one else could'. What he says reminds us that these forms of words may be given meanings such that what is meant by the former does not imply what is meant by the latter. And we are not without any idea as to what these meanings are. On the other hand he presents what he has to say in a way which obscures the fact that these forms of words may be given meanings such that what is meant by the former does imply what is meant by the latter. We may encounter someone who says 'When Q says "How blue the sky is" or "The after-image I see is green" I don't and couldn't know what he means. So when Q says "How blue the sky is" or "The after-image I see is green" I don't and couldn't know what his experience is and nor could anyone else.'

I am suggesting that what T means by 'When Q says . . . then he knows what his experience is but no one else could' does not imply what he, T, means by 'When Q says . . . he knows what he means but no one else could'. What he says indicates this and this reminds us that these forms of words can have meanings such that what is meant by the former does not imply what is meant by the latter. And we are not without any idea as to what these meanings are. On the other hand what he says may give the impression that these forms of words are never given meanings such that what is meant by the former implies what is meant by the latter. And this is not so. We have in P someone who gives to the words 'When Q says . . . he knows what his experience is but no one else could' and the words 'When Q says . . . he knows what he means but no one else could' meanings such that the former implies the latter. And we have an idea what these meanings are. P talks in a way which may obscure the fact that someone else, e.g. T, may give to the forms of words he uses meanings such that what is meant by the first does not imply what is meant by the second.

8. What P says when he says (1) 'When Q says "How blue the sky is" or "The after-image I see is green" then he knows what his experience is but no one else could' is independent of what he says when he says (2) 'When Q says "How blue the sky is" or "The after-image I see is green" then he knows what he means but no one else could' in the sense that a person may give meanings to P's first form of words and to his second form of words such that what is meant by the first does not imply what is meant by the second.

On the other hand what P says when he says (1) is relevant to what he says when he says (2) in that what he means by (1) implies what *he* means by (2).

As to Q. In his first challenge he asks a number of questions which include one which carries the suggestion that what P meant when he said 'When you say "How blue the sky is" or "The after-image I see in green" then you know what you mean but no one else could' is something which could not be true (or the suggestion that P's meaning is incoherent).

P in his reply combats this suggestion by representing what he, P, meant by his first disturbing words as implied by what he now expresses in the words 'When you say "How blue the sky is" or "The after-image I see is green" you know what your experience is but no one else could know what your experience is.'

Q in his second challenge asks a number of questions which include one which carries the suggestion that what P means by his second disturbing pronouncement is also something which could not be true. He does not point out that P's forms of words can be used in such senses that what is meant by the second does not imply what is meant by the first and in such senses that what is meant by the first does not imply what is meant by the second. I do not say he should have done so. But people like T and F bring this out. It is something which deserves to be brought out. If, however, someone says 'What P says in the second place about the privacy of experience doesn't imply what he said in the first place about the privacy of language'; or says 'What P says in the first place about the privacy of language doesn't imply what he says in the second place about the privacy of experience'; or says both these things – then although what he says brings to mind what deserves attention, it also obscures the connexion between what P means by his first pronouncement and what P means by his second.

9.  Q is not Wittgenstein. Nor is P the person Wittgenstein is talking to. For instance if someone were to say to me 'Doesn't Wittgenstein meet such a pronouncement as "When you say 'How blue the sky is' or 'The after-image I see is green' you know what you mean but no one else could know what you mean" with this question, among others, "What would it be for me to have a way of knowing whether I am right when I say 'How blue the sky is' or 'The after-image I see is green' although neither you nor anyone else could know how I know whether I am right?" ' then I would not deny this. Wittgenstein though he does not use *just* these words, does not ask *just* this question, comes close to doing so in a way Q does not.

This being so, someone may naturally feel inclined to say : 'Well then, Wittgenstein presents the following argument :

(i)   It is absurd to say of someone, M, that he has a way of knowing whether he is right when he says such things as "How blue the sky is" or "The after-image I see is green" although no one else could know what that way of knowing is.

(ii)  That implies that it is absurd to say of someone, M, that he knows what he means when he says "How blue the sky is" or "The after-image I see is green", although no one else could know what he, M, means.

Therefore,

(iii) it is absurd to say of someone, M, that he knows what he means when he says, "How blue the sky is" or "The after-image I see is green" although no one else could.'

A person who says this may go on to say 'In this argument (i) does not imply the conclusion (iii).'

In reply let me say two things :

First, a person may give to the words which follow (i), i.e. the words 'It is absurd to say of someone, M, that he has a way of knowing . . . ' a meaning which does not imply what to him is meant by the words which follow (iii), i.e. 'It is absurd to say of someone, M, that he knows what he means. . . .' This gives a sense in which a person may without inconsistency assert (i) and deny (iii). [Also a person may give a meaning to (iii) which does not imply what to him is meant by (i).] On the other hand a person may give to the words which follow (i) a meaning which *does* imply what to him is meant by the words which follow (iii). Such a person may then meet the argument by saying that (i) is false. On the other hand he may say 'I see that (i) is true. And I now see that (iii) is true.'

Second, although Wittgenstein's question in response to a strange pronouncement, readily puts into one's head the argument represented as his, he does not present that argument. He does not assert (i) or (ii) or (iii). He avoids doing so. And one may think that he does so because he is aware of how far from fixed and clear is the use of the words which follow (i) and (iii).

# 3

# SOLIPSISM AND LANGUAGE

## JOHN W. COOK

In writing about Wittgenstein's discussion of the idea of a private language, it seems necessary to begin by clearing away numerous confusions that have grown up around the subject. This is my first task. But I have found that in order to do this properly it was necessary to presuppose *some* familiarity with the way in which Wittgenstein finally deals with this question – I mean his way of showing that language cannot be cut off from human *activities*. As a result, Part I of this essay is filled with rather vague allusions to matters which are taken up in detail in Part II. Worse yet, these allusions are couched in a certain jargon ('language-game', 'connexion', 'grammar') that is not altogether harmless. I can only plead that proceeding in this way seemed like a useful first step, given the state into which the discussion of this topic has fallen. Hopefully, by the end of Part II most of this jargon will have have fallen away. Wittgenstein ended his lectures one term by remarking that the only seed he was likely to sow was a certain jargon. I should not like the present essay to contribute to that predicted state of affairs.

Much of what I have said in Part I could be thought of as an answer to the question 'Why does Wittgenstein speak of a private *language*?' The answer to this question, however, does not get us very close to the source of what is at issue here. If I had to say briefly what that source is, and what Wittgenstein thought it was, I could do no better than to quote this passage from W. T. Stace: 'Your colour red, instead of being similar to mine, may possibly resemble what I should call toothache. That we speak familiarly of our sensations proves nothing to the contrary.'[1] These remarks seem to me to express as well as anything could

[1] *The Theory of Knowledge and Existence* (London, 1932), p. 31.

37

that idea which Wittgenstein is concerned with in his discussion of private language. I will get around to examining this idea in Part II, but the reader will do well to keep it in mind throughout Part I.

I

Perhaps the best way to describe Wittgenstein's discussion of the idea of a private language would be to say that he wrote the passages in question (I refer specifically to the 'diary' passages)[2] with tongue in cheek. By this I mean that he did not for a moment intend that we should take seriously or try to make sense of the conditions he lays down (256) for the keeping of this diary. The question that he is asking himself here does not require that we make sense of these conditions. Why this is so I shall now try to explain.

The first thing to be clear about is that Wittgenstein's question does not concern the possibility of describing in ordinary terms someone's inventing a name for a certain sensation and using it in his private diary. There is no difficulty, that is, about describing the following sort of case. A young actress making her debut is mildly distressed at the funny feeling in her stomach as she waits in the wings before going on stage. (Somehow she has never heard of stage jitters.) She mentions it to no one and after the performance enters the following lines in her diary : 'Debut tonight. Frightening but exciting. Had a funny feeling in my stomach before going on stage – felt like butterflies fluttering about inside.' The next night she again writes in her diary : 'Second performance tonight. Had "butterflies" again', and in subsequent entries in her diary she uses 'butterflies-in-the-stomach' to refer to this funny feeling. She never uses this expression in speaking to other people, suspecting that they will think it silly. She has never heard others use this expression.

There is nothing of philosophical interest in such a story, and it is certain that Wittgenstein had no such case in mind when

---

[2] *Philosophical Investigations* (3rd edn, New York, 1968), Part I, Sections 256, 258, 260. Hereafter all references to this book will be placed in the text and unless otherwise indicated will refer to the sections of Part I.

discussing the idea of a private language.[3] We can see this from the way in which he introduces the subject :

> But could we also imagine a language in which one could record or express his inner experiences – his feelings, moods, and the rest – for his own use? Well, can't we do so in our ordinary language? – But that is not what I mean. The words of this language are to refer to what can be known only to the speaker; to his immediate, private, sensations. So another cannot understand the language. (243).[4]

What Wittgenstein is excluding as irrelevant here is any sort of mere secrecy or covert use of words that could be described without recourse to such philosophical phrases as 'immediate, private, sensation' and 'what can be known only to the speaker'.[5] My story of the actress involves only what Wittgenstein here calls 'ordinary language', i.e. no philosophical description is given of

---

[3] I bother to mention such a case only because some philosophers seem to have thought that Wittgenstein did intend to present a real case of someone keeping a diary. They are misled, partly, by taking out of context the lines that read : 'Let us imagine the following case. I want to keep a diary about the recurrence of a certain sensation' (258). Judith Jarvis Thomson, for instance, quotes these lines and then goes on to ask what would make the sign used in the diary such that 'it was logically impossible for anyone but LW to know what it meant? For suppose that we were to watch LW very carefully every day for several years, and suppose we were to notice the following regularities in his use of the word. . . .' Here she imagines us to notice that LW holds his cheek, furrows his brow, gingerly touches his tongue to his tooth and then winces, and so on. ('Private Languages' reprinted in *Philosophy of Mind*, ed. Stuart Hampshire [New York, 1966], p. 118). What she is forgetting is that we have already been put on notice (256) that the author of this diary is not endowed with (it is not part of his nature to have) any 'natural expressions of sensation'. After all, the diary case was invented solely for the purpose of exploring the question 'how, then, can I want to use language to get between pain and its expression?' (245).

[4] I have altered Miss Anscombe's translation of these lines in several places, eliminating the word 'person' in three places and also the words 'vocal' and 'private'. The German does not call for these words. My reasons for insisting on a more literal translation will be given below.

[5] In notes made for his own use preparatory to lecturing on this subject Wittgenstein alludes to this distinction as follows : 'Now compare secrecy with the "privateness" of personal experience ! In what sense is a thought of mine secret? If I think aloud it can be heard. – "I have said this to myself a thousand times but not to anyone else." ' ('Wittgenstein's Notes for Lectures on "Private Experience" and "Sense Data" ', *The Philosophical Review* [July, 1968], p. 314). Hereafter I shall refer to these notes as 'Notes'.

what the actress writes in her diary. Further on in the discussion
Wittgenstein himself describes a similar case : 'Let us now imagine
a use for the entry of the sign "E" in my diary. I discover that
whenever I have a particular sensation a manometer shows that
my blood-pressure rises. So I shall be able to say that my blood-
pressure is rising without using any apparatus' (270). Presumably,
what we are to imagine here is someone who, in quite familiar
ways, could talk to a doctor about his symptoms and could understand advice such as 'Take two of these capsules whenever you
begin to feel lightheaded.' In this respect he is like my actress,
and Wittgenstein's account of his use of the sign 'E' resembles
my story of the actress's use of 'butterflies-in-the-stomach' in so
far as neither contains a philosophical description that turns it
into a 'private language' story. In neither case, that is, do we have
the claim that the word (or sign) used refers to 'what can be
known only to the speaker, to his immediate, private, sensations'.[6]

How, then are we to tell a suitable 'private language' story? –
The answer is : Don't even try! But does Wittgenstein not try?
In a sense he does, and it is important to recognize just what sort
of attempt he makes. Unfortunately, mistranslations of several
passages obscure Wittgenstein's purpose here, allowing the English reader to think that the sentence 'I want to keep a diary about
the recurrence of a certain sensation' (258) is to be understood as
having been spoken (or written or thought) by a man, a human
being. For instance, in Sec. 260 Miss Anscombe translates 'So
hätte sich also, der das Zeichen in der Kalender eintrug . . . ' as
'then did the man who made the entry in the calendar. . . .' The
original does not, however, specify that it is a *man* keeping the
diary. The word 'Mensch' is carefully omitted here, as it is also

---

[6] My explanation here of Wittgenstein's use of 'ordinary language' in
Sec. 243 might be objected to as follows: 'The mere absence of that philosophical phrase (as you call it) from the two stories is not sufficient to dis-
qualify them from containing instances of private language, for after all in
both cases it is a sensation (or feeling) that gets named, and sensations are
private.' This would be a mistaken objection, however, for beginning in Sec.
244 Wittgenstein proceeds to undermine the idea that sensations are
private. In his 'Notes' (p. 314) he remarks: 'The "private experience" is a
degenerate construction of our language. . . . And this grammatical monster
now fools us; when we wish to do away with it, it seems as though we
denied the existence of an experience, say, toothache.'

in the initial formulation of the question about a private language (see footnote 3 above). But if it is not a *man* keeping the diary, who – or what – is it, then? – Well, perhaps it is a stone – or the soul that some stone has (cf. 283). Wittgenstein writes: 'Aber wie, wenn ich keine natürlichen Äusserungen der Empfindung, sondern nur die Empfindung besässe? Und nun assoziiere ich einfach Namen mit den Empfindungen und verwende diese Namen in einer Beschreibung' (256). Now this tells us about the author of the diary, but *what* does it tell us? Miss Anscombe translates the first sentence as 'But suppose I didn't have any natural expression for the sensation, but only had the sensation?' This translation of 'besässe' ('besitzen') as 'have' is misleading, for it suggests that the absence of the natural expression of sensation is, or might be, a temporary condition, as if we were to imagine here something like a mute and helpless paralytic, lying in bed amusing himself with making up names for sensations. But this is not at all what Wittgenstein intended, as the verb 'besässe' shows. The sentence should be translated: 'But suppose that I were endowed with no natural expression of sensation but only with the sensation?' What we are being asked to suppose, then is that this (what?) is not a temporary condition but a permanent, natural state. We are being told what *kind* of being the author of this diary is, namely, one not endowed with natural expressions of sensation. The statement is intended as a metaphysical one. If it is to be compared with anything, the right sort of comparison would be with Hume's way of summarizing the consequences of his sceptical doubts at the end of Book I of the *Treatise*: 'I am confounded with all these questions, and begin to fancy myself in the most deplorable condition imaginable, inviron'd with the deepest darkness, and utterly depriv'd of the use of every member and faculty.'[7] Hume does not, of course, mean that he has begun to think of himself as a helpless paralytic, lying in a darkened room, and it is nothing like this that Wittgenstein has in mind either.[8] What is meant, rather, is something that might

---

[7] *A Treatise of Human Nature*, ed. L. A. Selby-Bigge (Oxford, 1951), p. 269.

[8] I confess to being uncertain how to construe the references to 'die Menschen' and 'einem Kind' at the beginning of Sec. 257. These references

best be explained as follows: 'I am here conceiving of myself as the sort of being that, although capable of getting dizzy, is incapable of staggering about or groping for support or, for that matter, lying still; and that, although capable of suffering pain, is incapable of wincing or groaning or, for that matter, of gritting my teeth and keeping a stiff upper lip.' I don't suggest that this tells us what the author of the diary *is*, nor do I mean to suggest that this even makes sense, but it does tell us what the author of the diary *is not*, namely, a man, a human being. And it is just this point that Wittgenstein is speaking to later on when he observes: 'only of a living human being and what resembles (behaves like) a living human being can one say: it has sensations; sees; is blind; hears; is deaf; is conscious or unconscious' (281). So if we ask: 'What are we to imagine in connection with this diary case?' Wittgenstein's final answer is: 'Nothing.'

What, then, *is* this idea of a private language? Where does it come from? In the years when Wittgenstein was writing *Philosophical Investigations* there would have been little, if any, puzzlement over this, and perhaps that is why Wittgenstein does not explain himself more fully. Most philosophers had heard of Russell's project of constructing an 'ideal language', and even if not all took an interest in the project, its possibility was not doubted. Among the requirements for this ideal language was the stipulation that its terms should not imply the existence of anything that Hume's scepticism had called into question, including human beings.[9] What, then, *could* its terms refer to? 'To

occur within quotation marks and so are not in Wittgenstein's own voice. (The third sentence of the section, 'Well, let's assume the child is a genius . . .', is clearly ironic and so does not concern me here.) It would be convenient to be able to say that the two sentences at the beginning of the section are to be thought of as spoken by a philosopher who is not yet in a position to appreciate the difference between a Cartesian ego (or a Humean bundle of perceptions) and a human being and who therefore uses 'Mensch' although it is one of the former he is thinking of. I suspect that Wittgenstein is here imagining such a philosopher and imagining him to be alluding to the subject matter of Sec. 244, but I don't know how to prove this. In favour of this interpretation, however, is the fact that the remainder of Sec. 257 contains the right sort of rejoinder to such a philosopher.

[9] 'To philosophize is to construct, in accordance with certain minimal requirements, an exact formal language capable of describing experience. . . . The philosophical formalism must be constructed without the assumption of

sensations, to immediate experience', was the answer. The assumption here was that Hume had been right in thinking that sensations or experiences 'have no need of anything else to support their existence' or, as Hume also put it, that they have no 'real connexion' with anything else. This comes to much the same as – or at least results from – thinking that (a) the only philosophically significant relationships among words are 'logical' relationships, those that can be dealt with in terms of formal implications and definitions; (b) some words (among them the names of sensations and various qualities) are indefinable; (c) these words get their meaning by being directly associated with what they stand for (sometimes called 'ostensive definition'); and therefore (d) in philosophizing about the things these words stand for (about sensations, colours, etc.) a philosopher is at liberty to break any connexions which, in ordinary language, their names have with other words – since these connexions are at best an accident of our grammar, and at worst are spurious theories of untutored common sense.[10]

The idea of a private language, then, is importantly connected with a certain idea of how words get defined or explained or learned or taught or get a meaning, and it is this that provides the focus for Wittgenstein's discussion. When approached in this way, his whole discussion hangs together very neatly, and features of it which are otherwise surprising or obscure lose their oddity. For instance, it becomes evident why Wittgenstein, having introduced the topic in Sec. 243, turns immediately in the next section to the question 'How do words *refer* to sensations?' and then proceeds to provide a reminder (admittedly sketchy) of how we learn a word such as 'pain' : 'Here is one possibility : words are

terms which would imply the existence of a self who understands this language; of other people or other minds who use and understand this language; nor of a real external world of existent things to which the terms of this language refer. Thus these minimal requirements reflect a complete Humean scepticism.' Thomas Storer, 'Linguistic Isomorphisms', *Philosophy of Science* (January 1952), p. 77.

[10] 'All our everyday words embody theories. But it is not impossible to whittle away the element of interpretation, or to invent an artificial language involving a minimum of theory.' Bertrand Russell, *An Inquiry Into Meaning and Truth* (London, 1940), p. 154.

connected with the primitive, the natural, expressions of the sensation and used in their place. A child has hurt himself and he cries; and then adults talk to him and teach [bringen] him exclamations and, later, sentences' (244). Here at the beginning of the discussion, then, we find an indication of what will prove to be his main line of attack on the idea of a private language : if the words by which we refer to sensations are connected with (or 'tied up with' [256]) natural expressions of sensation, if there is a 'grammar of the word "pain" ' which the naming of it presupposes (257), then in the use of this word we have no private language. Or what comes to the same thing, if the word 'pain' does have such connexions, then we cannot 'try to use language to get between pain and its expression' (245), i.e. cannot propose to invent a language which allows us to refer to pain but which does not commit us to there being any expression of pain. Or to put the matter in still another way, if names of sensations are connected with the manifestations of sensations in human life, then philosophers are not at liberty to break these connexions when philosophizing about sensations – are not at liberty, for example, to suppose that what I call pain may be what you should call dizziness (cf. 272), which is the paradigm expression of the idea of a private language.

Another point that becomes clear when seen in the light of the foregoing is that when Wittgenstein asks us to imagine the diary case ('Let us imagine the following case'), he is not seriously asking us to first imagine certain conditions and then to inquire whether, given these conditions, language is possible. Instead, he introduces the diary case, which, incidentally, he borrowed from Moritz Schlick,[11] simply for the purpose of illustrating, or explor-

[11] It appears that Schlick's lectures entitled 'Form and Content', delivered at the University of London in 1932, served as a catalyst for much of Wittgenstein's discussion of this topic. In a section entitled 'Communication with One's Self' Schlick remarks that his theory of language is consistent with the possibility that he alone exists, for 'I can express facts to myself and communicate with myself – in fact, I do so every time when I take down something in my note-book or commit something to memory.' He goes on to remark that 'for the essence of communication it makes no difference whether the note-book is what the metaphysician would call "a mere dream", or possesses what he might call "objective reality" '. Moritz Schlick, Gesammelte Aufsätze (Vienna, 1938), p. 178. – This was very likely

ing, the question 'How, then, can I want to use language to get between pain [or any other sensation] and its expression?'[12] That is, given the way that I learned the word 'pain', how can I think that I could 'directly' name a sensation in a way that has no connexion with the expression of the sensation so that the name refers to something that only I can know about? The diary case simply fills out this question in a more or less familiar way (cf. Descartes writing his *Meditations* while supposing that he has 'no hands, no eyes, no flesh, no blood, nor any sense'), so that the question becomes: How can I imagine that I am endowed with no natural expression of sensation but that nevertheless I could invent a name for keeping a record of a sensation? The point of this is not to try to make sense of 'endowed with no natural expressions of sensation' but rather to get ourselves to ask whether, in giving a philosophical account of naming a sensation, we can rightly say that, although certain matters do not turn up in the account (are excluded from the account, no matter how), a sensation has been named. Wittgenstein's intention, then, was something like this: Let us take the case of the child and parents described in 244, strip the case of everything that passes between parent and child that could have any bearing on the child's use of the word 'pain' (let us not worry about how we are thus to strip the case – if a metaphysical picture will help here, so be it),

the inspiration for Wittgenstein's diary case, but it should be observed that Wittgenstein's 'supposition' that he has no natural expression of sensation (no 'body', if you will) is not the same thing as what Schlick is allowing when he allows that his note-book may be a 'mere dream'. Schlick's 'supposition' comes to no more than a philosophical willingness to interject the phrase 'I'm dreaming' (or the word 'seems') into one's remarks wherever syntax permits. But this ubiquitous use of, say, 'seems' would merely turn the word into a *façon de parler* and so would not create the case that Wittgenstein wants here. For what he wants is not a case in which he 'seems' to have natural expressions of sensation but a case in which he does *not* have natural expressions of sensation, i.e. a case in which the account in Sec. 244 of a child learning a word from his parents just wouldn't apply to him – not even with the word 'seems' liberally sprinkled through its sentences. And again, if we ask, 'But what sort of a case *is* this?' the answer is 'You're not supposed to worry about that' or 'It's *no* sort of case.'

[12] I have altered Miss Anscombe's translation of Sec. 245. The position of the word 'denn' in the sentence indicates that it is to be translated as 'then' and not 'for'; it refers the reader back to the reminder in the preceding section about learning names of sensations, so that it has the sense of: 'Given what we have now been reminded of.'

and then let us see whether we can still give an account which adds up to a description of the child's naming a sensation. The imagined diary case is not, then, as some have supposed, the first step in an argument of the *reductio ad absurdum* form but merely an (admittedly devious) heuristic device. There is, in fact, no argument here at all. Rather, we are being invited to consider a certain deliberately restricted description and being asked whether we could recognize from this description alone that a sensation has been named.

Another point that now becomes perfectly clear is Wittgenstein's reason for asking: 'What reason have we for calling "E" the sign for a *sensation*?' (261, Wittgenstein's emphasis). The point of this question is already indicated in Sec. 260 where he asks: 'Then did the one who made the entry in the calendar make a note of *nothing whatever*? . . . For a note has a function, and this "E" so far has none.' The point, then, of asking the first question is this: whether 'E' is the name of a sensation, rather than, say, of a song, depends on its function, on the way it enters into reasons or excuses or warnings or something of the sort. In short, it depends on its role in some language-game. Here is where the well-known manometer passage becomes relevant. For there Wittgenstein asks the same question, and answers that we can call 'E' the name of a sensation in *this* case because of 'the kind of way this sign is employed in this language-game' (270). He means that the man will now say from time to time, either aloud or to himself, 'There's E again; I'd better take my pill', that he might also say or write in his diary, 'Haven't had E all week; those pills must be working' or perhaps 'Have had E every day this week; it's time to see the doctor again,' and so on, and given this use of 'E' what *should* we call E if not a sensation? This is how we *use* the word 'sensation'. But now it is just this sort of role in various language-games that gets excluded from the diary case with its disembodied author. (I will discuss this in more detail below.) So, as Wittgenstein says, what reason have we for calling 'E' the sign for a sensation? None, apparently.

We can gain a better appreciation of the heuristic value of Wittgenstein's disembodied author by returning to a point made earlier in explaining the alleged virtues of an 'ideal' Humean language. One of its virtues was supposed to be that it differs from ordinary language in respect to the fact that the latter allows or encourages inferences which are grounded, not on 'real connexions' between things, but on accidents of our grammar. The Humean, in other words, recognizes that there are certain connexions in our grammar, but he thinks that they should not be there, that they do not reflect the true nature of things. A proponent of this view, then, might acknowledge that as far as our grammar is concerned there are connexions between sensations and human beings, but he would insist that these must be excluded from an ideal language.[13]

He might even go so far as to admit that in our language there is a connexion between a particular sensation (or the name of a particular sensation) and certain expressions of sensation, so that whereas we exclaim with a wince or a start, 'Ouch, that hurt!' we would never exclaim, 'Ouch, that tickles.' But having admitted this, a proponent of this Humean view will want to argue as follows: 'I admit', he will say, 'that in ordinary language words like "tickle", "hurt", "dizzy", and so on have a grammar that ties them to living human beings and to particular manifestations in human behaviour, but this fact does not prevent me from constructing a private, Humean, language in which these grammatical ties are broken. For I can invent a language of my own by restricting its vocabulary in such a way that one could not, when speaking (or thinking in) this language, mention either human beings or human behaviour, although many of the words of the language could be used to refer to sensations and other experiences. These words would be indefinable in the sense that

[13] Hume had insisted that since all perceptions (which for him included all sensations) 'may be consider'd as separately existent', it follows that 'there is no absurdity in separating any particular perception from the mind; that is, in breaking off all its relations with . . . a thinking being.' (*Treatise*, op. cit., p. 207.) Accordingly he would be disdainful of our asking, for example, 'Who's dizzy?' if we had overheard someone say, 'The dizziness shouldn't last much longer.' Hume would probably have said that our question 'Who's dizzy?' wrongly assumes a necessary connexion between dizziness and someone who is dizzy. A modern Humean would say that an ideal language would not permit an inference of the kind that our question here depends on.

anyone who undertook to use this language would have to give a meaning to these words for himself. Thus, if "zap" is a sensation word in this language, then one who so uses it must give a meaning to "zap" by associating it with some particular sensation of his. He can then use the word in giving descriptions, such as "Zap is now increasing in intensity" and "This zap has now lasted for five minutes". And the possibility of thus naming and using the names of sensations independently of any implied reference to human beings and human behaviour shows that sensations *are* private and that a genuinely private language is possible.'

Now what are we to make of this description of a 'language'[14] and of the claim that is made about it, namely, that its possibility demonstrates the privacy of sensations? It seems to me that for the most part the description or specification of the language is both unproblematic and uninteresting, for as far as I can see it does not differ significantly from my story of the actress who invents a word for referring to her stage jitters. By this I mean that it does not differ from the latter case in a way that justifies the claim made for it – the claim that its possibility demonstrates the privacy of sensations. (I can even imagine a philosopher, who was intent on refuting what he took Wittgenstein to be saying, perversely using this 'language' to keep a diary.) What I should want to deny is the claim that if someone has managed to associate a word of this language – say, 'zap' – with pain, for example, he has thereby (because of the restrictions on the vocabulary and grammaɪ of the language) managed to define 'zap' in a way consistent with Humean scepticism. Someone who thinks that the specifications for this language are of a Humean character is failing to realize, among other things, that in the case of the word 'zap' he has done nothing more than to substitute this word for 'pain' and to resolve to use 'zap' in only a certain few of the cases in which we use 'pain' i.e. 'zap in my knee' is ruled out but 'The zap is getting worse' is not. But this invention of a new word

[14] There is undoubtedly something odd in calling such a thing 'a language'. It is certainly not a language in the sense that French and English are languages. If it can be called a language at all, it is only in the sense that George Orwell called Newspeak a language. In what follows I will disregard this oddity.

with a restricted use does not leave it independent of the original word 'pain'.

A useful comparison for this case would be the following: a wife may invent a pet name – say, 'Honey Bun' – for her husband, which she then uses only in directly addressing him or calling him but never in referring to him in conversation with other people. It certainly does not follow that her use of this pet name is independent of the whole 'public' practice of using people's names; her capacity for inventing such a name is partly parasitic on her capacity to use people's names in the more usual ways. The fact that she deliberately restricts its use does not entail that if she were now to abandon the restrictions, if she began using it publicly so that it eventually became the man's public nickname, it would have changed its meaning in the sense of now having a *man* as its bearer whereas before it did not. After all, we said at the outset that it was her pet name for her *husband*. Now, similarly, if certain words in our supposedly Humean language are specified by the philosopher as being names of *sensations*, then even though their use is deliberately restricted, by comparison with the ordinary use of 'pain', etc. it does not follow from this that they are used *independently* of the grammar of these everyday words. (For instance, the use of 'zap' as described above, is not independent of the use of 'pain'.) The very possibility of *specifying* this imagined use of words presupposes their connexion with our everyday use of words. (So the imagined language is not really a Humean language; we might call it 'pseudo-Humean'.) But more important than this is the fact that if – or in so far as – we can agree that someone actually uses this language, that he has really 'associated' a word of the language with a sensation, we are thinking of him as someone who already uses words like 'pain', 'tickle', 'dizzy', 'chills', and so on. This is Wittgenstein's point when he remarks that 'a great deal of stage-setting in the language is presupposed if the mere act of naming is to make sense. And when we speak of someone's having given a name to pain, what is presupposed is the existence of the grammar of the word 'pain'. . . .' (257). To be a genuinely Humean language, what would have to be shown is that the possibility of associating its words with something (Can we say 'with sensations'?) does not presuppose that the speaker of this language has any prior command of certain words ('pain', 'tickle', etc.) of our everyday language. But how is one to show this? How, that is, could one be sure that the description of the naming of sensations does not covertly presuppose a prior mastery of the use of words like 'dizzy' and 'pain'?

It is just here, I believe, that Wittgenstein, in trying to think through this whole issue, found it useful to introduce the diary and its disembodied author. His aim, in other words, was to try to capture in a metaphysical picture a case in which the description of the naming of sensations ('And now I simply *associate* names with sensations and use these names in descriptions' [256]) would not covertly presuppose the circumstances of human life that surround actual cases of naming things – for example, the circumstances that are found in my story of the actress who writes in her diary about her stage jitters. By supposing an author of the diary who is 'endowed with no natural expressions of sensation' Wittgenstein ensures that his imagined private language will not turn out to be what I called above a pseudo-Humean language. In his 'Notes' Wittgenstein did not ensure against this, did not imagine a disembodied speaker, and as a result some of his remarks, which otherwise closely resemble remarks in *Philosophical Investigations*, seem to rule out the wrong thing or to rule out too much. For example, he writes :

> But can't you, . . . at least for yourself, give an *ostensive* definition of 'toothache'? Pointing to the place of your pain and saying 'this is . . .'? Can't I give a name to the pain I've got? Queer idea to give one's pain a name! What's it to do with a name? Or what do I do with it? What do I do with the name of a person whom I *call* by the name? What connexion is the name to have with the pain? The only connexion so far is that you had toothache, pointed to your cheek, and pronounced the word 'moo'. 'So what?'

What is said here is pretty odd, both because the target of these remarks is unclear and because it appears to be concerned with an ordinary human being (he can point to his cheek.) At one point it looks as though he is only saying that since we can already talk of pain it is a queer idea to suggest giving it a name. But a few sentences later it looks rather as though he is ruling out cases of the kind illustrated by my story of the actress and by his own example of the man with high blood-pressure. That is, it looks as though he is here denying that anyone could invent a new word for talking about his sensations. This is what he managed to avoid in the *Investigations* by explicitly directing his comments against a metaphysical picture in which we 'assume the abrogation of the normal language-game with the expression of a sensation' (288).

Let us return to Wittgenstein's question: 'What reason have we for calling "E" the sign for a *sensation*?' This means: if we suspend our objections to the metaphysical picture of the disembodied author of the diary and grant what this picture requires, what reason does this leave us for saying that a *sensation* has been named? 'For', as Wittgenstein adds, ' "sensation" is a word of our common language, not one intelligible to me alone' (261). That is, just as the wife in my above example cannot do just *anything* with 'Honey Bun' and still be said to have given her husband a pet name, since 'husband' is, after all, a word with a quite particular use, so too the author of our imaginary diary can't do just anything with the sign 'E' and still be said to have given a *sensation* a name. So how *does* this disembodied author use 'E'? As soon as we try to answer this question in such a way as to make it appear that 'E' is the name of a sensation, we begin to turn the author of the diary into a man and not a disembodied being. For we have to imagine *something* like what Wittgenstein describes in the manometer passage, where the man's noticing a correlation of E with the manometer reading enables him to dispense with the manometer (and any other equipment) in determining that his blood-pressure is rising. That E is a sensation (or that 'E' is the name of a sensation) is made clear in *this* case because of the kind of story we tell, a story about a man, his concern with his blood-pressure, the discovery which enables him to dispense with equipment, and finally the way we can imagine him to use 'E' in *saying* things. For example, he may say, 'There's E again; I had better take my pill', and 'I haven't felt E for at least a week; those pills must be working', and 'Had E this morning; but I was out of pills', and 'Had E every day this week; perhaps I had better see the doctor again', and so on. Here we have at least *begun* to make 'E' look like the right sort of word, but the kind of detail that is relevant here is excluded *per hypothesis* in the diary case with its disembodied author. He cannot, for example, use 'E' as part of a reminder to take his pills or as part of a reason to see his doctor or in stating his reason for not playing tennis or anything else of the sort. (Remember that this is not meant to be a solipsistic account of the more usual sort, where you are allowed to tell the usual sorts of stories about people provided only that 'seems' is liberally sprinkled through the account given. See footnote 11 above.) Wittgenstein tells us that the author is to 'associate names with sensations and use these names as descriptions' (256). But what sort of descriptions is he supposed to give, and what makes them to be *descriptions*? Significantly, Wittgenstein does not give us examples; he merely imagines this author to write 'E' in his diary. But let us try to imagine some descriptions consistent with this being a disembodied author. How are we to do this? Will it suffice to invent some *sentences* in the diary, for example, 'E is pulsating' or 'E is getting worse'? These, of course, are words from our common language, and they seem to smack too much of human life. 'Pulsating' has an obvious derivation ('pulse') that our disembodied author cannot be allowed. And as for 'worse', when we say a pain is getting worse, we generally seek relief, i.e. take aspirin or codeine or lie still or go to the doctor, and if we don't get relief, then there may be groaning and even writhing. So the word 'worse', as used here is certainly not free of the unwanted connexions with human life. But if we begin to trim away all these connexions, what do we have left? What would be the difference between our imaginary author's using it to mean what we mean and his using it to mean what we are saying when we say 'The pain is better now'? Can I privately demonstrate to myself the difference, perhaps by pinching myself harder and harder and as

I do so saying to myself 'Now the pain's getting worse'? Could I in this way privately explain to myself what our disembodied author will mean by 'worse'? No, for here we are back to the pseudo-Humean language. That is, although I can pinch myself and say those words, this does not go nearer to showing that I could say that my pain was getting worse if there had not been all the usual surroundings of human language. Well, suppose we give up the word 'worse' and imagine a different sentence in the diary, for example, 'E is changing.' Will this escape the above difficulties? It is true, of course, that 'changing' does not bring along with it the sorts of things that 'worse' does, but just for this reason it will not do the job we want it to do. For we were asking how our disembodied author could so use 'E' that we could begin to justify the claim that 'E' stands for a sensation. But the sentence 'E is changing' could hardly help us identify 'E' as the name of a sensation, for it is by no means a peculiarity of sensations that they change. It would appear, then, that we cannot accompish what we set out to do here. We cannot find the right sort of language-game for 'E' and so cannot call it the sign for a sensation. As Wittgenstein remarks in his 'Notes' (p. 291): ' "To give a sensation a name" means nothing unless I know already in what sort of a game this name is to be used.'

There is an even graver difficulty here. In the last paragraph we were considering what sorts of *sentences* might turn up in the diary. But what we call a 'sentence' is not somehow prior to and independent of people talking, asking questions, giving warnings, making complaints, giving instructions, and so on – and *these* are activities of human life. But since activities of this sort have been ruled out of the diary case *per hypothesis*, we really are not entitled to talk about sentences in this case either. If we tend to overlook this point, it is probably because we have a certain picture of human language or speaking – indeed, the very picture that lies behind the whole problem. Wittgenstein addresses himself to this point when he writes:

I should like to say: you regard it much too much as a matter of course that one can tell anything to anyone. That is to say:

53

we are so much accustomed to communication through language, in conversation, that it looks to us as if the whole point of communication lay in this: someone else grasps the sense of my words – which is something mental: he as it were takes it into his own mind. If he then does something further with it as well, that is no part of the immediate purpose of language. (363).

It is this picture of language, among other things, that Wittgenstein meant to correct with his metaphor 'language-*games*' (7, 23) and with his example of the builder and his helper (2). And the idea of a private language comes in for special attention because it is a particularly intractable version of this general idea about language. The reason for this is obvious: the picture of sensations as private objects provides special inducement to think of meanings as mind-made connections, as something in the mind. This is virtually inescapable if we find ourselves asking 'How can another person know what I mean by "red" or "tickle"?' or 'How can I know what others call "pain"?' The very questions imply that I have some special access to my own meanings for these words. These are the questions, then, that we must now directly confront.

## II

In my introductory remarks I quoted the following lines from W. T. Stace: 'Your colour red, instead of being similar to mine, may possibly resemble what I should call toothache. That we speak familiarly of our sensations proves nothing to the contrary.' Here we find Stace prepared to say that even if we use 'red' and 'toothache' in speaking to one another, still what we mean by them is essentially private: only I can know what I call 'toothache'. It evidently makes no impression on Stace that a person who has a toothache may occasionally wince or even cry out in evident distress and that, if the toothache is severe, he will do what he can to relieve the pain. If we do notice this, however, Stace's remarks become singularly odd. For he seems to be thinking that there could be nothing in what a person says that shows whether he is speaking of a colour or a pain, and yet if someone says, 'This toothache is getting worse; I'll need some codeine', or if someone excuses himself from a party, saying, 'I'm sorry to have to leave early, but I have a terrible toothache', how could either of these be a remark about a colour? If Stace were right, then whatever a person says using the word 'red' would still make sense if that word were everywhere replaced by 'toothache'. But if I say, 'I have decided to paint the door red, so I'll need a quart of red paint', this would surely no longer make sense if 'red' were replaced by 'toothache' – unless, of course, we think of a context in which someone is given to coining fanciful names for colours, in which case it will no longer serve Stace's purpose. (If someone regularly uses 'toothache' as the fanciful name for a colour, saying things like 'Man, that's a toothache necktie!' and 'I painted three walls black and the fourth I painted Chinese toothache', I am surely going to recognize that he is speaking of a colour and not a pain in his jaw.)

It would seem, then, that somewhere Stace has gone wrong. But where? The answer, pretty clearly, is that Stace is not think-ing of these words as being essentially connected with human activities, as playing very different roles in different language-games. For Stace, the paradigm use of 'red' would be illustrated by that sentence so frequently encountered in the philosophical writings of a few years back : 'Here now red'. He is thinking, in other words, that the very same thing that one person 'reports' or 'describes' with the words 'Here now red' may be what another person 'reports' or 'describes' in the words 'Here now toothache', and if this is the only sort of thing that they do with these words, then there is no way for them to discover that what one calls 'red' the other calls 'toothache'.

It might now occur to someone that Stace has simply chosen his examples badly, that he could have made his point successfully if he had left out the word 'red' and stuck to bodily sensations. Let us consider this.

If I have been reading a book to one of my children, I could understandably excuse myself from reading further by explaining that I had a headache, but it would not be understandable, or at least not in the same way, if I said that I had to stop reading because of a numbness in my foot. Of course, numbness might be a sign of something else (a thrombosis, say) that requires attention, and in that case mention of the numbness would, in an indirect way, provide an excuse; but then the significance of the numbness has to be explained in a way that a headache does not. On the other hand, my saying that my foot had gone numb would readily explain my walking a bit oddly after getting up from a chair, whereas my saying that my nose itched wouldn't explain such a thing at all. Again, I might warn someone, saying, 'Hold on to something when you stand up, because you may get dizzy,' but it would not make any obvious sense to someone if I said to him, 'Hold on to something when you stand up, because your scalp may tingle.' Or again, my request to someone to scratch my back could be explained by my saying that my wool sweater had made my back itch, but not by my saying I had a toothache – or even a backache. And whereas someone might tell a young actress that she will get over her 'butterflies' once she is accustomed to performing on stage, no one could tell a child that he will stop getting hurt once he is accustomed to spraining his ankle or hitting his thumb with the hammer. A doctor may reassure a child about a vaccination by saying, 'It won't hurt; it will only itch', but it would hardly be reassurance to be told, 'It won't itch; it will hurt'. And people can be threatened with pain in a way they can't be with tickling. We describe pains as sharp, stabbing, and throbbing, but these won't do as descriptions of itching or chills. And whereas we exclaim 'Ouch, that hurts!' there is no exclaiming 'Ouch, that tickles!' Finally, we understand someone who complains of an annoying tickle in his throat, but we could make no sense of someone's saying, 'My throat is dizzy', and whereas we can sympathize with someone who says he has a sharp pain in his shoulder, we could only wonder at someone who said he had a wave of nausea in his shoulder.

What these remarks can remind us of is that words such as 'headache', 'tingle', 'dizzy', 'itch' play significantly different roles in excuses, warnings, explanations, and so on. It was this sort of point that Wittgenstein was making when he wrote :

The concept of pain is characterized by its particular function in our life.

Pain has *this* position in our life; has these connexions. (That is to say : we only call 'pain' what has *this* position, *these* connexions.[15]

What we do about and because of pain is quite different from what we do about and because of dizziness or tickling, and our uses of these words differ accordingly. It is this that we have lost sight of if we think that what I mean by 'pain' may be what others mean by 'tickling'. Indeed, I have already gone wrong if I think that there is such a thing as what *I* mean by these words. They are words of a common language. As Wittgenstein remarks, 'You learned the *concept* pain when you learned language' (384).

This brings us back to the point which, earlier, I said was the crux of the problem : our ideas about how we learn these words, how they get a meaning. In the lectures that I referred to above, Schlick gives this account : 'A definition gives the meaning of a term by means of other words, these can again be defined by means of still other words, and so on, until we arrive at terms that no longer admit of a verbal definition – the meaning of these must be given by direct acquaintance : one can learn the meaning of the words "joy" or "green" only by being joyful or by seeing green.'[16] Russell, too, had something like this in mind when he wrote :

> Let us begin with 'meaning', and let us take the word 'hot' for the purposes of illustration. I shall suppose a schematic simplicity in the experiences by means of which I learnt the meaning of the word in childhood : there was an open fire in my nursery, and every time I went near it someone said 'hot'; that they used the same word when I perspired on a summer's day, and when, accidentally, I spilled scalding tea over myself. The result was that I uttered the word 'hot' whenever I noticed sensations of a certain kind.[17]

[15] *Zettel* (Oxford, 1967), Sections 532 and 533.
[16] 'Form and Content', op. cit., p. 194.
[17] *An Inquiry into Meaning and Truth* (London, 1940), p. 157.

We also find Russell explaining that 'a child understands the heard word "red" when an association has been established between the heard word and the colour red; he has mastered the spoken word "red" if, when he notices something red, he is able to say "red" and has an impulse to do so.'[18]

Now what are we to think of such an account? It is intended to be a philosophically instructive account of how we acquire our mother tongue and begin to talk. But is it? Wittgenstein writes: 'If you trained someone to emit a particular sound at the sight of something red, and another at the sight of something yellow, and so on for other colours, still he would not yet be describing objects by their colours' (p. 187). Let us consider this in detail.

I will suppose that I have a bank of coloured lights that I can switch on and off. In front of these lights I line up a number of children who have not yet learned any colour words, and as I turn the coloured lights on and off I pronounce the words 'red', 'green', etc. always pronouncing the same word for the same colour. Can I in this way teach them the names of colours? Well, there may be some difficulty here in getting them to pay attention, getting them to 'notice the colours', but let us for the moment overlook this difficulty and suppose that somehow, by means of encouragement and by rewarding them with sweets, I manage eventually to get the children to say the right word each time. That is, without my first having to pronounce it for them, they say 'red' when I turn on the red light, 'green' when I turn on the green light, and so on. Now surely what I have done here is to teach them the names of colours. Or have I?

To answer this question, let us change the example slightly. Suppose that instead of pronouncing an English word each time that I turn on a coloured light, I sing a note of a diatonic scale. There are eight lights, and I correlate each one with a note in the octave, singing 'do', 're', 'me', etc. The training here proceeds as before, with the children imitating me and being rewarded with sweets. Soon they are all well trained, and I can get them to sing the scale and even simple tunes by switching the lights on and off in the appropriate order.

[18] ibid., p. 29.

Now what have the children in this example learned? Here I am not so tempted to say that they have learned the names of colours. But how does this case differ importantly from the first one? Surely it is not a relevant difference that 'do', 're', 'me', and so on are not the names of colours in English, for they might be in some other language. Nor is it especially relevant that the children learn to sing these at certain tonal intervals. After all, some cultures have whistle languages, so why should there not be names of colours sung at intervals? The one relevant difference, then, seems to be the use to which this training was put : by using the lights as signals, I get the children to sing simple tunes in unison. Here we have a recognizable activity that we are not tempted to identify with the use of colour words.

In the light of this let us reconsider our first example. No mention was made there of the use to which the training was put. Let us suppose, then, that having trained the children to pronounce 'red', 'blue', etc. on cue, I now use this training to get them to chant word salads. That is, by switching the lights on and off in various sequences, I get them to produce chants, for example, 'red, green, blue, green, red, green, yellow, green, blue, blue, red, green, blue'. Let us also suppose that these chants are part of a formal ceremony performed in our culture, that we regard 'red', 'green', 'blue', etc. as sacred sounds, to be pronounced only in these chants and only by those who have learned them in their years of innocence; and let us finally suppose that later on, in other more usual ways, we teach them other words as the names of colours. Now with all of this detail added to our original example, it should be perfectly clear that we had no right to suppose, on the basis of the little that was said there, that the children were being taught the names of colours. Moreover, we cannot even begin to say what, if anything, they have learned if our description stops, as Russell's does, at the point at which the children have merely made an 'association'. And it is worth adding that it would have made no difference if the 'association' had been extended to coloured flash cards and coloured handkerchiefs. Adding this to the description still does not make it add up to a description of children learning colour words.

59

To complete the picture, let us consider how the training described above differs from the way in which we actually learn colour words. Most obvious is the fact that in my imagined case the activity which the training leads to, the performing of ritual chants, is not an activity in which the colour words play a part. I mean that this activity is not like the activities of using crayons to colour a picture, sorting objects by their colour, choosing an object for the sake of its colour, or like any of the other activities in which children take a spontaneous interest in colours. It is in connexion with activities of this latter sort that children learn colour words and begin to talk about the colours of things. Hence, if we are to describe a case in which it is colour words (none other) that are learned, what is essential is that we describe it as a case in which, as part of such activities, people *say* things to one another, for example, 'I'll colour the barn red', 'Paint the sky blue', 'Would you like a green sucker?', 'Bring the red ball', 'If you mix blue and yellow, you'll get green', 'You can't paint over purple with yellow', 'Use a bright colour here – perhaps orange', 'Those trees only look blue; there's a haze in the air', 'That tomato isn't ripe enough – it's not red yet', and so on. It is only by reminding ourselves of the actual use of colour words that we can begin to see why the children in my story who learned to chant were not speaking of colours. If we are to give a description that is supposed to show that someone has learned colour words, then it is not enough that there be some pairing ('association') of 'words' with coloured lights or with the colours of other objects, for if that is the extent of the description we give, then the 'words' may yet be nonsense syllables like 'do', 're', 'me'. And most important of all, it is essential that we imagine activities in which children would have a spontaneous interest in colours, so that we can imagine them having something to say, for we will have succeeded in describing a use of language only if we have included 'language-games' such as asking questions, giving instructions, making recommendations, pointing out mistakes, making requests, and so on. Now it is just this that is missing from Russell's account of learning (the word?) 'hot'. His account tells us neither what anyone did nor what anyone said; there was just a parrot-like repetition of 'hot'. Although he tells us that he spilled tea over himself and that someone said 'hot', he does not tell us that any concern was shown for him, that there was an expression of sympathy, that his burns were treated, that he was cautioned in the future about the tea or the soup that was served to him, nor even that the spilled tea made him cry. And again, when he speaks of going near the fire and hearing 'hot', he doesn't speak of anyone holding him back, of anyone saying 'Don't get near the fire; it's hot', or of his later asking apprehensively about other objects, 'Is it hot?' Now the fact that Russell makes no mention of such matters, that he gives no indication that he even grew up among people who talked, should leave us thoroughly puzzled about what, if anything, he had learned when he finally came to say 'hot' on certain occasions.[19] For all that his description tells us, he may have simply picked up an oath that was occasionally hurled at him.

How did Russell – and how do the rest of us – fall into giving the kind of account he did? Perhaps it is because we think of examples in which adults learn new words, as when someone tells me the name of an odd shade of colour. What happens in such a case is perhaps that I ask, 'What is that colour called?' and someone answers 'Mauve' or 'That's puce'. Now it is tempting to think that all that happens here is that a colour and its name are brought together and that this conjunction is somehow registered in me. But how? It is here that we are inclined to bring in the word 'association', and we tend to think of this as if the mind had some peculiar faculty for focusing on and picking out the colour (as opposed to the object or its shape or its texture) and for holding in conjunction the colour or its image and the name. But if we think of the case in this way, postulating some peculiar mental faculty, it is because we are disregarding the fact that, being an adult, I am already familiar with the use of colour words and that in the case in question I have for some reason taken an

---

[19] Remarking on a similar example of his own, Wittgenstein writes: 'What seemed to be a definition didn't play the role of a definition at all . . . and all that remains of our private language game is therefore that sometimes without any particular reason I write the word "red" in my diary.' ('Notes', p. 291.)

interest in the colour or had it called to my attention. That I should be able thus to take an interest in a colour or have it called to my attention and to ask its name is owing to the fact that I have already learned colour words in the way described above, i.e. in connexion with such activities as painting, colouring, sorting, arranging, choosing things for their colour, and so on where there is something to talk about, something to say or ask. One forgets, says Wittgenstein, 'that a great deal of stage-setting in the language is presupposed if the mere act of naming is to make sense' (257). When we are trying to think about what is involved in learning a word, we think of cases in which adults learn a new word and then, in asking about what happens in such cases, we think only of what is happening at the time the word is learned, not of the surroundings, whose bearing on the case is certainly not easily described. But when we neglect these surroundings and try to condense their function into some peculiar mental faculty which can pick out and focus on a colour or sensation or whatever and attach a label to it, we buy a great deal of philosophical trouble, for it is here that we invent philosophical notions of meaning or rules or concepts on ideas. That is, these notions are brought in just because we think that what needs accounting for is a mind learning words rather than a child starting to talk. One result of this is that we think of the learning involved as requiring recognition and hence memory. We can see this in the following passage from Locke's *Essay* :

> When children have by repeated sensations got ideas fixed in their memories, they begin by degrees to learn the use of signs. And when they have got the skill to apply the organs of speech to the framing of articulate sounds, they begin to make use of words to signify their ideas to others. These verbal signs they sometimes borrow from others, and sometimes make themselves. . . .[20]

What we find here is that Locke has removed language from the scene of human activities and located its source in the mind, where ideas get fixed in our memories. Now it is this picture of

[20] John Locke, *An Essay Concerning Human Understanding*, II, xi, 8.

language when applied in particular to sensation words that is
under discussion in those remarks of Wittgenstein's that have
occasioned most disagreement on the subject of 'private language'.
I refer to his remarks about the incoherence of the idea that the
private use of words depends on memory (258) or private rules
(259). Let us now turn to that discussion.

### III

Wittgenstein's discussion of this point is meant to sharply juxtapose
two very different ways of thinking about sensation words : on the
one hand, that familiar idea which was illustrated above by the
quotation from Stace, that no one can know what another means
by 'toothache' or 'tickle', and on the other hand, the alternative
to this which Wittgenstein himself sets before us. The latter consists of his (admittedly sketchy) reminder that 'words are connected with the primitive, the natural, expressions of the sensation and used in their place. A child has hurt himself and he
cries; and then adults talk to him and teach him exclamations
and, later, sentences' (244). The other is identified simply as 'the
abrogation of the normal language-game with the expression of a
sensation' (288). But by now we can recognize what this difference
is. It is the difference between human beings who talk, who *say*
things, and disembodied beings, minds, who, by getting ideas
fixed in their memories, 'associate' words with sensations.[21] That
is, we are to contrast that 'form of life' in which there is a place
for exclaiming ('Ouch, that hurt!'), reproaching ('Be careful, that
hurt!'), asking apprehensive questions ('Will it hurt?'), complain-
ing, comforting, diagnosing, and so on, with the supposed use of
words by a being of some sort who, although 'endowed with no
natural expression of sensation', nevertheless 'associate[s] names
with sensations and use[s] these names in descriptions' (256).
(These 'descriptions', as we have already seen in connexion with
Stace's remark, must be something like 'Here now pain', 'Here

[21] When Wittgenstein speaks of 'rules' here (259), he does not, I assume,
intend that we should think of something that could be written down, as the
rules of chess can be; the notion of a rule here is just what Locke is thinking of when he speaks of ideas, whatever that is, cf. Sec. 139.

now dizziness', etc.) Now what does Wittgenstein say about these two very different cases?

Trying to think himself into the position of the disembodied author of the imagined diary, he allows that he wants to 'keep a diary about the recurrence of a certain sensation'. This, of course, is already allowing too much; unless he could speak and use certain words, he could hardly be supposed to form an intention to keep such a diary. But never mind; let us see what sort of description can now be given of what this disembodied author does. What he does, we are told, is to associate the sign 'E' with a certain sensation. And how is that done? The author tells us: 'I speak, or write the sign down, and at the same time I concentrate my attention on the sensation – and so, as it were, point to it inwardly.' And now come the decisive comments:

> But what is this ceremony for? for that is all it seems to be! A definition surely serves to establish the meaning of a sign. – Well, that is done precisely by the concentrating of my attention; for in this way I impress on myself the connexion between the sign and the sensation. – But 'I impress it on myself' can only mean: this process brings it about that I remember the connexion *right* in the future. But in the present case I have no criterion of correctness. One would like to say: whatever is going to seem right to me is right. And that only means that here we can't talk about 'right' (258).

Now if this were meant to be an argument, it would be an extremely odd one. For not only does Wittgenstein here allow the one who keeps the diary to *use* the word 'sensation', but he even allows him, at the beginning of the passage, to use the phrase 'the recurrence of a certain sensation'. But if all of this is *granted* to the author of the diary, then surely no argument could *dis*allow his coining a word for noting down the recurrence of a sensation. As an argument, this passage plainly concedes too much. But is it an argument? Surely we are meant to read it only as the sort of dialogue that a philosopher is likely to have with himself at a certain stage of thinking about the whole puzzle concerning the use of sensation words. And what we are meant to recognize in this dialogue is the way in which the philosophical notion of 'association' begs all the questions without solving any of the problems. I remarked at the end of the preceding section that that notion of 'association' which comes into philosophical accounts of learning words is the notion of a peculiar mental faculty which can somehow pick out and focus on some particular kind of thing, say a colour or a sensation, and then hold it together with a word. And I also remarked that this results from trying to concentrate into a mental capacity that which is, in reality, the function of what Wittgenstein calls 'the stage-setting in the language'. Now it is just this notion of association that is at work in the above bit of philosophical dialogue. That is, here we have a philosopher, Wittgenstein himself, for whom all the stage-setting does exist, trying to operate with this notion of association, and *inevitably* that which only the stage-setting, i.e. a human childhood etc. could provide, namely, the mastery of the words of the dialogue itself, gets admitted illicitly into the story. In this way, as I said, the philosophical notion of association begs all the questions, for as Wittgenstein remarks, the word 'sensation' is 'a word of our common language, not of one intelligible to me alone. . . . So in the end when one is doing philosophy one gets to the point where one would like just to emit an inarticulate sound' (261).

However, not only have all the questions been begged, none of the problems have been solved either. For if we take seriously the supposition that this is a disembodied being whose 'words' or 'signs' play no role in any language-games, and then ask ourselves how this notion of association is supposed to account for whatever he is supposed to do with these signs, we really find ourselves in difficulties. For on the one hand, we want to speak of memory here, as Locke does, for this seems to be the only way of saying that there is not just something random here but a real association of word and object, and yet, on second thought, what difference could there be between a completely private randomness and a completely private 'memory'? That is, given the supposition that this is a disembodied being who neither does nor seems to participate in any form of life, there could *per hypothesis* be nothing whatsoever that differs between a supposed case in which he remembers and a supposed case in which he is mistaken. It rather looks as though Locke thought that there just is this faculty called 'memory', so that whatever is 'fixed in the memory' *could not* be mistaken. But this only raises the question of how it is to be decided what is 'fixed in the memory', so the idea of an infallible faculty of memory accomplishes nothing here. The issue here does not turn on any notion of verifiability, for we have not yet managed to describe the author of our diary in such a way that we could think of him as having any words at all, and so we haven't managed to attribute to him anything about which we could ask 'Is it verifiable?' The problem, rather, is one of trying to describe a faculty of memory or association in complete independence of any human – or human-like – activities. And what we soon discover is that we do not know what we are doing when we try to do this. After all, the metaphysical vacuum in which we have placed the author of the imagined diary is nothing like, for example, the classroom in which a teacher gets to know who his students are by associating the names on his class roster with the students who answer the roll call. In the latter case remembering and forgetting and mistaking one student for another make a difference in the lives of these people, in what they are doing, so that there is a point to remarks like 'I've forgotten your name' and 'Now I remember'; but in the case of our disembodied author nothing could make such a difference, and so in our attempt to endow him with memory we cannot even get a foothold.

Wittgenstein's actual remarks on this matter in the passage quoted above appear to be directed at a particular aspect of Schlick's solution to the problem of other minds. The interesting thing about Schlick's position is that although he is in some sense a dualist, he seeks to avoid the problems of dualism by also embracing a form of logical behaviourism. That is, he allows, on the one hand, that there are private mental contents, but on the other hand he proposes to analyse propositions in such a way that no words refer to these private entities.

In defending this view, Schlick finds it necessary to offer an account of first-person statements that renders them suitably behaviouristic. He is concerned, in particular, with statements like 'This is the same colour again', for since Schlick sees nothing wrong with the traditional causal theory of perception, such a statement seems to be one that refers to a private, immediately given sense quality. In order to maintain his behaviourism Schlick wants to avoid this conclusion, and his way of doing this is what Wittgenstein seems to have taken particular notice of. I will now try to summarize the relevant points.

In order to understand Schlick's position, it is essential to recognize that he, like Locke, thinks that the use of a word depends on memory or recognition. He writes: 'In order to give a name to the colour I am seeing I have to go beyond the immediacy of pure intuition [of the colour], I have to think, be it ever so little. I have to recognize the colour as that particular one I was taught to call "blue". This involves an act of comparison or association. . . .'[22] Now the problem for Schlick is how to reconcile this with a behaviouristic analysis of first-person statements, for it would seem off hand that if the use of a colour word depends on recognition, and if what is recognized is a private, mental quality, then the colour word must *refer* to that private, mental quality. To avoid this consequence, Schlick proceeds to give an analysis of what it means to speak of recognition or memory here. His account begins as follows:

> When I keep in mind the colour of a green object, and to-morrow I am shown another object and am asked whether it has the 'same' colour as the first one, my memory will give a more or less definite answer to the question. The question has a good meaning, of course, but can it be said to refer to 'same-ness of content'? Most certainly not! This follows from the way in which the answer given by memory is tested. For in a certain sense we must admit that our memory may 'deceive' us. When do we say that it has done so? If there are methods of testing its judgment, and if all these methods fail to verify

---

[22] 'Form and Content', op. cit., 195.

it. Such methods are : 1) looking again at the object in question and taking into account, on empirical grounds, the probability of its colour having changed in the meantime; 2) comparing my present judgment with a description I wrote down during the first observation; 3) comparing it with the description given by other people.[23]

Schlick goes on to say that 'the criterion of the truth of the judgment [that it is the same colour again] is the agreement of all these different propositions; and if we say that the colour is truly the same, that my memory has not deceived me, we mean nothing but that there is this formal agreement between the descriptions based on memory and on observation.'[24] The conclusion he wants to draw from this is that the meaning of the statement 'This is the same colour again' does not include a reference to a private, ineffable quality – or, as he puts it, the statement does not 'refer to sameness of content'. This, then, is his behaviouristic analysis of a case in which the colour is that of an external object and memory can be tested in the ways he enumerates.

However, Schlick goes on to consider another sort of case, namely, 'a case in which there [is] nothing else with which the judgment of our memory could be compared.' He does not tell us what sort of case this might be, but his discussion suggests that he may have been thinking of a case in which someone has an image and says 'I have a green image.' In such a case, he wants to say, the memory or recognition on which the use of 'green' depends cannot be tested by various observations, and this precludes his analysing the statement itself in the way that he analysed the statement in the previous case, i.e. as meaning nothing but an agreement of several descriptions. But with that analysis of memory thus excluded, it would seem that Schlick must acknowledge that the recognition involved here is a recognition of the private mental 'content' and that therefore this example refutes his behaviouristic solution to the problem of other minds. To avoid this conclusion he needs to show that the recognition involved in the image case is not really a recognition of

[23] ibid., pp. 178–9.
[24] ibid., p. 179.

'content', i.e. of the privately given quality. He argues for this in the following way :

> If we knew of a case in which there were nothing else with which the judgment of our memory could be compared, we should in this case have to declare it impossible to distinguish between a trustworthy and a deceptive memory; we therefore could not even raise the question whether it was deceptive or not : there would be no sense in speaking of an 'error' of our memory. It follows that a philosopher would be uttering a meaningless question if he were to ask : 'Is it not possible that the colour I am seeing now seems to me to be green, while actually it is red?' The sentence 'I am seeing green' means nothing but 'there is a colour which I remember has always been called green.' This recollection, this datum of my memory, is the one and only criterion of the truth of my statement. I recall it so, and that is final; in our supposed case I cannot go on asking : do I remember correctly? for I could not possibly explain what I meant by such a question.[25]

It is not easy to see how this gets Schlick around the difficulty he is trying to avoid. Perhaps what he means to say here is that in the image case there really is no recognition, properly so called, and hence no recognition of a private mental content. This would seem to be the point of the final sentence of the above quotation, where he says that in the case in question we cannot ask 'Do I remember correctly?' It is at least clear that Schlick, thinking that the use of a word must depend on memory, finds himself acknowledging that in the present case it is 'impossible to distinguish between a trustworthy and a deceptive memory', so that there is only an untestable memory 'datum' that serves as the 'criterion' for the use of the word 'green'. In other words, in attempting to preserve the idea that the use of a word depends on recognition, he has to settle for saying that in the image case 'green' just means 'what I seem to remember as the colour called "green".'

Now it is clear that Wittgenstein not only rejects this conclusion

[25] ibid.

to which Schlick has been driven but also rejects the starting point which drives him there. That is, he rejects the idea, shared by Locke and Schlick, that the use of a word depends on recognition as a criterion or justification. In response to the question 'How do I know that this colour is red?' (381), he rejects the suggestion that one recognizes the colour (378–80) and then dismisses the question itself by saying 'It would be an answer to say "I have learnt English".' 'To use a word without a justification', says Wittgenstein, 'does not mean to use it without right' (289).[26] Addressing himself to the particular case Schlick discusses, he writes: 'What is the criterion for the redness of an image? . . . For myself, when it is my image: nothing' (377). But why does Wittgenstein reject that view? One of his reasons can be seen from those lines quoted above from Sec. 258, where he is, in effect, pointing out the untenability of Schlick's position. Notice, first, that the account that Schlick gives of the rather special use of 'green' in describing one's own image is the account that he would have to give of all first-person uses of words like 'pain', 'tickle', 'dizzy', and so on. Now since Schlick has insisted that his own theory of language is compatible with the supposition that he alone exists and that his notebook is 'a mere dream' (see footnote 11 above), we can think of the dialogue in 258 as a dialogue with Schlick. The dialogue, then, proceeds in three steps. First it is pointed out that on Schlick's view giving oneself a private ostensive definition of the sign 'E' would have to mean that one could bring it about that one would remember the connexion *right* in the future.[27] Secondly, it is pointed out that in the case

---

[26] Wittgenstein had already made this point in *The Blue and Brown Books*, where he wrote: 'When someone asks me "What colour is the book over there?" and I say "Red", and then he asks "What made you call this colour 'red'?", I shall in most cases have to say: "Nothing *makes* me call it red; that is, *no reason*. I just looked at it and said, 'It's red'." ' (p. 148; see also p. 3.)

[27] Schlick himself remarks: 'The marks in [the notebook], whether "real" or "imagined" (whatever that may mean) do express something either correctly or incorrectly' (op. cit., p. 178). By 'correctly' he means remembered, and by 'incorrectly' he means that his memory has deceived him, and in both cases he means that the memory 'datum' can be tested. Hence, in the image case, where the memory cannot be tested, Schlick is not entitled to talk of the word being either 'correct' or 'incorrect'.

of the disembodied author of the diary Schlick's memory criterion comes to this : whatever is going to seem right is right. And finally, Wittgenstein observes : 'And that only means that here we can't talks about "right" '. This last step is just a way of pointing out that, in the passage quoted above, Schlick makes a mistake when he says merely 'there would be no sense in speaking of an "error" of our memory'. He ought to have added: 'And one cannot speak of correctness here either.' But this means that Schlick ought to admit that in the case of words like 'pain' and 'tickle' no sense can be made of his idea that the use of words requires memory as a criterion.

To drive home his point, Wittgenstein drops the case of the disembodied being and asks us to consider the case of a man ('einem Menschen') 'Whose memory could not retain what the word "pain" meant – so that he constantly called different things by that name – but nevertheless used the word in a way fitting in with the usual indications and prerequisites of pain.' 'Here', says Wittgenstein, 'I should like to say : a wheel that can be turned though nothing else moves with it, is not part of the mechanism' (271). That is, if like Schlick, we think that the use of the word 'pain' depends on memory and also think of memory as a mere 'datum' which determines nothing, then when we try to apply this picture to a real human being, we find it to be utterly unusable.

This leaves us with the question of what Wittgenstein proposes to put in place of an account like that shared by Locke and Schlick. His answer is this : 'What I do is not, of course, to iden-tify my sensation by criteria : but to repeat an expression. But this is not the *end* of the language-game : it is the beginning' (290). To understand this it is important to bear in mind that this account is meant to contrast with the diary case, where we had assumed 'the abrogation of the normal language-game with the expression of a sensation' (288). So Wittgenstein's point about merely repeating an expression is a reminder about the normal language-game and comes to something like this : If we take notice of the fact that before a child uses the word 'pain' – before he ever says, for example, 'I have a pain in my side' – there is a complicated history in which, at first, he does nothing more than wail and that later on, after a good deal of baby talk passes between mother and child ('don't cry; Mamma kiss the owie', 'Ouch! did you bump your head?' and so on) he begins to cry 'Owie, owie' and to exclaim 'Ouch!'; and that later, after a variety of other episodes in which his parents talk to him (for example, he pinches his finger despite a warning and his father says, 'That hurt, didn't it?') his exclamations become 'Ouch! That hurt!' – if, then, we take notice of all of this, we shall no longer be inclined to think that when he uses 'hurt', for example, he has to *recognize* something and that without a criterion he might pick out the wrong something. After all, who is going to think that after the exclamation 'Ouch!' there might follow the words 'That tickled' or that someone might exclaim 'Ouch! I'm dizzy'? Just as no recognition or criterion is required in order to say 'Ouch!' so none is necessary for adding 'That hurt!' or for explaining one's exclamation by saying 'I've got a pain in my side'. It is in this sense, then, that words for sensations are tied up with the natural expressions of sensation (256). And it is from this initial connexion that there develops the further use of such words as 'pain', 'headache', in various warnings, excuses, threats, and so on.

Once this is recognized, we can no longer think that perhaps people don't all mean the same thing by 'pain' and 'tickle' and 'dizzy'. For that seemed to make sense just because we thought we could use language 'to get between pain and its expression' (245). But if this is no longer plausible, then the idea of a private language has been dissolved.

# 4

# WITTGENSTEIN ON PSYCHOANALYSIS

CHARLES HANLY

The attitudes of many contemporary philosophers to psychoanalysis has been characterized by a dichotomy with a positive
and negative side. On one side of the dichotomy lies psychoanalytic theory; on the other side of the dichotomy lies psychoanalytic insight and therapy. The attitude towards psychoanalytic
theory has been largely antagonistic. The attitude towards psychoanalytic empirical phenomenology and theory has been more
often positive. This dichotomy is to be found in Ryle's *Concept of
Mind*,[1] and in a more explicit systematic form in MacIntyre's *The
Unconscious*.[2] In one respect the attitude is altogether appropriate, since it differentiates clinical observation and therapy
about which philosophers have no expertise from psychoanalytic
theory about which philosophers may claim expertise arising out
of their investigations into the logic and epistemology of theories
generally. Nevertheless, two questions must be raised : can a sound
examination of psychoanalytic theory be carried out in the
absence of clinical experience? Is the positive attitude toward the
descriptive (case studies) and therapeutic components of psychoanalysis a superficial one which rests on a more fundamental negative attitude which then animates and influences the philosophical
critique of psycholanalytic theory? The purpose of this paper is
to explore these questions by means of an investigation of Wittgenstein's understanding of psychoanalysis. In turning to Wittgenstein, one turns to the source of, perhaps, the major ideological
influence upon the contemporary philosophical critique of psychoanalytic theory.[3]

[1] G. Ryle, *The Concept of Mind*, London, 1949.
[2] A. C. MacIntyre, *The Unconscious*, London, 1958.
[3] It should be pointed out that there is also a significant and growing body
of philosophical work which does not fall under this description. Among the
philosophers who are contributing to a more constructive approach are
Lewis Feuer, John Hospers, Morris Lazerowitz, and J. O. Wisdom.

The principle sources for Wittgenstein's understanding of psychoanalysis are the *Lectures and Conversations*,[4] Moore's report on Wittgenstein's lectures,[5] and Malcolm's biographical memoir.[6]

It may be thought that they are not an adequate source for his ideas on psychoanalysis. After all they are only reports of what he said in lectures rather than propositions that he wrote down himself for the purpose of publishing his thoughts. Yet there is a special appropriateness about an access to his thought through his lectures. In his later work, Wittgenstein focused attention on the context of communication in which words are used to articulate meaning – on the speaker speaking (the thinker thinking) in a concrete life situation. Lectures are a specific form of publication,[7] if they are, as Wittgenstein's lectures appear to have been, fresh investigations of philosophical problems. Hence, the use of language to teach as distinct from the use of language to construct formal, theoretical papers can have a communcative efficacy of its own. It will have a special importance for anyone interested in understanding Wittgenstein's understanding of psychoanalysis because of the greater likelihood that underlying attitudes will be articulated in it.

Wittgenstein once informed Malcolm that he had been 'greatly impressed' by Freud's work. He went on to caution Malcolm, 'unless you think *very* clearly psychoanalysis is a dangerous and a foul practice, and it's done no end of harm and, comparatively, very little good. (If you think I'm an old spinster – think again!) All this, of course, doesn't detract from Freud's extraordinary scientific achievement.'[8] These sentences state the dichotomy defined above in its reverse form. Freud's scientific achievement is applauded and his therapeutic work is denounced. But the more standard form of the dichotomy is also to be found in statements Wittgenstein made about psychoanalysis. Wittgenstein

[4] C. Barrett ed., *Lectures and Conversations*, Oxford, 1966.
[5] G. E. Moore, 'Wittgenstein's Lectures in 1930–33', *Mird*, LXIV, pp. 1–27.
[6] N. Malcolm, *Ludwig Wittgenstein: A Memoir*, London, 1958.
[7] Wittgenstein so regarded his lectures. Many of his philosophical conversations were also significant philosophical investigations, at least on his side.
[8] *Ludwig Wittgenstein: A Memoir*.

cautioned his pupils that a study of psychoanalysis imposes unusal demands for conceptual clarity on the student because of the way psychoanalytic theory is formulated and he spoke elsewhere of psychoanalytic cures. It is this form of the dichotomy that has been philosophically most influential. It follows, however, that Wittgenstein's attitude to psychoanalysis was inconsistent and subject to reversal. This fact, along with the more expressive language in which Wittgenstein has communicated his attitude indicates that the conceptual dichotomy, at least in Wittgenstein's case, is the intellectual expression of a psychological ambivalence.

What were some of the main elements in Wittgenstein's understanding of psychoanalysis?

1. Wittgenstein believed that the criteria for validating a psychoanalytic explanation (interpretation) are one or other of the following: its acceptance by the patient; its therapeutic efficacy; its agreement with certain rules of experience which when satisfied establish that an explanation is the correct one, independently of its acceptance or rejection by the individual whose behaviour or experience is being interpreted.

2. Wittgenstein was especially struck by Freud's discovery that dreams are meaningful. This fact led Wittgenstein, given his philosophical interest in language and meaning, to view dreams as languages. These two points represent the most important areas of sympathetic understanding in Wittgenstein's grasp of psychoanalysis. Unfortunately, a closer scrutiny of them shows Wittgenstein's understanding to be partial and distorted. The inadequacies in his understanding led him into numerous errors.

Wittgenstein was familiar with the fact that Freud operated with three criteria for validating psychoanalytic interpretations and, hence, indirectly for validating psychoanalytic hypotheses: the acceptance of the interpretation by the analysand; its therapeutic efficacy; its corroboration by subsequent free associations – 'the rule of experience'. However, the concept of therapeutic efficacy is governed by the significance one attaches to the first and, particularly, the third criterion. If acceptance by the analysand and corroboration by free associations are thought to be the products of the persuasions of the analyst, then therapeutic efficacy must also be thought to rest upon suggestion. Although there is no evidence that Wittgenstein ever worked out the logic of the interconnection of these criteria, the evidence that is available indicates that he believed the first and third criteria to be forms of persuasion. Logic requires that the second criterion (therapeutic efficacy) also be understood in terms of the influence of suggestion.

Freud took the view, concerning the first criterion, that the only plausible motive for the acceptance of a psychoanalytic interpretation of his behaviour by someone not in analysis is its truth, because the interpretation will inevitably be felt as something of a blow to the individual's self-esteem. The second criterion only applies to a psychoanalysis. There a perturbative factor does operate as a result of the transference which, as Freud discovered, could produce pseudo-acceptance of psychoanalytic interpretation and pseudo-remission of symptoms. The production of associations that will please the analyst is a symptom of a new formation of the illness (the transference neurosis) and one that can be detected since the 'analyst' who is being pleased is a fantasy of the patient and not the analyst who is carrying out the analysis. This symptom can be subject to analytic interpretation as well as any other.

Because distortions in the process of free association caused by the transference phenomena can be detected and corrected, once the transference is identified as such and dealt with, Freud was able to find the basis needed by psychoanalysis for the validation of interpretations by means of the observation of free associations. In this respect psychoanalysis is more fortunate than the physics of sub-atomic particles for which there is no defence against the intrusions of the observer and no method for determining the nature and extent of the observer's influence.

Wittgenstein did not differentiate in his various comments on verification in psychoanalysis between interpretations out of analysis and interpretations in analysis. But even if he had done so, it is unlikely that he would have reached a better understanding of the problem. He still would have had to penetrate more deeply into the psychodynamics of free association and he may not have been able to do so. Psychological insight was not one of his many intellectual gifts. In addition, Wittgenstein appears to have had a motive for reducing the validation of psychoanalytic interpretation to a form of persuasion to a point of view.

Indeed, Wittgenstein postulated two different explanations as to why people credit psychoanalytic interpretations and theories. According to Wittgenstein there is in people a craving for the uncanny which causes them to be charmed by the idea of unconscious memories, fantasies, thoughts, and impulses giving significance to dreams, parapraxes, and neurotic symptoms; and there is also a craving for the iconoclastic which causes people to be charmed by psychoanalysis because it opposes social taboos and prejudices regarding sexuality. Although these postulated causes may account, in part, for a certain kind of fascination with psychoanalysis among some persons, they cannot account for its scientific interest. In any case, Wittgenstein appears not to have had any empirical evidence for these hypotheses – something that must arouse some doubt about the sources of Wittgenstein's conviction that they could perform the explanatory role assigned to them. Wittgenstein was a severe sceptic about scientific hypotheses, as his attitude to the hypotheses of the evolution of species shows.[9] Somehow, Wittgenstein's own hypotheses by which he sought to explain away the scientific claims of psychoanalysis managed to escape the purview of this scepticism.

As we have seen, Wittgenstein attributed the acceptance of psychoanalytic interpretations in analysis to the suggestive power of the psychoanalyst. Had Wittgenstein pressed this notion a little further he would have realized that it rested on the bizarre idea that Freud's genius consisted of an unlimited capacity for self-persuasion despite which he really had 'discovered phenomena and connexions not previously known.'[10] Apart from its inconsistency the inappropriateness of these ideas is illustrated by a letter Freud once sent to Einstein who had written to Freud that although he had always admired his theories, he had only recently

[9] C. Barrett, op. cit., p. 26.
[10] G. E. Moore, op. cit., p. 15.

come across evidence that convinced him of their truth. Freud wrote in reply:

'Of course I always knew that you "admired" me only out of politeness and believed very little of any of my doctrines although I have often asked myself what indeed there is to be admired in them, if they are not true, i.e. if they do not contain a large measure of truth.'[11]

Wittgenstein's causal explanations of the sources of conviction about the truth of psychoanalysis are themselves testable hypotheses. It is assumed here that empirical investigation would not turn up a more significant correlation between these phenomena than is presented to common observation of people. It would appear that an operative factor in the formation of his opinion about psychoanalytic verification and in the corresponding disturbance of his understanding of it, was a wish to assimilate its methodological procedures to his own.

Wittgenstein believed that Freud was confused throughout his work about the difference between hypothesis formation and 'merely a good way of representing a fact'. Accordingly, he thought that Freud's major contribution was the taxonomy of mental phenomena, 'the enormous field of psychical facts which he arranges'.[12] As a result of so representing psychoanalysis to himself, Wittgenstein was able to assimilate Freud's work to his own in so far as he thought of his own work as an arrangement or synopsis of ideas which enables us to clear up our thinking when it is in a muddle. Wittgenstein said of his method of analysis in philosophy, 'I am in a sense making propaganda for one style of thinking as opposed to another. I am honestly disgusted with the other. Also, I'm trying to state what I think. Nevertheless I'm saying: "For God's sake don't do this".'[13] However, Freud always had a clear grasp of the logical difference between the description and classification of concomitant phenomena and the hypotheses that explain their concomitance. More and better descriptions

---

[11] E. Jones, *The Life and Work of Sigmund Freud*, London, 1961, p. 506.
[12] G. E. Moore, op. cit., p. 20.
[13] C. Barrett, op. cit., p. 28. This point is corroborated by Moore in 'Wittgenstein's Lectures in 1930–33', op. cit., p. 27.

and different arrangements of the descriptions of the facts of hysteria would not have added anything to the understanding of its genesis or the method of its therapy. Evidently, Wittgenstein had a need to simulate the method of psychoanalysis in his own philosophical style. This point is logically connected with Wittgenstein's thinking about dream interpretation which is a crucial test because of the centrality of dream interpretation in psychoanalysis.

To summarize the results of the argument thus far : Wittgenstein was unable to grasp the basis for objectivity in psychoanalytic interpretation and validation; consequently, he saw psychoanalysis as a form of persuasion; as a result, he assimilated psychoanalytic method to his own philosophical method.

Freud's discovery that dreams are meaningful struck Wittgenstein as both true and significant. Two pieces of evidence appear to have imposed this view on the philosopher. His inner experience taught him that dreams often have an enigmatic quality – a promise of a meaning to be disclosed. In this respect, dreams are different from memories which are stimulated into consciousness by the cognitive or emotional demands of waking life.[14] Once, while visiting an art exhibition in Vienna, Wittgenstein saw a picture which he took to be akin to a dream. Subsequently, his sister described the painting to Freud who confirmed that its subject matter and composition contained elements that are frequently found in dreams. Wittgenstein summarized the results of this experience as follows :

You would not say of *every* painting "this is a dream". And this does show that there is something like a dream language.'[15]

But this very general, rather vague recognition that dreams are meaningful was about as far as Wittgenstein was able to proceed towards a comprehension of this aspect of psychoanalysis. He did perceive that dream interpretation is a scientific activity in that the psychoanalyst having been told the content of a dream can formulate hypotheses which will predict what associations

[14] C. Barrett, op. cit., p. 47.
[15] ibid., p. 43.

will occur with various dream elements and which can be tested against the associations that actually occur. Additionally, Wittgenstein may have grasped something of the associative process itself. He spoke of the work of interpretation which the dreamer must do and appears to have had some perception of the importance of memory associations in undoing the dream work and doing the work of interpretation by association.

But even here Wittgenstein's understanding was so seriously limited as to verge on distortion. His statement that the work of interpretation done by the dreamer 'still belongs to the dream itself' is ambiguous. It may mean that the associations in which the meaning of the dream is contained are themselves a part of the dream – the latent or unconscious part. It may also mean that the work of interpretation by the dreamer is itself an extension of the dreaming. The first meaning is compatible with a correct understanding of psychoanalytic dream interpretation; the second is not. The second meaning confuses dream interpretation with secondary revision, i.e. the waking reflection on the dream which is itself an extension of and the final phase of the dream activity and which may include thoughts about its meaning. For example, a young man dreamt that he was standing on a balcony overlooking a square in which angry men were shouting at him and throwing things. After waking he formed the idea, having reflected on the dream, that it referred to his recently acquired maturity associated with graduating from the university – fortitude in the face of difficulties (the angry throng) and a broad perspective on society and the world (his location on the balcony). Anyone but the dreamer would perceive something dubious about the interpretation at once. It is too self-congratulatory. He had placed himself above other men in courage and wisdom. More significantly, the dreamer, when he began the *work* of interpretation by association, produced associations the central theme of which was rivalry and hostility to other males bound up with determined efforts to preserve an infantile relationship to his mother. The menacing figures in the square, represented one or other of these jealous relationships of rivalry. It follows that Wittgenstein's understanding of dream interpretation was ambiguous. Which side of the ambiguity more likely represents his grasp of the subject can be decided by taking into account his view of psychoanalytic validation and its application to dream interpretation. As we have seen Wittgenstein believed psychoanalysis to be a form of persuasion. This notion in turn vitiates his apparent grasp of one of the predictive elements in psychoanalysis, viz. the validation of interpretive hypotheses by predicting the content of associations. Thus Wittgenstein correctly points out :

'There are various criteria for the right interpretation : e.g., (1) What the analyst says or predicts, on the basis of his previous experience; (2) What the dreamer is led to by *freier Einfall*. It would be interesting and important if these two generally coincided.'

But he then goes on to add erroneously :

'But it would be queer to claim (as Freud seems to) that they *must always* coincide.'[16]

To be sure such a claim would be 'queer', but Freud never made such a claim or even seemed to do so. Astonishingly, Wittgenstein himself laid claim to a bizarre capacity for free association which might establish their coincidence if anyone could properly lay claim to such a capacity. He claimed that he spontaneously produced himself the associations to Freud's dreams reported by Freud and, had confirmed Freud's interpretation by arriving 'at the same results as those he reaches in his analysis'.[17] This claim tells us a great deal about the nature of Wittgenstein's understanding of psychoanalysis.

Freud carefully differentiated between symbolic and non-symbolic dream elements. The distinction was an empirical distinction based on the fact that most dream elements have chains of associations bound to them while a few do not. (This phenomenon shows up in the patterns of free associations.) The elements that do not have associations were termed symbols. Their meaning had to be derived by inference from the associations to the non-symbolic elements. These symbolic elements occur repeatedly in

[16] ibid., p. 46.
[17] ibid., p. 50.

dreams of different persons but they vary over time and space according to culture. They are the 'universal' elements in dreams. The non-symbolic elements are individual in nature, arising out of the personal life-experiences of the dreamer. The meanings of these elements are to be found in the memory, fantasy, feeling, and thought associations which arise out of the personal pattern of instinctual development and the vicissitudes in the life experience of the individual. Therefore, it is not possible for one person to reproduce genuinely the associations of another's dream. The prediction of the contents of free association is possible in specific terms only for individuals and not for the species. Hence Wittgenstein's 'thought experiment' must have been a psychologically artificial process guided by inferential thinking – a psychoanalytically spurious form of interpretation, and governed psychologically by a wish to identify with Freud for the purpose of vicariously taking over his discoveries (a kind of unconscious theft).

This notion that he could simulate in himself the work of associative interpretation to which Freud had subjected his own dreams is an adjunct of the idea that psychoanalysis is a form of persuasion. Hence, it tips the scale against assuming that Wittgenstein had a sound understanding of dream interpretation despite the ambiguity of his statement of it.

Furthermore, Wittgenstein understood the way dreams are significant through an analogy with language. This analogy led him to formulate a set of misleading metaphorical arguments designed to show that there are 'many different sorts of dreams, and that there is no single line of explanation for all of them'.[18] If dreams are languages, then since there are many different sorts of language, there are many different sorts of dream. Again, if dreams are games that dreamers play, then since 'there is no one cause or one reason why children always play', there is no one cause or one reason why dreamers dream. Further, if dreams are games, the game of dreaming might be like putting paper figures together to form a story; then some elements in a dream might not be significant because a child playing the game of 'cut-outs' might put in a picture in its entirety, although he only wanted

[18] ibid., p. 47.

part of it and would include the rest 'just because it was there'. Also, if dreaming is like writing stories, then since not all stories are allegorical, are we to say that not all dreams are symbolic or meaningful? Wittgenstein is not clear as to what inference is to be drawn. Finally, if dreaming is like talking, then there is no one reason why people talk. Sometimes children babble and adults talk for the sake of talking.

The point of these metophorical arguments is similar to the point of the doctrine of multiple hypotheses employed by the Epicureans. The purpose is also similar – to combat mythological thinking and the attitude of religious certainty and to promote naturalistic thinking and the attitude of scepticism. Scepticism according to the Epicureans was best promoted by demonstrating that a variety of hypotheses of the same conceptual type (naturalistic) could explain those natural phenomena which had become the focal points of superstitious dread and religious belief – birth, death, famine, earthquakes, eclipses, etc. Wittgenstein believed psychoanalysis to be dangerously mythological and a sceptical attitude towards it could be promoted by advancing arguments in favour of a multiplicity of causes and a corresponding uncertainty of interpretation.

The metaphors themselves are dubious. Normal speech is an ego function. It is reality adapted. Dreaming is an inhibited ego function which reverses the psychic process involved in verbally articulated thought, whether spoken or not. Writing stories was likened by Freud to day-dreaming. Day-dreaming is similar to, but also different from, night dreaming in being more reality adapted (a day-dream 'takes off' from one's real life situation and is more influenced by the aims of the ego). Consequently, story writing which involves a further adaptation of psychic to natural and social reality will often contain adventitious material and conjuctions of events just as the world does, but it does not follow that the same is true of dream formation. The evidence is to the contrary – in dreams nothing is adventitious. The same will also be true of the play of children when the play requires the use of instruments and materials that resist perfect reduction to the game's rules and to the child's intent in playing the game.

When this constraint is not present it is surprising how children will invent games and carry them out in a rigorously expressive way. I once observed three boys, ages three to four, from different families in my neighbourhood, all of whom had in common that a new baby had arrived in his family. They had spontaneously come together to play 'baby-saving'. A step leading to a patio was converted into a harbour, the patio itself was a sea and they took turns at being 'captain' and 'crew' of a phantom ship that cruised the sea. On each expedition the 'captain' announced 'Baby overboard!' which was the signal for one of the 'sailors' to dive in to the rescue. The rescue having been effected the 'captain' would return the vessel to port and relinquish his place to another and ready himself for his turn at aquatic heroism. Finally, Wittgenstein could not have been familiar with the mechanisms of displacement in dream work or he would have seen that the composition of 'collages' by children, when they incorporate extraneous material because it goes along with things they want, actually represents something that takes place in dream work and is one of the sources of the confused quality of the manifest dream.

But quite apart from the inadequate psychology behind Wittgenstein's metaphors, the arguments rest on a conceptual confusion. It is necessary to differentiate between the hypotheses that state the type of explanation of a phenomenon and the hypotheses that state the explanations of occurrences of the phenomenon. Freud postulated that dreaming (contrary to earlier medical and folk ideas) is caused psychologically, although organic factors and conditions may also play a part (e.g. auditory, tactile, or kinaesthetic stimuli), and that the dynamic psychological factor is an ungratified wish. Hence, the postulate that describes the type of cause recognizes two types of factor, one organic, the other psychological, and states that the second factor will always be present and is sufficient in itself, without organic factors, to produce a dream. In this sense, Freud's formula postulated a single type of causation for dreams. But also there are as many causes for dreams that people have as there are ungratified wishes. Consequently, Freud's hypotheses that state the explanations of occurrences of dreams state many different causes according to the associations. The question then arises: is there a multiplicity of types of causes? To that question the answer is clear. Psychoanalysis has produced an abundance of evidence to show that each element of a dream will have associations bound to it which will indicate its significance and that dreams are caused by ungratified wishes. Wittgenstein produced only some intrinsically doubtful metaphors and no falsifying observations to support his case.

Wittgenstein's view of validation in psychoanalysis and his misconceptions about psychoanalytic dream theory join at this point. The idea that some counter metaphors could suffice to contradict Freud's theory of dreaming must have appeared plausible to Wittgenstein because he believed that all he had to contend with, on Freud's part, was an equal and opposite metaphor. But before examining in more detail Wittgenstein's notion that psychoanalytic theory is based on a bad metaphor, it is worth considering other specific issues in the psychology of dreams.

Wittgenstein had an imperfect grasp of the crucial difference between the manifest and the latent dream content. He objected to Freud's interpretation of dreams on the ground that it treated the manifest dream as an appearance and the unconscious processes that cause it as the reality. Accordingly, Wittgenstein complained that Freud insisted on finding the 'coarsest sexual' meaning in a beautiful dream in which the dreamer 'descended from a height, saw flowers and shrubs, broke off the branch of a tree, etc'.[19] But psychoanalysis does not deny that the qualities of the manifest dream are other than they appear to be or that they may insert themselves into the on-going conscious life of the individual. Psychoanalysis does show, however, that when this happens a range of more or less serious psychological liabilities may be incurred. For Freud discovered what has been confirmed many times over by practising psychoanalysts, that the manifest dream is only one part of the dream process – in fact, its end product – and that it is a distorted representation of thoughts, images, memories, and impulses that have a different character of

[19] ibid., p. 23.

85

their own. The differentiation between the manifest and latent dream expresses the nature of an intra-psychic conflict. This conflict cannot be understood simply by denying to the manifest dream qualities that it actually possesses. However, the terminology of appearance and reality is appropriate for two reasons, both of which appear to have eluded Wittgenstein : the sentiment and aura of beauty that invests certain dreams may be an artificial defence against very ugly proclivities – it may be a cover-up for an unhealthy sexuality; if so, to co-operate with it is further to deny to the individual any prospect of achieving a healthy sexuality and the authentic beauty of person that is its concomitant. Assuming that the associations establish this conflict, then irrespective of how refined, lofty, and spiritual the manifest dream and connected waking fantasies may be, they are derivative phenomena. Causal efficacy lies with the disordered impulses which will produce hysterical, obsessional, or other symptoms. The analogy which Wittgenstein drew between dreaming and using language by means of which he sought to understand dream formation was not sufficiently apposite to protect him from serious inadequacies of comprehension.

Because Wittgenstein failed to grasp the difference between the manifest and latent dream, it was inevitable that he should perceive Freud's interpretation of dreams as a dangerous and gratuitous attack on the 'higher' – on those things 'whereof one cannot speak' and about which 'one must be silent'. Wittgenstein felt compelled to come to the rescue of beautiful dreams and the innocence of hysterical women. But this compulsion is no more humane in its consequences than the efforts of a misguided person who, wishing to protect a friend from the anxiety of having to face up to a diagnosis of cancer, thereby encourages a delay in treatment until a condition that was initially operable has become terminal. In contrast, Freud's attitude was scientific, therapeutic, and helpful even in the face of painful problems. Wittgenstein's belief that psychoanalysis is a gratuitous attack on 'higher things' was, from the logical point of view, made possible by his being unable to realize that psychoanalytic investigation involves more than, and something quite different from, imposing a certain organization and arrangement of the facts – a *gestalt* which invests the phenomena in question with a certain, observationally un-verifiable, inter-subjective significance.

Given these misconceptions, Wittgenstein was bound to specu-late about a third causal explanation of why people find psycho-analysis credible. It is the very repulsiveness of psychoanalytic interpretations that causes people to accept them : 'it may be the fact that the explanation is extremely repellant that drives you to adopt it'.[20] Here Wittgenstein toys with an idea that was passionately affirmed in a more general form by Plato – a sensual appetite for the repulsive[21] – as the explanation for the acceptance of the analysts' allegedly debasing interpretations.

A further significant misunderstanding arose out of Wittgen-stein's difficulty with dream theory which is linked to his appre-hension about the debasing influence of psychoanalytic interpre-tations. He erroneously attributed to Freud a monistic theory of the instincts. We are to believe that, according to Freud, sexuality is directly or indirectly the cause of all behaviour. The idea that psychoanalysis presupposes a behavioural pan-sexualism is not an original idea. It was held among others by Jung, but is an erroneous view. Psychoanalysis hypothesizes the predominance of sexuality in the formation of hysterical symptoms. But Freud's earliest formulations of the aetiological differentiation between hysterical and obsesssional neurosis stressed the contribution of aggression in the formation of the latter. Sexuality and aggression were in turn differentiated from the ego instincts. Freud's obser-vations taught him that parapraxis and dreams, unlike hysterical symptoms, are not always motivated by sexual wishes. The ideas that sexuality is inevitably inimical to the higher things of life and that it insinuates its influence everywhere are ideas that are generated out of unconscious reactions to Freud's work. These ideas then impose themselves on the interpreters of his writings in much the way that the dream work imposes secondary revision on the dreamer.

Before generalizing the results of this examination of Wittgen-

[20] ibid., p. 24.
[21] Plato, *Republic*, IV, 439–440.

stein's understanding of psychoanalysis, it is worth taking up one more detailed point concerning the psychology of dreams because it illustrates a connexion with Wittgenstein's more technical philosophy. According to Wittgenstein, Freud felt compelled to find a single cause for dreaming which would be the essence of dreaming, hence the theory that dreams are hallucinatory wish-fulfilments. Wittgenstein's counter arguments to show that dreams have many different causes have already been elucidated and examined. He also attacked the notion of an hallucinatory wish-fulfilment. Two arguments are presented : one dealing with dream as wish-fulfilment and the other with its hallucinatory aspect. Wittgenstein cites the usual evidence of anxiety dreams. One cannot be too critical of Wittgenstein on this score, because unanalysed experiences of anxiety dreams to which all people are periodically subject make the evidence, and therefore the argument, appear convincing to many people. Nevertheless, the psychoanalysis of anxiety dreams regularly show their dynamic relationship to unconscious wishes. The evidence of these analyses was available to Wittgenstein. The fact that he preferred the evidence of his own introspection – the surface of his own consciousness – to the results of objective methods of inquiry is unfortunately one of the things that made Wittgenstein a 'true philosopher'.

Concerning the hallucinatory nature of the wish-fulfilment, Wittgenstein made a linguistic-conceptual point based on the following rule for the use of the word 'camouflage' : if the word 'camouflaged' can be appropriately used to describe an activity then the activity in question cannot be said to accomplish its end. Presumably, it will have accomplished some other tangential end. Thus if the effort in sleep to gratify a wish results in a distorted hallucinatory experience which camouflages the wish, the wish cannot be said to be gratified. But the grammatical restriction is surely unnecessarily extreme to the point of being mistaken. One would have thought that camouflage is a useful means of accomplishing certain wished-for ends. If the activity in question is to surround a fortress and take it by surprise, to camouflage the soldiers and 'make Birnam wood come to Dunsinane' is a means of accomplishing rather than frustrating it. Taking medicine in the form of sugar-coated pills is still taking medicine. Dreaming in distorted forms about murdering someone is to fulfil a wish vicariously, to which the subsequent waking depression and guilt bear eloquent testimony. The symptoms of hysteria successfully camouflage the sexual cravings that are released through them. It is doubtful whether the recommended use of "camouflage" would be suitable in non-psychoanalytic contexts. More fundamentally, the logical grammar of language must be adapted so as to express reality and cannot be soundly used to define *a priori* what can and what cannot take place. Language is ontologically neutral. The objectivity of Wittgenstein's persuasions about what can be meaningfully said appears to have been compromised by unstated and no doubt unconscious thoughts about what ought and ought not to be.

Given Wittgenstein's views on these specific issues, it is not surprising that he should have been able to find little difference between psychoanalysis and mythology.

'Freud refers to various ancient myths . . . and claims that his researches have now explained how it came about that anybody should think or propound a myth of that sort. . . . He has not given a scientific explanation of the ancient myth. What he has done is to propound a new myth.'[22]

This statement refers to some hypothesis Freud had advanced to explain the genesis of an ancient myth. However, other statements can be found which indicate that Wittgenstein generalized this view to other elements of the psychoanalytic theory.

'The attractiveness of the suggestion, for instance, that all anxiety is a repetition of the anxiety of the birth trauma, is just the attractiveness of a mythology.' . . .

'Much the same could be said of the notion of an *"Urszene"*. This often has the attractiveness of giving a sort of tragic pattern to one's life. It is all the repetition of the same pattern which was settled long ago. Like a tragic figure carrying out the decrees under which the fates had placed him at birth. Many people have, at some period, serious trouble in their lives – so serious as to

[22] C. Barrett, op. cit., p. 51.

lead to thoughts of suicide. This is likely to appear to one as something nasty, as a situation which is too foul to be a subject of a tragedy. And it may then be an immense relief if it can be shown that one's life has the pattern rather of a tragedy – the tragic working out and repetition of a pattern which was determined by the primal scene.'[23]

However sound Wittgenstein's insight into unstated inadequacies in Freud's hypothesis concerning the explanation of a myth may have been, the form in which he states the criticism and his extension of it to other elements in the psychoanalytic theory rests on an error. Freud did not assert 'that all anxiety is a repetition of the anxiety of the birth trauma'. On the contrary Freud's mature formulation of the psychoanalytic theory of anxiety in 1926 makes it clear that his understanding of anxiety was not the one attributed to him.

'In man and the higher animals it would seem that the act of birth, as the individual's first experience of anxiety, has given the effect of anxiety certain characteristic forms of expression. But, while acknowledging this connexion, we must not lay undue stress on it or overlook the fact that biological necessity demands that a situation of danger should have an affective symbol, so that a symbol of this kind would have to be created in any case. Moreover, I do not think that we are justified in assuming that whenever there is an outbreak of anxiety something like a reproduction of the situation of birth goes on in the mind. It is not even certain whether hysterical attacks, though they were originally traumatic reproductions of this sort, retain that character permanently.'[24]

Again it must be assumed that some cause was operative in Wittgenstein's thinking about psychoanalysis which denied him the privilege of thoroughly understanding it. Perhaps, the cause is hinted at in the references to serious trouble in life leading to thoughts of suicide. But this point will be taken up later.

Wittgenstein believed that the intellectual fabric of this myth-

[23] ibid., p. 51.
[24] S. Freud, 'Inhibition, Symptom and Anxiety', *Standard Edition*, vol. XX, pp. 93–4.

making function of psychoanalysis was the influence of nineteenth-century mechanistic physiology. Wittgenstein claimed, at least, to have no quarrel with Freud's observations – roughly the clinical, descriptive, phenomenological work. He did not believe that these observations provided an empirical basis for a coherent, comprehensive psychodynamic theory of unconscious and conscious mental functioning. Psychoanalytic theory was based on the choice of a mechanical metaphor. Thereafter, the metaphor imposed itself on the organization of the evidence and the formation of the hypothesis. Dream associations came to be viewed as linking mechanisms driven by the force of ungratified wishes according to general laws that must have general application.

It is perfectly true that Freud often chose mechanical metaphors to represent various facets of the relationships among the diverse functions of the human personality that he was gradually uncovering. He also used animistic metaphors. What is at issue are the implications of the choice. Does it imply the adoption of the tenets of nineteenth-century physiology? Does it imply a psychogenetic priorism? Is the statement of such invariance and inevitability in psychological phenomena as is found in psychoanalysis a consequence of the metaphors rather than a consequence of the clinical observations? These are some of the substantive issues.

Freud was schooled in nineteenth-century mechanistic physiology. But he had to abandon at least one of its major tenets in order to formulate psychoanalysis at all. That is to say, he had to postulate the decisive influence of psychogenetic as against physiological factors in the aetiology of the neurosis. At the same time, he was logically obliged to adopt a theoretical language that could describe and explain the facts of mental life in terms of both efficient and final causes. In doing so Freud uncovered the psychological roots in human nature of the identity between motives and causes that is built into ordinary as distinct from some philosophical language. On the other hand, Freud did not postulate that all dream elements, all parapraxies or all neurotic symptoms had to have a psychological significance and, hence, a psychogenisis according to some metaphysical law. Freud, the neurologist, was well aware that brain tumours can cause depression and that disturbances in mental functioning can be caused by organic malfunctioning. These were matters to be investigated. The investigations of the psychogenetic roots of dreams and the neuroses pointed to universal although not absolutely invariant phenomena. This generality of the phenomena was stated in the formulation of the theoretical postulates. Freud did not confuse the metaphors in which he often stated his theory with the theory itself. Metaphorical constructs were used as an aid to communication.[25] The operation of the sexual instinct subject to frustration is very like the pressure of a torrent against an obstacle and it is not like the choice of a word to express a thought. The implacability of unanalysed psychopathology expressed in recurrent patterns of self-destructive or inhibited behaviour demands causal analysis just as much as any natural process. It is appropriately represented in mechanistic metaphors. Neither mental health nor mental disease are chancy, intrinsically nebulous phenomena. They appear to be so only because we believe that they can be known completely by means of introspection and empathy. Thus Freud chose mechanical metaphors not because he was the intellectual victim of a philosophically perverse scientific tradition but because such metaphors were appropriate to the nature of the phenomena.

Because of his view that the theoretical formulations of psychoanalysis were governed by an unsuitable metaphor, Wittgenstein was unable to clearly grasp the most central and important concepts of psychoanalysis – repression and the unconscious. According to Moore, Wittgenstein accused psychoanalysis of misleading us into 'thinking of the difference between a "conscious" and an "unconscious" hatred as like that between a "seen" and an "unseen" chair'.[26] But the sin against philosophy, if such it be, is different from, and greater than, Wittgenstein has supposed. It is not just that people can hate without knowing it; it is rather that people often cannot know that they hate. This difference is

---

[25] S. Freud *Introductory Lectures on Psychoanalysis, Standard Edition,* vol. XVI, pp. 295–7.
[26] G. E. Moore, op. cit., p. 15.

not just the difference between a seen and an unseen chair; it is the difference between a chair that can be seen and is seen and one that cannot be seen because some agency does not want it seen. The dynamic connexion between repression and the unconscious escaped Wittgenstein's conceptualization. Along with it must have gone a refusal to bring under clear scrutiny the realities of intra-psychic conflict in people. Accordingly, Wittgenstein had to reject the idea that anything could be taking place in the mental life of an individual of which he was not aware at the time it was taking place and which could cause him to laugh at a joke, commit a psychological error, dream, or act out a neurotic disorder. This being the case, the crucial psychoanalytic concepts of repression and the unconscious would have to appear to Wittgenstein as mythological in nature. Credence in them would have to be the result of persuasion, not observation.

It is not altogether fair to expect Wittgenstein to have had a clear and thorough grasp of psychoanalysis. Many scientists and humanists do not. In persons unfamiliar with the subject, ignorance is no fault and prejudice against it is tolerable and comprehensible even if not admirable, as simple scepticism would be. But Wittgenstein once saw himself as 'a disciple of Freud' and 'a follower of Freud'. And he took up the subject in his lectures in order to teach his pupils something about psychoanalysis. Consequently, one must be surprised by the obvious lacunae and distortions in his understanding of the subject. Wittgenstein's ideas about psychoanalysis are important to philosophy because of the great and justifiable influence Wittgenstein has had, based on his original contributions to other branches of philosophy. Unfortunately, Wittgenstein's ideas about psychoanalysis have also exerted an influence on other philosophers who have attempted to construct systematic philosophical critiques of psychoanalysis. They will also, if not corrected, discourage and inhibit the development of more constructive efforts to establish useful relations between the two disciplines. The case of Wittgenstein's approach to psychoanalysis proves the importance of an adage for our times, modelled on Plato's formula for political wisdom in the Republic. Good order will only prevail in the state of philosophy when philosophers become scientists or when scientists become philosophers or, more particularly in this sphere of philosophical inquiry, when philosophers become psychoanalysts or psychoanalysts become philosophers.

Why is this so? Psychoanalysis is two things. It is a theory and it is a therapy. One can become attracted to and interested in the psychoanalytic theory because of an unconscious need for psychoanalytic therapy. If so, the intellectual interest in the subject becomes compromised at many points by the impact on the unconscious of what is learned about psychopathology, including defences against treatment which are maintained in an unconscious state. Gaps and distortions in the understanding of the theoretical abstractions inevitably result. It seems evident that Wittgenstein's well-known, fatalistic, tragic outlook was not so much a result of any abstract thought process as the expression of his personal experience of life. His statement about suffering and thoughts of suicide in the passage cited above appears to have a personal reference in the light of the Engelmann correspondence and Malcolm's *Memoir*. Chronic depression and recurrent thoughts of suicide are symptoms that demonstrate a need for therapy. The psychological denial of this need meant that Wittgenstein had to be his own physician. Subsequently, he could identify his philosophical work as a therapeutic instrumentality aimed against conceptual confusions that lead thought astray. The defence could be made complete by applying the instrument to psychoanalysis itself in the form of Wittgenstein's philosophical critique. If our thesis is correct, the intrinsic value of the philosophical instrument should not be tested against its application by Wittgenstein to psychoanalysis. Its application was disturbed by the unconsciously determined ambivalence Wittgenstein had toward the subject.

[26] G. E. Moore, op cit., p. 15.

# 5

# WITTGENSTEIN AND ETHICS

THEODORE REDPATH

There is rather little about ethics in Wittgenstein's published writings. He also seldom said anything on the subject in his lectures at Cambridge. There is somewhat more about it in his manuscript and typescript remains, but not much in the way of extended discussion. It seems pretty clear that he held the view that ethics could not be discussed in the same kind of way in which he discussed logical or even metaphysical problems. Anyone, however, who knew Wittgenstein at all well, even for a short period, could scarcely fail to realize that he had extremely strong moral convictions, which he often expressed with a punch which could be devastating to those whose behaviour he was attacking, or whose views did not coincide with his own.

Now, among Wittgenstein's literary remains there is a very interesting typescript of a paper on ethics, evidently written to be read to a society in Cambridge, and probably actually read to The Heretics in 1929 or 1930. This paper has recently been published in *The Philosophical Review*.[1] The paper both shows how deeply serious was Wittgenstein's attitude to moral issues, and also throws a good deal of light on why he distrusted systematic treatment of ethics. I want to examine the paper in some detail, to try to get to grips with its salient positions, and finally to express my own view as to their validity.

[1] *The Philosophical Review*, Ithaca, New York, Vol. LXXIV, January 1965, pp. 3–12. It is there followed by some 'Notes on Talks with Wittgenstein' by Friedrich Waismann, and by a piece entitled 'Some Developments in Wittgenstein's View of Ethics' by Mr Rush Rhees, of University College, Swansea, one of Wittgenstein's literary executors. I am grateful to Professor G. H. von Wright for permission to quote extensively from Wittgenstein's paper.

Wittgenstein starts his paper by announcing that he feels that he will have 'great difficulties' in communicating his thoughts to his audience. He goes on to specify these difficulties. The first was the lack of 'precision and subtlety' in his English. The second was a feeling that many of his audience might have come 'with slightly wrong expectations', and he then explains his reasons for choosing the subject of ethics :

> When your former secretary honoured me by asking me to read a paper to your society, my first thought was that I would certainly do it, and my second thought was that if I was to have the opportunity to speak to you I should speak about something which I am keen on communicating to you and that I should not misuse this opportunity to give you a lecture about, say, logic. I call this a misuse, for to explain a scientific matter to you it would need a course of lectures and not an hour's paper. Another alternative would have been to give you what's called a popular scientific lecture, that is, a lecture intended to make you believe that you understand a thing which actually you don't understand, and to gratify what I believe to be one of the lowest desires of modern people, namely the superficial curiosity about the latest discoveries of science. I rejected these alternatives and decided to talk to you about a subject which seems to me to be of general importance, hoping that it may help to clear up your thoughts about this subject (even if you should entirely disagree with what I will say about it).

From this passage it is amply clear that Wittgenstein thought the subject of the nature of Ethics one of general importance, and that he also considered (quite rightly, in my view) that it was possible to say something worthwhile about it within the scope of an hour's paper.

Wittgenstein goes on to mention a third difficulty, that of a hearer of a philosophical lecture understanding both what is being said and what the speaker is driving at. Wittgenstein asks the audience to be patient and to hope that they will in the end see 'both the way and where it leads to'. I do not want to comment on this but to go on to the body of the paper.

Wittgenstein starts by adopting Moore's definition of ethics in *Principia Ethica* as 'the general inquiry into what is good', but then he slightly widens the term to include what he believes to be 'the most essential part of what is generally called aesthetics', and he offers a Galtonian picture of ethics by enumerating a 'row of synonyms' intended to enable the audience to see 'the characteristic features they all have in common', which are 'the characteristic features of ethics'. This 'row of synonyms' is presented as follows:

'Ethics is the enquiry into what is valuable'
'Ethics is the enquiry into what is really important'
'Ethics is the enquiry into the meaning of life'
'Ethics is the enquiry into what makes life worth living'
'Ethics is the enquiry into the right way of living'.

Wittgenstein then goes on to say that 'the first thing that strikes one about all these expressions is that each of them is used in two very different senses', one 'trivial or relative' and the other 'ethical or absolute'. Actually he only goes on to exemplify this with regard to three of the expressions, namely 'good', 'important', and 'the right way'; but we need not take him up on this. He exemplifies the relative sense of 'good' by 'a good chair', meaning a chair which serves a certain predetermined purpose; and 'a good pianist' meaning (*sed quaere*, though we need not quarrel with this) a pianist who can play pieces of a certain degree of difficulty with a certain degree of dexterity. He exemplifies the trivial sense of 'important' by saying that 'it is important for me not to catch cold' means that catching a cold would produce certain describable disturbances in my life; and the trivial sense of 'the right road' as the right road relative to a certain goal. He contrasts the relative, trivial sense of the terms with the ethical sense as follows:

Supposing that I could play tennis and one of you saw me playing and said 'Well, you play pretty badly', and suppose I answered 'I know, I'm playing badly but I don't want to play any better', all the other man could say would be 'Ah, then that's all right'. But suppose I had told one of you a preposterous lie and he came up to me and said 'You're behaving like a beast' and then I were to say 'I know I behave badly, but then I don't want to behave any better', could he then say 'Ah, then that's all right'? Certainly not; he would say 'Well, you *ought* to want to behave better'. Here you have an absolute judgment of value, whereas the first instance was one of a relative judgment.

This may seem reasonable enough, but one could well have the thought that a real enthusiast for tennis might quite easily have been far from believing or saying that it was quite all right for the poor player Wittgenstein not to want to play any better, and might, indeed, have used the very form of words of the moral stricture and rejoined : 'Well you *ought* to want to play better'. We might have said that in such a case the tennis enthusiast would have been making an absolute judgment of value. But, if this would have been Wittgenstein's view, then the difference between the tennis case and the lying case would not be in respect of the type of activity (playing tennis and lying) about which the judgments were made. In which case was it not misleading to contrast these cases, since the choice of them would so readily suggest that it *was* the contrast of the activities that contributed wholly or largely to the essential difference beween the judgments made about them? If, on the other hand, Wittgenstein's view would have been that the tennis enthusiast's judgment 'Well, you *ought* to want to play better' would *not* be an absolute judgment of value, but only a relative judgment, then 'Ah, then that's all right' was *not* 'all the other man could say', even by way of making a relative judgment. In which case was it not misleading to make the contrast between the relative and the absolute judgments of value seem to depend on whether 'the other man' 'would' (or 'could' – it is interesting that Wittgenstein uses both terms) reply 'Ah, then that's all right' or would (or 'could') reply 'Well, you *ought* to want to . . . better'? Either way Wittgenstein's contrast is not wholly satisfactory.

Wittgenstein goes on, however, to sum up what he takes to

be the essential difference between judgments of relative value and judgments of absolute value :

> The essence of this difference seems to be obviously this : Every judgment of relative value is a mere statement of facts and can therefore be put in such a form that it loses all the appearance of a judgment of value : Instead of saying 'This is the right way to Grantchester' I could equally well have said 'This is the right way you have to go if you want to get to Grantchester in the shortest time', 'This man is a good runner' simply means that he runs a certain number of miles in a certain number of minutes, and so forth.

This passage is also open to objection, since although 'This is the right way to Grantchester' would very often, and perhaps even most often, mean 'This is the way you have to go if you want to get to Grantchester in the shortest time', it might sometimes mean 'This is the way you have to go to Grantchester if you want to have the most pleasant walk.' The translation of 'This man is a good runner' may seem a harder nut to crack, but, as it stands, it is not right either, since the man might be a good sprinter but wholly unable to run even *one* mile, and if the context concerned the choice of a man to run a short distance very quickly, to rely on the formula offered by Wittgenstein might be catastrophic. But, though his specific formulations will not do as they stand, it could well be said that his general account of the nature of relative judgments of value holds water – every judgment of relative value is a mere statement of facts, and can therefore be put in such a form that it loses all the appearance of a judgment of value.

Now, let us consider this with reference to the two judgments Wittgenstein has mentioned. 'This is the right way to Grantchester' would certainly seem to be a judgment relative to some purpose – to get there most quickly, to have a pleasant walk or drive, to have the best view of the village, and there might be other purposes. Likewise 'This man is a good runner' would for instance also seem to be a judgment relative to some purpose – to win or do well in a race of some distance or other, to take a message quickly and surely, to demonstrate a style of running. At least it would seem to be relative to some standard – the Alverstone standard, the standard of other runners recognized as 'good' in the community, and so on. But is it so certain, then, that there *is*, in contrast, as Wittgenstein suggested, an absolute ethical judgment, for example 'This is a good man', which has no relation to any purpose or standard? As we shall remember, Wittgenstein has already given an example of what he considers to be an absolute judgment of value, namely, 'Well, you ought to want to behave better'. It is, therefore, particularly interesting to follow the subsequent evolution of his argument, as we shall see. His immediate continuation runs, however, as follows :

Now what I wish to contend is, that although all judgments of relative value can be shown to be mere statements of facts, no statement of fact can ever be, or imply, a judgment of *absolute* value. Let me explain this : Suppose one of you were an omniscient person and knew all the movements of all the bodies in the world dead or alive and that he also knew all the states of mind of all human beings that ever lived, and suppose this man wrote all he knew in a big book, then this book would contain the whole description of the world; and what I want to say is, that this book would contain nothing that we would call an *ethical* judgment or anything that would logically imply such a judgment. It would of course contain all relative judgments of value and all true scientific propositions and in fact all true propositions that can be made. But all the facts described would, as it were, stand on the same level, and in the same way all propositions stand on the same level. There are no propositions which, in any absolute sense, are sublime, important, or trivial. Now perhaps some of you will agree to that and be reminded of Hamlet's words: 'Nothing is either good or bad, but thinking makes it so'. But this again could lead to a misunderstanding. What Hamlet says seems to imply that good and bad, though not qualities of the world outside us, are attributes of our states of mind. But what I mean is that a state of mind, so far as we mean by that [a] fact which we can describe, is in no ethical sense good or bad. If for instance in our world-book we read the description of a murder with all its details physical and psychological, the mere description of these facts will contain nothing which we could call an *ethical* proposition. The murder will be on exactly the same level as any other event, for instance the falling of a stone. Certainly the reading of this description might cause us pain or rage or any other emotion, or we might read about the pain or rage caused by this murder to other people when they heard of it, but these will simply be facts, facts and facts but no ethics.

Let us look into this passage. What are we to say to the contention that 'no statement of fact can ever be, or imply, a judgment of *absolute* value'? Let us take one of Wittgenstein's examples, the case of a murder, and let us suppose that the murder took place in England. Then the question we have to consider is whether the following statement, couched in the antique phraseology of Coke's *Institutes*, either is itself what Wittgenstein has called 'an ethical judgment' or implies such a judgment : 'X unlawfully killed Y on such and such a day, Y being a reasonable creature, in being and under the Queen's peace, and X did so with malice aforethought either express or implied, the death following within a year and a day.' Now I think we may readily admit that this statement neither is nor 'implies' (by which Wittgenstein clearly means 'logically implies') an 'ethical judgment', since the propounder of the statement that X 'murdered' Y (according to the legal definition) might, for all we know, have considered the murder to have been morally justified. Suppose, however, that he did *not* consider the murder to have been morally justified, and made this clear by the tone in which he referred to it, uttering the statement 'X *murdered* Y' with a fury which would leave no one hearing him in reasonable doubt as to his moral attitude, are we then to say that his statement 'X *murdered* Y' does not imply 'X ought not to have murdered Y'? It will probably be clear enough that Wittgenstein's answer would very likely have been that 'X *murdered* Y' would in that case not be a mere statement of fact, but also the expression of a moral attitude to the fact. But now suppose we put the statement in another form : 'X committed the atrocious act of murdering Y', we then raise the matter in a way in which it has divided modern ethical philosophers, and in which it affords fair colour to both sides. For certainly it seems reasonable enough to say 'Well, the act either was atrocious or it was not, and surely to say either is to make a statement of fact'; while, on the other hand, it does not seem absurd to rejoin that whichever one says one is really simply expressing an attitude to the fact of the murder when one calls the act 'atrocious', and not making any statement additional to the statement that it was a murder. One side is holding that the term 'statement of fact' covers this case of the assertion of atrocity, and the other is holding that it does not. There may well be points in favour of both sides, but, as some philosophers have clearly realized, there may not be any overriding reason for preferring one side to the other. When he wrote this paper, however, Wittgenstein was far from holding such a view. 'Facts, facts, and facts' were, for him, in bleak contrast with 'ethics'.

I want now to pass to another part of the last quoted passage. This is where Wittgenstein says that 'there are no propositions which, in any absolute sense, are sublime, important, or trivial'. That statement is, of course, closely connected with his statement that the 'big book' would not contain anything that we would call an ethical judgment, or anything that would logically imply such a judgment, but it is not the same statement, and it is worth separate discussion. Here Wittgenstein is not simply saying that there would be no ethical judgments or no absolute judgments of value in the big book. He is saying that no absolute judgments of value could be *made about* any of the statements in the big book. Now this would involve saying that, in the case where X told a preposterous lie, and admitted that he was behaving badly, but brazenly asserted that he did not want to behave better, 'the other man' could not make the absolute value judgment that he ought to want to behave better, or, in other words, could not make the absolute value judgment that the proposition that he did not want to behave better was important and ethically wrong. Now this would seem to involve Wittgenstein in contradiction. As we shall see later, Wittgenstein seems to have realized something of the sort, but calls the contradiction a 'paradox'.

More immediately, however, Wittgenstein goes on to make some remarks which are of considerable interest but far from easy to understand :

And now I must say that if I contemplate what Ethics would really have to be if there were such a science, this result seems to me quite obvious. It seems to me obvious that nothing we could ever think or say should [would] be *the* thing. That we cannot write a scientific book, the subject matter of which could be intrinsically sublime and above all other subject matters. I can only describe my feeling by the metaphor, that, if a man could write a book on ethics which really was a book on Ethics, this book would, with an explosion, destroy all the other books in the world. – Our words as we use them in science, are vessels capable only of containing and conveying meaning and sense, *natural* meaning and sense. Ethics, if it is anything, is supernatural, and our words will only express facts; as a teacup will only hold a teacupful of water and if I were to pour out a gallon over it. – I said that so far as facts and propositions are concerned there is only relative value and relative good, right, etc. And let me, before I go on, illustrate this by a rather obvious example. The right road is the road which leads to an arbitrarily predetermined end and it is quite clear to us all that there is no sense in talking about the right road apart from such a predetermined goal. Now let us see what we could possibly mean by the expression '*the* absolutely right road'. I think it would be the road which *everybody* on seeing it would *with logical necessity* have to go, or be ashamed for not going. And similarly the absolute good, if it is a describable state of affairs, would be one which everybody, independent of his tastes and inclinations, would, *necessarily*, bring about or feel guilty for not bringing about. And I want to say that such a state of affairs is a chimera. No state of affairs has in itself, what I would like to call, the coercive power of an absolute judge.

A great deal could be said about this passage, but I must confine myself to a few points. First, it is possibly worth asking what sort of thing Wittgenstein thought the 'book on ethics, which was really a book on ethics', would be; and did he really think that there could be such a book, or did he think there could not? Clearly enough, he did not think that a *scientific* book on ethics would be possible, since a *scientific* book, as he understood the idea, would only contain what he considered to be 'mere statements of fact'. But what would he have said about a book like the *Nicomachean Ethics*, which, besides factual statements and analyses of ethical statements of various kinds, also contains many absolute judgments of value? Would he have said that that was not really a book on ethics? If so, how could he have supported such a view? One kind of support I can imagine at the moment would be to deny that Aristotle's book does really contain absolute judgments of value, and to say that what appear to be such are really simply expressions of personal opinion. But are they any more so than Wittgenstein's own *paradigm* case of an absolute judgment of value: 'You ought to want to behave better'? Another kind of support (and it is the only other kind I can think of at the moment) would be to agree that Aristotle's book does really contain absolute judgments of value, but to deny that it is a *scientific* book on ethics. This would bump up against the objection that 'scientific' statements need not perhaps be confined to what Wittgenstein has called 'mere statements of fact', and also the objection, already mentioned, that it may not be correct to exclude absolute value judgments from the realm of 'fact'. But, in any case, whatever may be the force of these objections, I do not believe that Wittgenstein would have been contented with denying that a *scientific* book on ethics could be written. It seems to me pretty clear that he believed that it would be impossible to write *any sort* of book on ethics. For what such a book would need to contain would not be merely personal opinions but judgments having absolute ethical validity. Moreover, the book would also have to be written in words, and words, according to Wittgenstein in this passage, will only express facts. Now these are two quite separate arguments against the possibility of the book on ethics; and the second one, from the nature of language, seems to me far weaker than the first. What is more, this argument is in conflict with the first of the two kinds of possible support I mentioned just now for the view that Aristotle's book was not really a book on ethics, namely, that what seemed to be absolute judgments of value were really merely expressions of personal opinion. For, if it is even possible for words to express personal opinions, then they can express something other than 'facts'. Wittgenstein's other argument against the possibility of a book on ethics seems to me much stronger, for if such a book were to have to express judgments having absolute ethical validity, then it would not perhaps be absurd to say that such a book could only be 'supernatural', would have the explosive character that Wittgenstein attributes to it, and could not be written by a human being as such (but only, let us say, by a human being directly inspired by God, or by God himself). Nevertheless, many of us are unlikely to admit that the term 'a book on ethics' can only be properly used in this strange and highly sophisticated sense, and are likely to want to continue to call precisely by that name the many attempts of fallible human beings to state their views on how people should behave.

Wittgenstein's criterion for 'the absolutely right road' throws considerable light on the way in which he was regarding the whole matter. 'The absolutely right road' would be 'the road which *everybody*, on seeing it, would, with *logical necessity* – have to go, or be ashamed for not going'. We may at once ask : 'What is there to prevent someone from knowing perfectly well what road he ought to follow, but feeling no shame at not following it?' How can human conscience be compelled to operate by logical necessity? Does a man cease to be a human being because he knows clearly what he ought or ought not to do, but does the opposite without any feeling of shame? Hardly, even though people might want to sting him by reprobating him as 'inhuman'. Indeed, we can properly say that there would be no point in their calling him 'inhuman' unless he were human. But though, for this sort of reason, I believe that Wittgenstein's criterion for 'the absolutely right road' is to be rejected, it is important to try to see why he proposed that criterion. And it seems to me not impossible that he proposed it for the very reason that it would make the whole concept of 'the absolutely right road' appear chimerical. For this it certainly would do. Let us, however, now enquire whether there is any other possible criterion of 'the absolutely right road'. It may be worth considering, for instance, the possibility that 'the absolutely right road' will be the road which, given all the circumstances, any person whatever ought to follow. We would, of course, always need to take account of the distinction, acutely indicated by Moore, between the two senses of 'right' in 'It is always right to do what one believes to be right' – the second 'right' having the meaning 'objectively right' (i.e. taking account of actual consequences); and the first 'right' not taking any account of actual consequences. The more absolute duty, presumably, would involve having true beliefs about what is likely to produce the best consequences, and therefore to act in such a way as *is actually likely* (not merely *seems likely*) to produce the best consequences. And so we may suggest that an alternative criterion to Wittgenstein's for 'the absolutely right road' might have been 'the road which, given all the circumstances, is most likely to lead to the best consequences'. There is, of course, nothing original about this – it is Moore's *agathistic utilitarianism*. But, whatever objections may be made against it, it does not make the concept of 'the absolutely right road' appear chimerical. Presently, I want to inquire why Wittgenstein could have wanted to make that concept appear chimerical; but before doing this I want to turn attention for a moment to what Wittgenstein proposes as the criterion for 'the *absolute good*', since I think this may throw light on that further enquiry.

You may remember that he wrote that 'if it is a describable state of affairs,' it would be 'one which everybody, independent of his tastes and inclinations, would *necessarily* bring about or feel guilty for not bringing about'. I do not wish to repeat the objections I made to the 'necessity' clause of Wittgenstein's definition of 'the absolutely right road'. What I am most concerned with now is the clause 'independent of his tastes and inclinations'. The conclusion of this clause suggests that for Wittgenstein what is good is far from being independent of people's tastes and inclinations. His idea would seem to have been that A will call 'good' a state of affairs which he is glad has been brought about, or wants to bring about. B, a state of affairs which he is glad has been brought about or wants to bring about, and so on : and that there is simply *nothing*, not merely that everybody would *necessarily* bring about or feel guilty for not bringing about, but even that everybody would, *in fact*, bring about or feel guilty for not bringing about. Now this may well be true; but it does not show that no 'absolute good' exists, since 'the absolute good' might, for instance, be a state of affairs which everybody *ought* to welcome or want to bring about. And this is clearly not at all the same as what they would, either *necessarily*, or *in fact*, bring about or feel guilty for not bringing about. Wittgenstein, indeed, has substituted for an ethical definition of absolute good a definition depending on logical necessity, and has also, by implication, excluded a definition of absolute good depending upon people's actual desires and inclinations. The first conception he has easily made to appear chimerical, and the second would readily seem to fly in the face of facts, since, as Wittgenstein was fully aware, people do not all desire or incline towards the same states of affairs. Indeed, Wittgenstein did not need to attack this second kind of possible definition, since its unsatisfactoriness would be obvious. We may now, however, ask more effectively the question why Wittgenstein could have wanted to make the concept of 'absolute good' appear chimerical. I should not be surprised if the answer lay, partly, at least, in a reaction against the absolutism of *Principia Ethica*. In any case, however, I am strongly inclined to believe that he was animated by a spirit of rebellion against any philosophy which presumed to dictate general values. This would certainly accord with my own recollection of a number of occasions on which he said, with regard to some moral issue, that it was a 'personal' matter. This was, as far as I can remember, usually, if not always, when there seemed to be what we might call 'a good deal to be said on both sides'; but that could possibly have been enough to discount 'absolute good' in his way of looking at things. But the question now arises whether it ought to be considered enough to discount 'absolute good' in *our way* of looking at things – and I am inclined to think that it ought *not* to be considered enough. For, although there might be many cases in which a number of states of affairs which could be brought about would be of roughly equal value, so that nobody definitely *ought* to aim at any particular one of these states, but would be perfectly decent if he were to aim at any of them he might wish to, might there not also be many cases in which one state of affairs would be so much better than any other which could be brought about, that everybody ought positively to try to bring about that state of affairs? And, if this is so, then there would be an 'absolute good'; and this distinctively ethical concept would be saved both from the naturalism refuted by Moore, and from what we might call the 'logicism' set up and then knocked down by Wittgenstein.

What is more, it is probably worth raising the question, though here one would be treading on dangerous ground, whether Wittgenstein himself might not have been brought to be satisfied with such a conception of 'absolute good'. For, in the next part of his paper, Wittgenstein very interestingly describes a number of experiences about which he was 'still tempted to use such expressions as "absolute good", "absolute value", etc.'. Of the first of these experiences he says:

> I believe the best way of describing it is to say that when I have it *I wonder at the existence of the world*. And I am then inclined to use such phrases as 'How extraordinary that anything should exist!' or 'How extraordinary that the world should exist!'.

Of the second he says:

> It is, what one might call, the experience of being *absolutely* safe. I mean the state of mind in which one is inclined to say, 'I am safe, nothing can injure me whatever happens'.

He then goes on to contend that 'the verbal expression which we give to these experiences is nonsense!' The arguments for such a view are, in some form, probably pretty familiar to readers, but I want to follow them out as stated in this particular paper. Wittgenstein's main point is that 'I wonder at such and such being the case' has only sense if I can imagine it not to be the case, and I cannot imagine the world not existing. Similarly, to be safe essentially means that it is physically impossible that certain things should happen to me, and therefore it is nonsense to say that I am safe *whatever* happens. And Wittgenstein generalizes as follows:

> Now I want to impress on you that a certain characteristic misuse of our language runs through *all* ethical and religious expressions. All these expressions *seem*, prima facie, to be just similes. Thus it seems that when we are using the word 'right' in an ethical sense, although, what we mean, is not right in the trivial sense, it's something similar, and when we say 'This is a good fellow', although the word 'good' here doesn't mean what it means in the sentence 'This is a good football player', there seems to be some similarity. And when we say 'This man's life was valuable' we don't mean it in the same sense in which we would speak of some valuable jewellery, but there seems to be some sort of analogy.

And later, taking up the argument again in general terms, he says:

> But a simile must be a simile for *something*. And if I can describe a fact by means of a simile I must also be able to drop the simile and describe the facts without it. Now in our case as soon as we try to drop the simile and simply to state the facts which stand behind it, we find, that there are no such facts. And so, what at first appeared to be a simile, now seems to be mere nonsense.

What are we to say about all this? It seems to me that we may first do well to ask the question whether it was true to say that the expressions in question, 'wonder', 'extraordinary', 'safe', 'good', for instance, do seem even prima facie to be similes. It is important to question this, for if they do not even *seem* to be similes at all, then the knockdown argument used by Wittgenstein in the passage last quoted would lose its relevance. (And even if they seem at first sight to be similes, but turn out to be something else, but not nonsense, then his argument would also fall wide of the mark.) Let us take the case of 'I wonder at the existence of the world'. Now I, for one, recognize, and many readers will probaby recognize, the experience expressed by these words. But if we say these words are we really using a *simile* for something else? What reason would there be for calling it a 'simile'? Well, from what Wittgenstein has said in the last two passages I have quoted, it would seem as if he probably regarded such a statement as a simile because it was *similar*, in some way, to saying something like 'I wonder at the size of that horse', where it would be perfectly easy to imagine a horse of smaller size at whose size he would not have wondered. But, if this was why Wittgenstein called 'I wonder at the existence of the world' a 'simile', he was using the term 'simile' in what is, at first sight at least, an unusual way. For what sort of things are usually called 'similes'? 'His face was as pale as a sheet', 'The wind blew the bus over like a toy', 'His character was as firm as a rock'. These are paradigm cases of the use of 'similes'. All of them make a comparison. But 'I wonder at the existence of the world' makes no comparison. Of course, Wittgenstein might well have replied that, though it does not do so explicitly, it does so implicitly, and that the sentence could be reworded as follows to bring this out: 'I wonder at the existence of the world rather like I might wonder at the size of an enormous horse'. I do not know whether this was the sort of justification Wittgenstein had in mind for calling 'I wonder at the existence of the world' a 'simile', but I cannot think of any better justification that he could have adduced. At all events, let us see what this would lead to. You will remember that he said that if I can describe a fact by means of a simile I must also be able to drop the simile and describe the fact without it. I suppose we can say, fairly enough, that the fact expressed by 'His face was as pale as a sheet' could be expressed by 'His face was white', and 'His character was as firm as a rock' by 'His character was extremely firm'. 'The wind blew the bus over like a toy' does not seem so easy to express without a simile, and I am even not sure that this can be done satisfactorily. If it cannot, then we may suspect that the generalization that if I can describe a fact by means of a simile I must also be able to drop the simile and describe the fact without it, may well not be valid. What, however, about 'I wonder at the existence of the world rather like I might wonder at the size of an enormous horse'? Can we express this without the use of a simile? My own answer to this is that we *can*, simply by saying: 'I wonder at the existence of the world'. For (and this is the curious thing), it is not 'I wonder at the existence of the world' that is the simile, but 'rather like I might wonder at the size of an enormous horse'; just as, in the paradigm cases, the similes were 'as pale as a sheet', 'like a toy', and 'as a rock'. In saying, therefore, that such expressions as 'I wonder at the existence of the world', 'How extraordinary that the world should exist', 'I feel absolutely safe', 'This is a good fellow', 'This is the right road' (to follow in a case of conduct), 'That man's life was valuable', and so on, are 'similes', Wittgenstein was himself misusing language. He had got things the wrong way round. He evidently thought that by being in some way similar in import to other, current expressions, an expression would thereby become a 'simile'; whereas, if anything, it would be the current expressions, such as 'I wonder at the size of that enormous horse', 'How extraordinary that that man should still be alive!' (e.g. if he had been severely wounded on several occasions), 'I feel safe now I am back at home after my visit to Belfast', 'This is a good football player', 'This is the right road to Grantchester if you want to get there as quickly as possible', 'That piece of jewellery is valuable', that would be the similes. And this is by no means a trivial point, but a crucial one; since if, as I hope is clear, such expressions as 'I wonder at the existence of the world', 'This is a good fellow', 'This is the right road to follow' (in a case of conduct) are *not* similes after all, then *even if* (as is very doubtful, to say the least) whenever I can describe a fact by means of a simile I must also be able to drop the simile and describe the fact without it, this is no argument in favour of its necessarily being possible, or even possible at all, to describe or express the experience or judgment they refer to in any other way than by those expressions themselves. I think I can honestly say that I believe I understand quite well what Wittgenstein meant by the words 'I wonder at the existence of the world'. I believe also that it is probable that a fair number of those who heard him read his paper also understood quite well what he meant; and I believe that, in fact, a great number of people would understand the words. Though, however, I believe these things to be so, and therefore that those words are not 'nonsense', in a perfectly good and familiar sense of that word, I do not think that one can let the matter rest there.

If my analysis is right, Wittgenstein made a crucial mistake in calling those expressions 'similes', but, as one would expect, Wittgenstein was not operating in shallow waters, but engaged on a deep philosophical investigation of considerable importance. Although he misexpressed his insight by calling the expressions 'similes', it is clear that he saw sharply – perhaps, indeed, *too* sharply – that there was some important difference of usage between the use of the central terms, 'wonder', 'extraordinary', 'right', 'good', 'valuable', 'safe', and so on, in the religious and ethical contexts, from their use in the other contexts he referred to. It might well not be misleading, indeed, to call their religious and ethical uses 'transferred uses' (or even 'metaphorical uses'), but the question would still remain whether these uses deserved to be called 'nonsensical'.

Let me, however, at this point return to the text of Wittgenstein's paper. The passage I am now going to quote follows, after a dash, the passage I last quoted :

Now the three experiences which I have mentioned to you [Wittgenstein had added a third to the two we have indicated – namely, feeling guilty] (and I could have added others) seem to those who have experienced them, for instance to me, to have in some sense an intrinsic, absolute value. But when I say they are experiences, surely, they are facts; they have taken

112

place then and there, lasted a certain definite time, and consequently are describable. And so from what I have said some minutes ago I must admit it is nonsense to say that they have absolute value. And I will make my point still more acute by saying 'It is the paradox that an experience, a fact, should seem to have supernatural value.' Now there is a way in which I would be tempted to meet this paradox. Let me first consider, again, our first experience of wondering at the existence of the world and let me describe it in a slightly different way : We all know what in ordinary life would be called a miracle. It obviously is simply an event the like of which we yet never have seen. Now suppose such an event happened. Take the case that one of you suddenly grew a lion's head and began to roar. Certainly that would be as extraordinary a thing as I can imagine. Now whenever we should have recovered from our surprise, what I would suggest would be to fetch a doctor and have the case scientifically investigated, and if it were not for hurting him I would have him vivisected. And where would the miracle have got to? For it is clear that when we look at it in this way everything miraculous has disappeared; unless what we mean by this term is merely that a fact has not yet been explained by science, which again means that we have hitherto failed to group this fact with others in a scientific system. This shows that it is absurd to say 'Science has proved that there are no miracles'. The truth is that the scientific way of looking at a fact is not the way to look at it as a miracle. For imagine whatever fact you may, it is not in itself miraculous in the absolute sense of that term. For we see now that we have been using the term 'miracle' in a relative and an absolute sense. And I will now describe the experience of wondering at the existence of the world by saying : It is the experience of seeing the world as a miracle. Now I am tempted to say that the right expression in language for the miracle of the existence of the world, though it is not any proposition *in* language, is the existence of language itself. But what then does it mean to be aware of this miracle at some times and not at other times? For all I have said, by shifting the expression of the miraculous from an expression *by means of* language to the expression *by the existence of* language, all I have said is again that we cannot express what we want to express and that all we *say* about the absolutely miraculous remains nonsense.

Personally I find this a splendid passage of profound interest; though I am far from satisfied with its drift and conclusion. Some things that are said seem to me so right, and others so wrong. I want to focus discussion, to start with, on two consecutive sentences :

The truth is that the scientific way of looking at a fact is not the way to look at it as a miracle. For imagine whatever fact you may, it is not in itself miraculous in the absolute sense.

The first of those two sentences is wholly acceptable if one takes it as substantially meaning that investigating something scientifically is not at all the same as wondering at it as a prodigy. On the other hand, the second sentence was clearly being presented by Wittgenstein as a reason for the point he was making in the first. But he had nowhere told his audience what 'miraculous' in the *absolute* sense meant. He had, indeed, reminded them roughly what was meant by 'miracle' 'in ordinary life' – 'simply an event the like of which we yet have never seen'. But what he had also done, which throws some light on the absolute sense, was something rather curious. He had said that by the scientific investigation of the lion's head case, 'everything miraculous' would have 'disappeared'; and by 'everything miraculous' he had clearly meant, *not* 'everything miraculous' in the 'relative sense', but 'everything miraculous' in the 'absolute sense'. Yet in the very next sentence he said that this showed that it was absurd to say that 'science has proved that there are no miracles'. This appears to me to be a violent contradiction. And the reason why that contradiction arose was, I believe, because Wittgenstein had, in saying that 'everything miraculous' would have 'disappeared', been thinking of what would *very often* happen in circumstances in which a prodigy is submitted to scientific investigation, that is, that the scientific investigator and the spectator would

114

cease to think of that 'prodigy' as a 'miracle' – would lose their wondering state of mind. But, in my submission, he went too far in assuming that that is what would necessarily happen, since it might well be possible, surely, still to wonder at the prodigy? (I do not see, for instance, that Leibniz *need* have lost any wonder he may have previously felt at the liquefaction of the blood of St Januarius, if and when he submitted it to chemical analysis.) In my view, then, the statement that in the lion's head case 'everything miraculous' would have 'disappeared' was wrong. And, if we reject it, the contradiction vanishes.

Unfortunately, however, the same kind of contradiction re-appears between the two statements which I quoted just now as a focus of interest. And that contradiction recurs there because to say 'imagine whatever fact you may, it is not miraculous in the absolute sense' is simply a generalization of the false statement made about the lion's head case. That the generalization does not hold I feel convinced from personal experience. I have from time to time had a kind of thought and feeling which may well be familiar to many people, namely, a sense of amazement that things really hold together and retain their identity for more than a split second – that a book rests quietly on my table, retaining its shape, colour, and size, that a blackbird hops across the lawn and does not disintegrate into a thousand parts after a moment's existence, and so on. I know perfectly well that these facts can be explained in a scientific way, but that does not in any way lessen my wonder at them when I feel it. So that I should want to say that I could not only imagine *countless* facts that would seem to me 'miraculous' in the *absolute* sense, but that I have already, from time to time, felt a number of facts, of the kind I have mentioned, to be 'miraculous' in that sense. I should therefore want to accept wholeheartedly Wittgenstein's statement that the scientific way of looking at a fact is not the way to look at it as a miracle; but to deny vehemently that one cannot imagine any fact as in itself 'miraculous' in the absolute sense.

I foresee, however, that it may be objected that I have omitted to give due weight to the words 'in itself'; and that Wittgenstein meant to lay considerable stress on them when he said that one cannot imagine any fact as 'in itself miraculous in the absolute sense'. Now, to such an objection I am inclined to answer as follows: If Wittgenstein *did* mean to lay considerable stress on the words 'in itself' when he said that one cannot imagine any fact as in itself miraculous in the absolute sense, it seems likely that this would have been because he had conceived of a 'fact' as something which could be 'scientifically described', and was not prepared to allow that 'miraculousness' could be part of a 'scientific description'. But what are we to take him to mean by a 'scientific description'? If it is a description which *necessarily* excludes any value element, then the matter is, of course, settled by the prescribed usage; but then Wittgenstein's point becomes philosophically insubstantial. If, on the other hand, it is any description which communicates knowledge (and Wittgenstein evidently wants it also to *be* this), then can we be so certain that it communicates no knowledge to say, for instance, that the existence of the world is 'miraculous', that is, worthy of wonder? Indeed, may there not be many facts which are worthy of the sort of wonder which consists in regarding them as 'miracles' in an absolute sense? And, if so, can we be so certain as Wittgenstein seems to have been, that it is better not to call their *being* worthy of that sort of wonder, *itself* a 'fact', rather than '*not* a fact'? Which we may prefer to call it, if, after careful consideration, we are of opinion that the matter deserves dispute or preference, may well depend, I believe, partly on our attitude to terminology, rooted in the history of our particular acquaintance with the language, and partly on our attitude to the relations between matters not involving values and matters involving values – for instance, whether to stress the difference or to stress the similarity. I should not be surprised if Wittgenstein, at the time he wrote this paper, was reacting strongly against the view of ethics which regarded it as one of the 'sciences', like physics, chemistry, or biology – a view embodied in the title by which the discipline of philosophy was at that time, and, indeed, until very recently, has been, known at Cambridge, namely, 'Moral Sciences'. On the other hand, as, indeed, comes out in Wittgenstein's paper, he had an intensely strong sense of values. Yet, even in speaking of the sort of experience, wonder at the existence of the world, which was his foremost case of absolute value, he says, in parentheses, in his paper, that 'this is an entirely personal matter and others would find other experiences more striking'.

Matters of absolute value, then, we may possibly say, were for Wittgenstein (in this paper at least), *personal* matters. Ethical matters, moral judgments, aesthetic judgments, were entirely a personal affair. If we were to say that this was Wittgenstein's view of the matter, however, we should need to be quite clear that it did not involve the view that one person should not subject another person to moral criticism, or a work of art to aesthetic (or moral) criticism, and so on. Wittgenstein often called behaviour of which he strongly disapproved 'indecent'. (We should also need to be quite clear that his view did not involve what has sometimes been called 'The Emotive Theory of Ethics'.) But, though Wittgenstein passed moral judgments, and sometimes asked his friends for their moral opinions, it is also, I believe, the case that he had what one might, perhaps not too misleadingly, call a 'religious attitude' to such matters. I mean that he was somehow aware that, however strong some moral conviction he had might be, and however much he might respect someone else's moral judgment, he was fully aware that he and everyone else were just human beings and not gods. For that reason there seemed to him a certain absurdity in making the kind of claims involved in the writing of an ethical treatise purporting to consist of universally valid moral judgments or scales of value. Such judgments and scales, in his view, could never be more than personal, and there was a certain pretentiousness or, at least, a profound misconception, in writing as if they were more. On the other hand, it is important to sense the pressures and true balance in Wittgenstein's attitude, and, for this reason, it will be necessary to accord due weight to a passage right at the end of Wittgenstein's paper, which I shall quote presently.

Meanwhile, however, I want to return to the *logical* aspect of Wittgenstein's contentions – what we might call his doctrine of 'inexpressibility', which is to me the least convincing element in his paper. He attempts to reinforce this position in a passage which immediately follows that in which he reasserted that 'we cannot express what we want to express', and that 'all we can say about the absolutely miraculous remains nonsense'. The ensuing passage reads as follows :

> Now the answer to all this will seem perfectly clear to many of you. You will say : Well, if certain experiences constantly tempt us to attribute a quality to them which we call absolute or ethical value and importance, this simply shows that by these words we *don't* mean nonsense, that after all what we mean by saying that an experience has absolute value *is just a fact like other facts* and that all it comes to is that we have not yet succeeded in finding the correct logical analysis of what we mean by our ethical and religious expressions. – Now when this is urged against me I at once see clearly, as it were in a flash of light, not only that no description that I can think of would do to describe what I mean by absolute value, but that I would reject every significant description that anybody could possibly suggest, *ab initio*, on the ground of its significance. That is to say : I see now that these expressions were not non-sensical because I had not yet found the correct expressions, but that their nonsensicality was their very essence. For all I wanted to do with them was just *to go beyond* the world, and that is to say beyond significant language. My whole tendency and I believe the tendency of all men who ever tried to write or talk ethics or religion was to run against the boundaries of language. This running against the walls of our cage is per-fectly, absolutely hopeless.

Now this is the crux. And we may first ask : What does Wittgen-stein mean by 'running against the boundaries of language'? The answer is that he simply means, after all, that language can only express 'facts'. And the boundaries of the realm of 'facts' he has *drawn* in such a way that the statement of a moral judgment, or any other absolute value judgment, cannot express a 'fact'. But, in doing this, he has *manufactured* the 'cage' against the walls of which he tells us that it is 'perfectly, absolutely hopeless' to run. Even, indeed, if we were to concede, as seems quite unnecessary, that the statement of a moral or other absolute value judgment cannot express a 'fact', it would not follow that it does not express *something*; unless, of course, we arbitrarily, and contrary to correct usage, lay down that the term 'express' is to be used in such a way that language *can only* 'express' 'facts', and not for instance, attitudes. Thus I cannot see that anything that Wittgenstein has said in this paper has shown that ethical judgments are *inexpressible*.[2]

On the other hand, Wittgenstein makes it amply clear at the end of his paper that, however 'hopeless' what he considers this 'running against the boundaries of language' might be, it did not deserve to be regarded with derision. His concluding words were these :

> Ethics, so far as it springs from the desire to say something about the ultimate meaning of life, the absolute good, the absolute valuable, can be no science. What it says does not add to our knowledge in any sense. But it is a document of a tendency in the human mind which I personally cannot help respecting deeply and I would not for my life ridicule it.

The attitude to ethics which Wittgenstein here expresses I, for one, find not only acceptable but admirable; but the view of language seems to me not only unconvincing but likely to encourage a disrespect and even ridicule for value judgments, which would run clean counter to Wittgenstein's own attitude. 'Nonsensical' is a strong word which most often bears a charge of contempt. Wittgenstein's view of language, we might say, seems to have led him to a position perilously close to another which would have been deeply repugnant to his moral consciousness.

[2] Nor, incidentally, do I believe that anything advanced in the *Tractatus* proves that point.

# 6

## ABOUT THE SAME

### GEORGE PITCHER

A naïve, but somehow compelling, picture of how we all originally learn to use language – or, as I should rather put it, of how we originally acquire the concepts of our language – is this : our elders point to things (objects, qualities, etc.) and repeat their names to us. We gradually learn to correlate the names with the things, or the kinds of things, and when we have done this, we know what the words mean. Augustine had some such picture, and Wittgenstein gives Augustine's account of it in the opening lines of the *Investigations*. The view of language-learning is not totally wrong, but it is drastically over-simplified and contains more than one *suggestio falsi*.

For one thing, the view betrays no sensitivity to the complications that surround the seemingly straightforward and unambiguous act of pointing to something. Wittgenstein describes these complications in a few convincing paragraphs. I shall not be concerned here with the well-known things he says about the possible misunderstandings that can always arise over what it is, exactly, that a person is pointing to, nor with his equally familiar remarks about how much a learner must already know before he can understand an ostensive definition or the teacher's subsequent attempts to free it from ambiguity. I am interested, rather, in an attack on the Augustinian picture that Wittgenstein launches at a more advanced point, as it were. Perhaps it is not quite accurate to characterize the passages I mean as constituting an attack on the picture, since they occur in a later part of the *Investigations* and are not explicitly directed against the Augustinian view of language-learning. Nevertheless they do set forth considerations that undermine a certain thesis that is implied, or anyway strongly suggested, by the Augustinian picture. These considerations,

120

moreover, seem to me to shed light on some of the important, but obscure, things Wittgenstein has to say about sensations.

The thesis that is implied, or suggested, by the Augustinian picture may be put too darkly – and too crudely – like this : we can see the universal in the particular. Let us suppose, for example, that a child is being taught, à la Augustine, what a *cat* is. His teacher points out several cats to him. The child eventually grasps the idea that what is designated by the word 'cat' is not a certain colour, nor any particular individual animal, nor a given mode of behaviour, nor any number of other possibilities, but rather a certain kind of animal. (To do this, he must of course know at least roughly what an *animal* is.) It is all too easy to think that once the child reaches this point, he *ipso facto* knows what a cat is, and, indeed, that he ought to have no further problems about applying the term 'cat' to new animals of that kind that may come his way. All he has to do, so it would seem, is to note whether the new animal is the *same*, in the relevant respects, as those animals, already seen by him, to which the term 'cat' was properly applied. The idea is, then, that being able to focus one's attention on a particular instance of a concept, i.e. on something that 'falls under' the concept, is tantamount to *having* the concept.

So baldly put, this idea does not bear a moment's serious examination. But suppose we make it slightly more sophisticated as follows : we now hold that if a learner observes several particulars that fall under a given concept, knowing that they do fall under it, he can abstract their relevant common features (viz., the essential ones) and thereby come to have that concept. Wittgenstein attacks this view on several fronts : thus his doctrine of family resemblance, for example, challenges the notion that there must be a property, or a cluster of properties, shared by all particulars that, as I have put it, fall under a given concept.

What Wittgenstein says about family resemblance, if it is valid, constitutes a powerful argument against these Augustinian pictures of concept formation. It might, however, be thought that the argument tells against those pictures only in so far as concepts of relatively complex things, but not where concepts of relatively simple things, are concerned.[1] For surely all *red* things, all *square* things, all *miles*, and so on, do have something in common. And so the Augustinian picture, even the cruder version of it, might seem to have something right about it, as long as its scope is limited to the concepts of relatively simple things (properties, relations, or whatever). Is it not entirely plausible to think that once a person realizes that 'red' designates this particular colour, that 'square' designates this particular shape, and that 'one mile' designates this particular distance, he has all he needs to enable him to apply those terms correctly to future things he may encounter that fall under those concepts? He need only note whether the new particular has the same colour, has the same shape, is the same distance, or whatever, as the original.

Whatever plausibility this last-ditch defence of the Augustinian picture may have derives from the presumption that sameness, at least in the case of relatively simple things, is what may be called a wholly natural, as opposed to a conventional, relation. And the presumption has a seductive appeal. It is, of course, a matter of convention that 'red', 'colour', 'square', 'shape', 'mile', and 'distance' are words in the English language. It is also a matter of convention that the word 'red' designates the attribute redness (or expresses the concept of redness), that the word 'colour' designates colour (or expresses the concept of colour), and so on. But given these purely linguistic conventions, it is not a matter of convention at all that this patch of red is, or is not, the same colour as that coloured patch; nor is it a matter of convention that the distance between points $x$ and $y$ – suppose it is a mile – is or is not the same as the distance between points $y$ and $z$. The actual colour of the two patches, and the two actual distances, settle the questions, not a linguistic or any other kind of convention.

What Wittgenstein finds wrong with all this is its talk of *the*

[1] I have no criterion for distinguishing the relatively complex from the relatively simple. I rely on intuitions alone, and trust that yours will agree with mine. Nothing of much importance hangs on any such agreement, however.

attribute of redness, *the* concept of redness, *the* concept of a mile, *the* concept of distance, and so on, as if these were the only possible concepts answering to those terms. He freely admits, and indeed insists, that we all have a strong tendency to regard our own concepts as the only ones, or anyway as the only natural or right ones. We regard them as forced on us by the nature of reality. In this, we are all terribly insular – and terribly wrong. Consider his example of teaching a pupil to continue the series 2, 4, 6, 8, 10, . . ., indefinitely by constantly adding 2 each time. (*Investigations*, Sec. 185 et seq. See also *The Blue and Brown Books*, p. 141 ff.) Given our concepts of addition and of two, it is not a matter of convention that what follows 1,000 in the series is 1,002 and not 1,004 or some other number. If the pupil is to go on in the same way after he reaches 1,000 he *must* hit next on 1,002, and not on any other number – but this is only so if he is to proceed in accordance with *our* mathematical concepts. And if we think our concepts are *the* (only) ones, or the only correct ones, then we need to unleash our imagination and let it roam more freely. So when the pupil adds 2 to 1,000 and gets 1,002, we would indeed say that he is doing the same thing he did in all the earlier steps – he is going on in the same way. But what counts as the *same*, here, is determined by our mathematical concepts which are ultimately a matter of how we all do in fact talk and act when we continue series, solve mathematical problems, and the like. These modes of procedure constitute one type of social *practice* or *custom*, and hence are, at bottom, conventional – in the sense that alternatives to them are conceivable.[2] Within some such framework of social practices or language-games, and only within them, sameness is determined by the way things really are. But to say this is to say that there is an element of convention – indeed, a profound element of convention – in all sameness.

There can be no doubt that the foregoing mathematical

---

[2] Or perhaps I should say, more weakly, only that the idea that there are such alternatives is an intelligible one. On this point, see Barry Stroud's perceptive 'Wittgenstein and Logical Necessity', *The Philosophical Review*, LXXIV (1965), 504–18.

example is highly controversial. Moreover, it raises questions in the philosophy of mathematics that I am not able to discuss with much confidence. Despite all this, I believe the example embodies a valid principle that is illuminatingly applicable to ordinary concepts of relatively simple things. I want to try now to show this by treating of some non-mathematical examples.

1. Start with middle C on the piano and play the diatonic scale of C upwards: after the seventh note, B, we say that you reach C again – not middle C, of course, but the C above middle C. It is the same note, only one octave higher. (See *The Blue and Brown Books*, p. 140 ff.) There is no absolute necessity in this: someone unfamiliar with our musical nomenclature, upon hearing middle C and the C above middle C, might well deny that they are both the same note. And would he be wrong to do so? Yes and no. Speaking from *within* the framework of the accepted musical nomenclature, one must indeed say that he would be wrong – for according to that nomenclature, the two notes are both Cs, and hence are both the same note of the scale.[3] But if we thus accuse him of an error, we ought to make no mistake about its nature. It is not necessarily the result of a failure to hear something that is 'really there'; he need not be labouring under any misapprehension whatever about the qualities of the two notes themselves – he need not be 'hearing them different' from the way we hear them. His error, to the extent that what he reports *is* wrong, may simply be based on ignorance of the conventions of our musical nomenclature. For the sameness of middle C and C above middle C consists at least partly in this: that they are both called 'C'. And that is a matter of convention. Not, of course, *pure* convention, as if any other convention would be just as reasonable or natural. I take it that with everything else remaining as it is, it would be wholly unnatural and pointless to call what we now call middle C and middle D 'the same note'.

[3] According to current usage in England, all pitches with the same letter-name are indeed considered as being the same note; middle C and its octave, for example, are called 'the same note but different tones'. In the United States, theorists are adopting Milton Babbitt's term 'pitch-class' to express the concept of all pitches with the same letter-name.

Nevertheless, one can think of other conventions that might be almost as natural as the actual convention, or at least that might come to seem so if one were to live with them for a time.[4]

There is a tendency to suppose that whatever is conventional is *ipso facto* wholly arbitrary. It seems to me that this is almost never the case, and that there is nearly always some good reason for adopting one convention rather than another. This is certainly true, at least, in the present case of the convention whereby every eighth note in a diatonic progression is called the *same* note, is assigned the same name. The whole theory of music stands behind that convention and would be vastly more complex and difficult without it. So the point of stressing the conventionality of the sameness of middle C and C above middle C is not at all to impugn it as arbitrary. It is rather to bring out the negative fact that despite the great 'natural similarity' the two notes have to our ears, they are not *in and of themselves* the same note. And that means : it is not true that, apart from fundamental musical theory and the nomenclature that is an integral part of it, middle C and C above middle C are the same note, just in virtue of their intrinsic natures. No doubt their instrinsic natures – i.e. the *sound* of them – help determine what musical theory shall be : but the fact remains that without that theory, and the conventions of musical nomenclature that are part of it, their sameness is non-existent.

2. In the previous example, the sameness-establishing convention was backed by a theory (viz., musical theory); let us turn now to one where the convention is backed by a way of life. I once read a clipping from a Hong Kong newspaper that said: 'The Chinese of old had miles of two lengths – one for going uphill, one for downhill.' This may seem perplexing : on the one hand, the news flash appears to be perfectly intelligible and we are even disposed, in the absence of knowledge to the contrary, to accept it as true. On the other hand, it appears to be self-contradictory : we think that there really cannot be *miles* of two different lengths,

---

[4] Nevertheless, it should be noted that recognition of the octave does seem to be a universal human phenomenon.

since a mile is defined as being exactly 1,760 yards long. But then we recall that we ourselves have nautical miles of (roughly) 2,000 yards as well as standard land miles of 1,760 yards: so why shouldn't the Chinese of old have had uphill and downhill miles of two different lengths if they wanted them? Implicit in this concession, however, is an assumption about what the Chinese practice actually was: the assumption, namely, that they considered the uphill mile and the downhill mile to be of *different* lengths, just as our nautical mile and our land mile are of different lengths. Very likely this assumption is true; but for the purposes of our inquiry, I want to indulge in a quite different interpretation of the data. I want to suggest that although the ancient Chinese certainly had what we, and like-minded people, would call miles of two different lengths, perhaps they considered their uphill mile and their downhill mile to be of exactly the same length. And if we ask '*What* length did they think they both were?', the answer would be: 'A mile of course.'

At this point, the following objection will be raised: 'But look here, nobody in his right mind can possibly maintain that one of those uphill miles is the same distance as one of the downhill miles; for it has been agreed that one is longer than the other. Let's say the uphill mile is 1,760 yards long and the downhill, 2,000 yards: now how could the uphill and the downhill miles conceivably be of the same length? Your interpretation is hopelessly confused.' One possible reply to this objection is that although the Chinese might, indeed, grant that the uphill mile is 1,760 yards long and the downhill one 2,000 yards long, nevertheless they could still insist that 1,760 yards uphill *equals* 2,000 yards downhill – the two distances are exactly the same, for one is uphill and the other is downhill. Here is an analogy that might help to make this reply plausible: we say that a dollar in a small town such as Oshkosh is equal to, or is worth, fifty cents in New York City. This means that the purchasing power of a dollar in Oshkosh is greater than it is in New York. Similarly, the Chinese can be understood as holding that the measuring power of a yardstick uphill is greater than it is downhill. Just as you need more dollars in New York than you do in Oshkosh to achieve the same (monetary) value, so you need to lay down the yardstick more times going downhill than you do going uphill to achieve the same (spatial) value – i.e. distance.

This, I say, is a possible interpretation (call it interpretation A) of the ancient Chinese practice that will serve to answer the objection. But there is another possible interpretation (call it interpretation B) that is more plausible and will also serve our particular purposes better. According to it, the Chinese did not determine distance by laying down yardsticks or by any similar procedure and hence they would not concede that a downhill mile contained a greater number of distance-units (e.g. yards) than did an uphill mile. Rather, they measured any given distance by observing how long it took a standard walker to traverse it; let us suppose that if such a walker walked in a standard way from point A to point B in one minute, they would say that the distance between A and B was one spell. If it took him five minutes, the distance would be five spells, and so on. Naturally, a standard walker goes a smaller number of (our) yards uphill in one minute than he goes downhill in the same time, so that the phrases 'up the road a spell' and 'down the road a spell' designated what we would call different distances – although *they*, of course, would say they designated the same distance (viz. a spell). An uphill mile and a downhill mile, according to the Chinese on this interpretation, were of exactly the same length – 15 spells, say – although *we*, with our way of measuring distances, would hold that their downhill mile was longer than their uphill one. Here again, then, we encounter the conventionality of sameness : given two stretches of road, the question of whether or not they are of equal (i.e. the same) length can only be settled by an appeal to the method of measuring distance – and that, as we have seen, is a matter of convention.

If we suppose that walking was the primary means of transportation in ancient China, their notion of a spell, with its consequence that an uphill and a downhill mile were of the same length,. would be seen to embody a convenient 'conceptual scheme' – one that for us, with our airplanes, trains, and automobiles, would not be so convenient. 'To imagine a language', as

Wittgenstein tells us, 'means to imagine a form of life'. (*Investiga-tions*, Sec. 19. See also Sec. 241.)

Wittgenstein would hold, I believe, that since the ancient Chinese measured distance differently, their concept of distance, or length, was different from ours.[5]

If this is right, then the moral of our example may be stated as follows : 'Given two stretches of road, or any two one-dimensional spatial magnitudes, it is perfectly possible for there to be two different ways of measuring length, and hence two different, but closely related, concepts of length (meanings of the word 'length') such that according to one the two magnitudes are different and according to the other they are exactly the same. Therefore, whether one one-dimensional spatial magnitude (e.g. the length of a stretch of road) is the same as another or not is in part a matter of convention.'

3. For a final example, let us consider sameness in connexion with colours. We say that light blue and dark blue are both shades of the same colour. Is there a necessity in this, or is there an element of convention at work here as there was in the previous examples? Well, to say that light blue and dark blue are shades of the same colour is to utter a mere tautology : for it is a tautology

---

[5] Is Wittgenstein's contention here valid? I shall in this paper assume so. But consider the following two claims :

(a) The ancient Chinese had different concepts of a *mile* and of *distance* from ours (or the meanings they attached to the words in their language that correspond to our words 'mile' and 'distance' were different from ours) *because* they measured distance in a different way.

(b) The ancient Chinese had the same concepts of a *mile* and of *distance* as ours (or the meanings they attached to the words in their language that correspond to our words 'mile' and 'distance' were the same as ours) – they simply *measured* distance in a different way.

What the relevant considerations are for making a choice between (a) and (b) are by no means clear. In any case, a discussion of the matter would take us too far afield; and so I shall merely follow Wittgenstein in his choice of (a). I hasten to add, however, that the points I am trying to make are in no way affected by this decision : they could be made equally well on the basis of (b).

Someone who accepts (b) would assert, and Wittgenstein would deny, that the meanings the Chinese assigned to the words in their language corresponding to our words 'length' and 'distance' are the *same* as those assigned by us to our words 'length' and 'distance'. Is there an element of convention involved in *this* sameness? Of course !

that light blue and dark blue are both shades of blue, and it follows from this that they are both shades of the same colour. So it *is* necessary – but uninterestingly so – that light blue and dark blue are both shades of the same colour. In order to have an interesting question, then, we must rephrase the original one as follows: Is it necessary that the colour we now call 'light blue' (dub it colour 1) and the colour we now call 'dark blue' (dub it colour 2) are both shades of the same colour, or could it be otherwise? There are no doubt good reasons why we call colour 1 and colour 2 shades of the same colour (viz., blue): for one thing, in order to get a paint of colour 1 and a paint of colour 2, one need only mix a paint of pure blue with white and black, respectively. But these reasons are not of sufficient weight, nor of the right kind, to produce unalterable necessity: they must, in fact, constitute merely good reasons for the adoption of a convention, because it is easy to describe states of affairs in which a totally different convention might well prevail, according to which colours 1 and 2 would *not* be shades of the same colour. For example, consider the following tribe – a variation on two described by Wittgenstein. (See *The Blue and Brown Books*, p. 134 ff.) There are two castes, one patrician, the other plebeian. The members of the first, and only they, wear what we call red and light blue (colour 1) garments, while the members of the second, and only they, wear what we call yellow and dark blue (colour 2) garments. In the language of these tribesmen, what we call red and colour 1 are both called simply *patrician*; yellow and colour 2 are both called *plebeian*. They have no separate names for what we consider to be the distinct colours of red and yellow, nor for colour 1 or colour 2. The tribesmen would not think that colour 1 and colour 2 had anything in common. They would certainly not judge that they were shades of a single colour; indeed, as far as one can determine from our story so far, they may not even have the concept of *two shades of the same colour*. Since colour 1 is patrician and colour 2 plebeian, the tribesmen would be inclined to think that they are as different as can be.

It may seem to you that the world of our mythical tribesmen has been too sketchily described, and that the plausibility of the example depends on the omission of certain important facts. For instance: 'Surely the tribesmen must notice some difference between what we call red and light blue (colour 1) – so how could they *not* have distinct names for the two obviously different colours?'

No doubt they notice a difference – but the difference counts for naught in light of the huge sameness-establishing fact that the two colours are, after all, both patrician. Why must all noticeable differences be enshrined in one's language? The people we are talking about may simply have no need to mark the difference between (our) red and (our) light blue: so having separate names for the two colours would appear to them to be utterly pointless.

Perhaps in their restricted natural environment these particular colours do not occur *at all*, much less singly: they always occur together and then only in patrician garments. Moreover, we can readily imagine that the tribesmen have no interest whatever in marking the difference between the two patrician colours. So why should, or must, they have distinct names for them? And even if (our) red and light blue do imbue objects other than patrician garments, the tribesmen may just have no interest in assigning distinct names to them. The colours of flowers, insects, fruits, and so on, play no part in their lives. All they care about, when it comes to colour, is the fact that patrician garments are what we call red and light blue (colour 1) and that plebeian garments are what we call yellow and dark blue (colour 2). This fact bulks so large that it governs their whole use of the relevant colour terms. It establishes, for them, an identity of colours that does not exist for us. To imagine this requires us to imagine a way of life quite different from ours: but there is no incoherence involved in describing that way of life.

Actually, the validity of the point about (our) red and (our) light blue having something in common for the tribesmen does not depend on their lack of distinct names for the two colours. For suppose they do have such names – 'patric', say, and 'ian'. Even so, given the overwhelming importance of the fact that the two colours figure in patrician garments, the relationship between patric and ian would be akin to the relationship between our maroon and our scarlet, for instance. Patric and ian would be two versions (to use a neutral term) of patrician – two patricians – as, for us, maroon and scarlet are two versions of red – two reds. So for the tribesmen, patric and ian (i.e. red and light blue) would have something in common, while (our) light blue and (our) dark blue would not.[6]

'But wouldn't these people notice that by mixing what we call a pure blue dye with a white one, something of (what we are calling) colour 1 – light blue – results, and that if they mix it instead with a black dye, they get (what we are calling) colour 2 – dark blue? If so, then surely they would have to get the idea that colour 1 and colour 2 are shades of the same colour.' The answer to this is that our tribesmen may very well not indulge in any such mixing of dyes. Or suppose they did, but that the mixing of their dyes produced the following odd chemical reactions: a colour 1 (light blue) dye mixed with a black one yields red, while a mixture of red and white dyes yields colour 1. (Similarly for colour 2 and yellow.) This might even lead the tribesmen to maintain (if they have the concept of *two shades of a single colour*) that (our) red and colour 1 are two shades of patrician, and that (our) yellow and colour 2 are two shades of plebeian. It would hardly cause them to regard colour 1 and colour 2 as being two shades of the same colour.

'But can't they just look and see that colour 1 and colour 2 are shades of the same colour?' We can look and see that, but they cannot: their concepts do not allow it. But then, equally, they also see sameness of colour to which we are quite blind. We might put the difference this way: for us, it is a merely contingent fact about red and light blue (colour 1) that they are the colours worn by the patricians – 'being the colours of patrician garments' is an *external* relation between red and light blue. But for the tribesmen, the fact is a necessary one, the relation internal.

These examples show that there is no answer to the question

---

[6] I mean they would have nothing *of a philosophically relevant or interesting sort* in common, however that sort is to be characterized (here I shall have to trust that your intuitions again square with mine) – for of course the two colours do share some predicates. They both occur in the garments of some caste or other, for instance.

whether or not two colours are different shades of the same colour apart from the conventions embodied in the colour-concepts of this or that language – concepts determined by the 'form of life' of the language users and by certain general facts of nature (such as facts about what happens when dyes of different colours are mixed). There is no sense to the claim that colours 1 and 2 just *are*, in and of themselves, shades of the same colour : according to our colour-concepts, they are indeed shades of the same colour – namely, of blue; but according to the colour-concepts of our mythical tribesmen, they are not.

We have been talking about *shades* of the same colour : but it is even more evident, I think, that there is a convention at work when different colours are called *hues* of the same colour – e.g. when we say that olive and pea-green are two hues of green, or that rose and scarlet are two hues of red.

At this juncture, the idea is liable to arise that the conventionality of sameness in connexion with colours must stop at a certain point. That is to say, although it may be conceded that it is partly a matter of convention that two different colours (e.g. colours 1 and 2) are called shades of the same colour, or that two different colours (e.g. rose and scarlet) are called hues of the same colour, still it will be thought that at least it cannot be a matter of convention *at all* that two patches of the same colour (e.g. two patches of colour 1) are said to have the same colour, or that their colours are said to *be* exactly the same shade of colour. It would seem that there can be no logical room for convention where there is absolute or perfect identity. In reply to this, I would say that although there may be less logical room than in the case of two different colours being called shades or hues of the same colour, nevertheless there is still *some* room. That is, one could describe societies or cultures with concepts of colour such that what we call two patches of exactly the same colour would be said by members of those societies not to have the same colour. Some of those describable societies would admittedly be uninteresting in that the word 'colour' would have a radically different meaning in their language. For example, suppose the members of a certain society refused to say that two surfaces were of the same colour unless their shapes were also the same : they would deny that what we would call a red triangular patch had the same colour as what we would call a red circular patch. This case is trivial because this society assigns a very different meaning to the word 'colour' : in their dictionaries, the entries for colour-words would have to contain an essential reference to the shapes of the coloured things. However, I think it is possible to describe a society whose colour-practices are such that they would sometimes deny that two patches, which we would judge to be of exactly the same colour, were of the same colour, and yet such that their concept of colour is at least interestingly close to ours – and perhaps it is even the same as ours.

Consider, then, a tribe whose colour-vocabulary is exactly like ours and who determine the colours of things just as we do – e.g. by merely looking or, in doubtful cases, by comparison with colour samples or other paradigms – but who spend almost all their lives in a jungle illuminated by an eerie light called *jungle light*. Most things are unchanged in colour when they are brought from sunlight into jungle light, but certain kinds of materials $x$ change slightly in colour when this happens to them. Hence it is quite possible that we should judge two pieces of cloth – one of kind $x$ and another of kind not-$x$ – to have exactly the same colour when the jungle tribesmen would judge them to be of different colours.

Here one is tempted to object : 'But of course under different lighting conditions, things appear to have different colours. We outsiders would agree with the tribesmen that under jungle light the two pieces of cloth had different colours, and conversely, the tribesmen would agree with us that in sunlight, they were of exactly the same colour. There is nothing surprising in this, and the example lends no support to the claim that there is an element of convention involved here in the sameness of colour.' But it is not evident to me that we and the tribesmen would have to agree in all our colour-judgments when we were all apprised of the relevant facts, although I think it *might* happen. It seems more likely, however, that we outsiders – especially if we spent very little time in the jungle – would insist that the two pieces of

133

cloth merely appeared to differ in colour in jungle light, but that this appearance was deceptive and the two pieces were really of exactly the same colour. (Compare the remarks of haberdashers about the colours of ties under their artificial light.) And it seems more likely that the tribesmen – especially if they spent very little time out of the jungle – would say the same thing, *mutatis mutandis*, about the colours of the pieces of cloth in sunlight. If this is a correct account of what would happen, then we would have two groups of people who disagree as to whether two patches of cloth were exactly the same colour, and their disagreement would not be attributable to any radical difference of meaning that the two groups assign to the word 'colour' or to the various colour-words, for there is no radical difference of meaning (and perhaps there is no difference at all). The disagreement results from their accepting different conventions as to what will count as standard conditions of lighting. So not only is it partly a matter of convention that two different colours are called two shades or two hues of the same colour, it is also partially a matter of convention that two objects (surfaces, or whatever) are said to have exactly the same colour.

To conclude, I want to apply the lesson contained in the three foregoing examples to the case of sensations – and in particular, to pain. The Augustinian picture is especially tempting here. Once a child realizes that the word 'pain' designates an unpleasant sensation, such as he gets when he hits his head against a stone wall or falls off his tricycle, then he knows what pain is. He does not, certainly, have to learn any more in order to be able to apply the word correctly to future sensations of his that may fall under the concept of pain : he has but to note whether they are the same (or feel the same) as the already experienced pains.

But if the principles involved in our three examples are valid, then this picture cannot be a true one. It is impossible for the child to focus his attention on one or two pains he now has, or has had, and, noting their quality, to be confident that he thereby knows what a new sensation must be like in order to be the *same* as these paradigms – i.e. to be the same kind of sensation, namely, a pain. For that to be possible, sameness (of kind) would have to be a totally natural relation : and our three examples have shown that it is not – it is at least in part a conventional one. A convention, of course, embodies a social practice, custom, or habit. So whether two different particulars, $x$ and $y$, count as the same $Z$ (i.e. the same kind of thing) is a matter, ultimately, of whether the people who speak the relevant language would call them, for one reason or another, the same $Z$. To know which of his future sensations are *pains*, then, the child cannot simply rely on some sort of intuitive feeling that they are intrinsically the same as his already-experienced paradigms : he must, rather, learn the appropriate convention that *establishes* the sameness.

This sameness-establishing convention cannot, it would seem, deal with nothing but the experienced, or felt, quality of pains. For how should any such convention be taught or learned? A teacher certainly cannot, for instance, note the actual felt qualities of a learner's sensations and inform him which ones are properly called *pains*, and which ones are not. For the same reason, the learner cannot learn the convention by observing the felt qualities of other people's sensations and noticing which of them they call pains.[7] How, then, could he possibly learn it ?

One suggestion might be this : 'It's quite simple : the learner first learns what "same" means in the case of colours, sounds, lengths, weights, and so on, and then applies what he learns to sensations. Nothing is more familiar than this sort of extrapolation in the learning and use of language. For example, a child learns what a blue book, a blue bottle, a blue blanket, and so on, are, and after a while he is able to apply the term "blue" correctly to new things. In the same way, why can't a child first learn what the same colour, the same sound, the same length, and so on, are, and then extend what he has learned to sensations?' This suggestion will not work. One cannot extend one's use of the notion of sameness as one can the notion of blueness.

[7] Indeed, the situations envisaged, and rejected, in this and the previous sentence are the worst sort of impossibilities – for their (attempted) descriptions are actually unintelligible.

The concept of sameness is essentially tied to other concepts in a way that few others are. One thing cannot be *merely* the same as another : it must be the same colour, the same shape, the same size, the same kind of animal, or whatever. And what counts as the same *x* varies as *x* varies, so that the movement from sameness of one kind (e.g. of colours) to sameness of another (e.g. of lengths) can hardly ever be made on the basis of general principles alone : new kinds of sameness must be learned one by one. Certainly from a knowledge of what counts as being the same colour, nothing can be inferred about what counts as being the same length or being the same shape or being the same kind of animal, and so on. Colours, lengths, shapes, and animals are radically different kinds of 'things' and so the various conventions that establish the sameness of these 'things' are incomparable. And even where there is some degree of affinity among different kinds of 'things', so that one might reasonably expect a corresponding affinity among the conventions that establish their several samenesses – as in the case of quantitative 'things' such as length and weight, for example – still the separate conventions of sameness *might* be totally different, for any number of reasons. Therefore, whether sensations are very like or very unlike colours, weights, shapes, and so on, there can be no sound extrapolation from what counts as the sameness of those 'things' to what counts as the sameness of sensations.

The assumption that it is in virtue solely of their inherent felt qualities that certain sensations are properly called pains thus seems to run into an insuperable difficulty; because there seems to be no way for a person to learn any convention that would unite sensations having a certain range of felt qualities as all being the *same* (kind of) sensation – e.g. as all being pains. But to say that there is no possible way for anyone to learn the required convention is to say that no one could possibly learn to apply the word 'pain' to any of his own sensations; and that is absurd. Therefore the assumption must be abandoned.

Well, how *could* someone in fact learn the convention that determines the sameness of (kinds of) sensations? The only way a person can do this – or at least the only way available at

136

present – is to learn under what sorts of (public) conditions the sensation-words can be properly used. Consider pain: he must learn what typical causes of pain are (e.g. knocking a part of one's body violently against a hard object, burning a part of one's body, the rending of one's flesh by a sharp object, and so on), what pain-behaviour is (e.g. holding or rubbing the affected part of one's body, moaning, crying, grimacing, rocking and rolling back and forth, and so on), and what pain-attitudes are (most notably, the person with a pain wants, more or less strongly, to be rid of it). What he learns, therefore, is this: 'pain' refers to the sensations that are caused in a certain range of different ways, that one has a particular sort of 'anti-attitude' towards, and/or that one feels when one behaves, or at least has an inclination to behave, in a certain range of different ways. It is in virtue of some combination of *these* characteristics of certain sensations, rather than in virtue of their inherent felt qualities, that the word 'pain' is properly applicable to them. (This is only a very crude account, of course, but I think that it is right in principle and that for present purposes it is not necessary to go into more detail.) The conventions determining sameness of sensations, then, pertain not at all to the felt qualities of the sensations themselves, but rather to the situations in which they occur, including the attitudes and behaviour (or inclinations to behaviour) of the people (or animals) experiencing them.[8] In other words, the felt quality of the sensation drops out as irrelevant: 'it cancels out, whatever it is' (*Investigations*, Sec. 293). If the only question at issue is whether or not the word 'pain' applies to a given sensation, then it does not matter what the intrinsic felt quality of that sensation is; for it is not, and could not be, that quality that determines whether the term 'pain' is applicable to it or not. Each person may think of sensations of a certain range of felt qualities (the qualities, namely, of his own pains) when he thinks or speaks of pain, so that the word 'pain' is associated in his mind with sensations of a certain range of felt qualities. (See *Investigations*,

---

[8] This is undoubtedly one of the considerations lying behind Wittgenstein's remark: 'An "inner process" stands in need of outward criteria' (*Investigations*, Sec. 580).

Sec. 256.) But for all anyone knows, each person may associate the word 'pain' with sensations of wildly different ranges of felt qualities – or perhaps everyone associates it with sensations having exactly the same range of felt qualities. There is obviously no way of telling which, if either, of these possibilities is actual, and this by itself is enough to show that it is not the felt quality of a sensation that determines whether or not the word 'pain' is applicable to it.

I believe that the points I have been trying to make about the conventionality of sameness as it applies to sensations shed light on the nature of the connexion between 'outward criteria' and 'inward' occurrences. I think they also help us to understand better some of the things Wittgenstein says about sensations and private languages. For example, in *Investigations*, Sec. 258 he imagines what would be involved in keeping a diary to record the recurrences of a certain (presumably new) sensation. 'I speak, or write the sign ['E'] down, and at the same time I concentrate my attention on the sensation – and so, as it were, point to it inwardly.' The diary is to record just the occurrences of one specific sensation – viz., sensation E. So whenever the diarist writes 'E' in his book, the sensation whose occurrence he thus records ought to be the *same* as the original sensation and the others that followed. But what is supposed to determine whether a new sensation is or is not the *same*, and hence whether 'E' is or is not applicable to it? We have ruled out sameness as a purely natural relation; and there just is no established convention in this case to determine what sameness is to be. Anything, therefore, goes : the diarist may do as he pleases. 'In the present case I have no criterion of correctness. One would like to say : whatever is going to seem right to me is right. And that only means that here we can't talk about "right".' In the absence of any convention, or rule, to establish sameness, there simply isn't any sameness : i.e. of any new sensation, it cannot be said either that it is, or that it is not, the same as the original sensation (over which the ritual of saying 'E' was first performed) and its followers. And so 'E' is not the name of a (kind of) sensation.[9]

[9] This reading of Sec. 258 derives from comments of Saul Kripke.

There are unclarities and other difficulties in the general sort of view I have been attributing to Wittgenstein. Much more needs to be said about it than I have space for here. Indeed, I have at most merely sketched the beginnings of what I take to be his view about the connections between language and sensations. I think, though, that the view here hinted at is a powerfully compelling one. The biggest problem it has to face seems to me to be this: how can such a view account for the privileged epistemological position each person enjoys with respect to reports concerning his own sensations? Wittgenstein, as we know, wrestled with this problem. To what extent he did so successfully is one among many questions that I must for the present leave unanswered.[10]

[10] My thanks are due to Richard Rorty for helpful comments on an earlier draft of this essay.

# 7

# PHILOSOPHY AS GRAMMAR AND THE REALITY OF UNIVERSALS

'You think that after all you must be weaving a piece of cloth : because you are sitting at a loom – even if it is empty – and going through the motions of weaving.' – *Wittgenstein*

The intellectual activity in which Wittgenstein was engaged during the last twenty or so years of his life and the results of which are embodied in such posthumously published works as *Philosophical Investigations* was one that he thought it appropriate, and yet misleading, to call 'philosophy' :

> If . . . we call our investigations 'philosophy', this title, on the one hand seems appropriate, on the other hand it certainly has misled people. (One might say that the subject we are dealing with is one of the heirs of the subject which used to be called 'philosophy'.) (*BB*, p. 28.)[1]

Certainly the reader of Plato and Aristotle, of Descartes and Kant, who takes up the *Investigations* for the first time finds himself in quite another world, as it were, but one that is somehow continuous with the world of traditional philosophy. The problems to which Wittgenstein devotes such manifest intellectual energy and imagination seem to be quite unlike those one has met with in Aristotle or Kant, say, and yet there is a dimly discerned but powerfully felt connexion between the two. Although it is most often a debatable question just how Wittgenstein's

[1] References to Ludwig Wittgenstein's *Preliminary Studies for the 'Philosophical Investigations' Generally Known as The Blue and Brown Books* (Oxford, 1958) will be indicated by the letters '*BB*' followed by a page number. References to Wittgenstein's *Philosophical Investigations*, G. E. M. Anscombe trans. (2nd edn. Oxford, 1958) will be indicated by the letters '*PI*' followed by a section number for Part I, a page number for Part II.

140

inquiries connect up with traditional philosophical issues,[2] the object of this paper is to explore one such connexion. It traces a few lines between some of the things Wittgenstein says in his *Philosophical Investigations* and in the 'preliminary studies' for it, and the age-old but notoriously unresolved controversy between realists and nominalists that is known as 'the problem of universals', in the hope of shedding some light on the nature of this 'problem' and its seeming insolubility.[3]

The key to Wittgenstein's view – or at least one of Wittgenstein's views – of 'the subject which used to be called "philosophy" ' as well as his own investigations, lies, as I see it, in the distinction he draws between empirical or experiential propositions, which make up natural history and natural science, and conceptual or what he most often calls 'grammatical' propositions – in an extended, or even metaphorical, sense of the word. For he denies that philosophy is science or natural history – philosophical statements are not empirical statements, and he holds that philosophical statements are in one way or another grammatical.[4] (Which is not to say that all grammatical propositions are philosophical.) By an 'empirical proposition' Wittgenstein seems to mean a proposition (1) that is about phenomena, about the world, which means that it is not directly or indirectly about the use or meaning of words (single words, phrases, and

---

[2] He mentions very few philosophers by name – Socrates (Plato), St Augustine, Frege, James, Russell, Moore – and he rarely cites passages from their works.

[3] 'The very word "problem", one might say, is misapplied when used for our philosophical troubles. These difficulties, as long as they are seen as problems, are tantalizing, and appear insoluble' (*BB*, p. 46). We shall see why this is so.

[4] These points are made in many ways at many places in both *BB* and *PI*, but the following are representative: on the contrast between philosophical and empirical propositions, *PI*, 85, 109; on that between the empirical and the grammatical, *PI*, 251, 295; on the characterization of his own investigations as conceptual or grammatical, *PI*, 90, 383, p. 230; on that of traditional philosophical questions – here St Augustine's 'What is time?' – as grammatical, *BB*, p. 26.

That philosophical propositions are grammatical in nature is not to be taken as a definition of 'philosophical proposition' or of 'philosophy', I gather, but rather as a description of many, if not all, philosophical statements, independently identifiable as such, which is intended to reveal something about their logical nature, i.e. their 'grammar'.

sentences or 'propositions'), and (2) that is confirmable or dis-confirmable by observation or experiment.[5] A grammatical pro-position on the other hand is one that is explicitly or implicitly verbal in import; it is directly or indirectly about the use or mean-ing of words. (To examine the grammar of the word 'to know' is to examine the use of the word 'to know', and 'a grammatical explanation' about a word is 'an explanation concerning the meaning of the word' (*BB*, pp. 23–4).) A proposition is explicitly grammatical if it mentions a word (or words) and says something about its (their) use; it is implicitly grammatical if it uses, but does not mention, a word (or words) but still expresses a rule, convention, or decision about verbal usage and imparts no infor-mation about the world.[6] Examples (drawn from the text of Wittgenstein) of explicitly grammatical remarks are: ' "I" is not the name of a person, nor "here" of a place, and "this" is not a name' (*PI*, 410); ' "Willing" is not the name of an action' (*PI*, 613); 'In "I have pain", "I" is not a demonstrative pronoun' (*BB*, p. 68). Examples of implicitly grammatical remarks are: 'Believing is not thinking' (*PI*, 574); ' "Observing" [i.e. what we call "observing"] does not produce what is observed' (*PI*, p. 187); 'A machine can't think' (*PI*, 360); (also *BB*, p. 47). These are all instances of what Wittgenstein calls 'depth grammar' as opposed to 'surface grammar' (*PI*, 664), surface grammar being 'what immediately impresses itself upon us about the use of a word', 'the way it is used in the construction of the sentence, the part of its use – one might say – that can be taken in by the ear.' ' "This" is a pronoun' is surface grammar, the sort of thing one can easily learn from a dictionary; ' "This" is not a proper name', however, although it would seem to follow from ' "This" is a

[5] Language is obviously a phenomenon, a feature of the world, and hence a topic of empirical statements, in the sense of statements that satisfy con-dition (2) alone. But we sometimes – as here – wish to distinguish between words and the world, i.e. between words and what they are most often used to talk about; in which case an understandable restriction may be placed on the scope of 'empirical proposition'.

[6] This distinction between explicitly and implicitly grammatical proposi-tions is not Wittgenstein's. It is my way of characterizing two kinds of pro-positions Wittgenstein calls 'grammatical'. Also what follows is an interpreta-tion of 'grammatical' in the light of Wittgenstein's examples and what he says about them.

pronoun', together with the surface grammatical claim that pro-per names, pronouns, verbs, etc. are all different parts of speech, is depth grammar, a claim that borrows its depth, so to speak, from the fact that some philosophers, e.g. Russell, have held that 'this' and 'that' are the only *real* proper names. (Similarly for ' "I" is a personal pronoun' as opposed to ' "I" is not the name of a person' or 'In "I have pain", "I" is not a *demonstrative* pro-noun'.)

The nature of explicitly grammatical statements seems obvious enough, but that of implicitly grammatical statements requires further scrutiny, not only because of its bearing on an under-standing of philosophy, but – a related point – because they are easily taken for, because they look like, empirical statements. Consider the following propositions: (1) 'Three men can't sit side by side on a bench a yard long' and (2) 'The colours green and blue can't be in the same place simultaneously' (*BB*, p. 56).[7] The language in which these propositions are clothed makes them look alike (*PI*, p. 224), but (1) is an empirical proposition and 'states a physical impossibility', while (2), which suggests 'the picture of physical impossibility', perhaps a picture of the two colours getting in each other's way, 'is not analogous to this [i.e. to (1)]; but is somewhat analogous to "3 times 18 inches won't go into 3 feet" ' – which 'is a grammatical rule and states a logical impossibility'.[8] How can the difference – the *grammatical* difference – between these statements be brought out?

One way to exhibit the difference is to ask of each whether and how it can be verified: 'Asking whether and how a proposi-tion can be verified is only a particular way of asking "How d'you mean?" The answer is a contribution to the grammar of the proposition' (*PI*, 353). Clearly we know how to verify (1). To show that it is true (or probably true) we would naturally either introduce known empirical facts about the dimensions of adult males or try to fit three men, the thinnest we could find, on a

---

[7] I take (2) to mean something like 'The same thing (area, surface) cannot be entirely and only blue and entirely and only green at the same time'.

[8] '(Compare the proposition "He is 6 inches taller than I" with "6 foot is 6 inches longer than 5 foot 6 inches." These propositions are of utterly different kinds, but look exactly alike.)' *BB*, p. 56.

bench a yard long. But no known facts about the colours blue and green, e.g. facts of spectroscopy, and no imaginable experiment with paints, coloured lights, transparencies, etc. would serve to verify – or, of course, falsify – (2). The truth of (2) – often classified as a synthetic *a priori* proposition – is guaranteed solely by the rules or conventions governing the use of the words that make up the sentence expressing it. The implicitly grammatical statement 'The same area can't be all blue and all green at the same time', although it is not logically equivalent to the explicitly grammatical statement 'The phrase "all blue and all green at the same time" – like the phrase "perfectly square and perfectly round at the same time" – has application to nothing, expresses a linguistic absurdity', still tells us *in effect* only what the second tells us. And since the second is a grammatical rule (in Wittgenstein's sense), the first is said to be a grammatical rule as well. An implicitly grammatical proposition, then, is a necessary or *a priori* proposition (whether 'analytic' or 'synthetic' makes no difference here), the sort of proposition that is often said to be 'true (false) by definition' or 'true (false) *ex vi terminorum*'. An explicitly grammatical proposition, being a proposition about how certain linguistic expressions are in fact used, is contingent. The two are therefore not logically equivalent. But they are related, and the former is said to be 'grammatical' for something like the following reason. To put it schematically, let $S_1$ be a sentence expressing an implicitly grammatical proposition, e.g. 'One's paternal grandmother is one's father's mother', and let $S_2$ be a corresponding explicitly grammatical proposition, e.g. 'The phrase "paternal grandmother" means one's father's mother'. Now if I know that $S_1$ expresses (as here) an *a priori* true statement, then I know that $S_2$ expresses a true contingent statement; and conversely. And the same holds, *mutatis mutandis*, for sentences expressing false propositions.[9]

Another, but clearly related, way to bring out the grammatical nature of a proposition that may seem to be empirical is to

---

[9] This interpretation of what Wittgenstein means by a 'grammatical proposition' helps to explain his remarks that '*Essence* is expressed by grammar' (*PI*, 371), and 'Grammar tells us what kind of object anything is' (*PI*, 373).

ask 'Can we imagine the opposite?' or 'What would it be like, if it were otherwise?' (*PI*, 251). To change the examples, this time affirmative ones, consider 'Every rod has a length' and 'This table has the same length as the one there'. We can imagine one table not having the same length as another; we know what it would be like if it were otherwise. But can we imagine a rod that has no length; do we know what it would be like for something to be a rod without length? Clearly not.

> Of course, here 'I can't imagine the opposite' doesn't mean : my powers of imagination are unequal to the task. These words are a defence against something whose form makes it look like an empirical proposition, but which is really a grammatical one (ibid.).

'Really a grammatical one' for the reasons already given. The implicitly grammatical 'Every rod has a length' *means something like* (Wittgenstein's own way of putting it) the explicitly grammatical 'we call something (or *this*) "the length of a rod" – but nothing "the length of a sphere" ' (ibid.); or ' "... has a length" is properly applicable to whatever "... is a rod" is properly applicable to'; or 'a sentence of the form "The rod is . . . feet long" makes sense' (cf. *BB*, p. 30).

That Wittgenstein thought of his own philosophical inquiries as grammatical in nature, as having to do with the ways in which words are used, is manifest at many points; e.g. *PI*, 90, 109, 383, 496, and *BB*, pp. 18, 27, 28, 125. Further, philosophical grammar, in Wittgenstein's sense, is intended to be *'purely descriptive'* (*BB*, p. 125). 'Purely descriptive' as opposed to what? In the first place, as opposed to 'explanatory' :

> Grammar does not tell us how language must be constructed in order to fulfil its purpose, in order to have such-and-such an effect on human beings. It only describes and in no way explains the use of signs (*PI*, 496; cf. *PI*, 124, 126, *BB*, p. 125).

In the second place, Wittgenstein has no interest in proposing new uses of words, in constructing what is sometimes called an 'ideal language', on the supposition that their everyday or ordinary uses are somehow defective :

It is wrong to say that in philosophy we consider an ideal language as opposed to our ordinary language. For this makes it appear as though we thought we could improve on ordinary language. But ordinary language is all right (*BB*, p. 28).

Philosophy may in no way interfere with the actual use of language; it can in the end only describe it. . . . It leaves everything as it is (*PI*, 124).

That philosophical grammar is purely descriptive does not mean that its method is 'merely to enumerate actual usages of words'; it may deliberately invent new ones, 'some of them because of their absurd appearance' (*BB*, ibid.), but these inventions, as in the case of Wittgenstein's ingeniously contrived 'language games', are intended to reveal features of the actual uses of words. They are not linguistic recommendations, proposals put forward for general adoption. Finally, and most important in my opinion, philosophical grammar is both purely descriptive *and philosophical* because of its difference from and at the same time its relation to traditional philosophical perplexities and 'theories'.

The work of the philosophical grammarian does not duplicate that of the lexicographer or the grammarian in the ordinary sense – or, if it does, it has a different point. The description of how a certain word, e.g. the word 'to know', is used, 'gets its light, that is to say its purpose, from the philosophical problems' (*PI*, 109), e.g. the problems of traditional epistemology. This is because these problems 'are, of course, not empirical problems'. Appearances sometimes to the contrary, philosophical problems are not solved, philosophical theories are not confirmed or disconfirmed, by introspection, or by observation, or by experimentation : 'they are solved, rather, by looking into the workings of our language. . . . The problems are solved, not by giving new information, but by arranging what we have always known' (ibid.), i.e. what we already know about the workings of our language. Hence, 'the work of the philosopher [i.e. of the philosophical grammarian] consists in assembling reminders for a particular purpose' (*PI*, 127). Reminders addressed to whom? To those who are philosophically puzzled, those who do not see that what baffles them is nothing that empirical information, information about the world, about phenomena, will resolve or set straight, but rather something that is in some way grammatical. And what is the purpose of the reminders? To clear up the problem, expose its grammatical nature, in such a way that the problem will not be solved, in the sense in which mathematical or scientific problems are often solved, but will dissolve or disappear: 'For the clarity we are aiming at is indeed *complete* clarity. But this simply means that the philosophical problems should *completely* disappear' (*PI*, 133). And this is why one might say that the word 'problem' is misapplied to philosophical perplexities: where there is nothing that can rightly be called a 'solution' there is nothing that can rightly be called a 'problem' either.

The assumption is clear: philosophical – or, as Wittgenstein often prefers to call them, 'metaphysical' – problems and theories are not empirical but linguistic or grammatical:[10] 'the characteristic of a metaphysical question being that we express an unclarity about the grammar of words in the *form* of a scientific question' (*BB*, p. 35). If they were not grammatical, then descriptive grammar would be irrelevant to them and Wittgenstein's investigations would indeed be misleadingly called 'philosophical'. Just *how* they are grammatical or linguistic, however, is something of which Wittgenstein had a number of – possibly conflicting – views.[11] For example, apart from his thinking of metaphysicians as uttering disguised nonsense (*PI*, 464) which the philosophical grammarian must expose or 'uncover' (*PI*, 119) – perhaps a hangover of a view of philosophy to be found in the *Tractatus* – Wittgenstein represents the metaphysician as making linguistic mistakes (e.g. *PI*, 383; *BB*, p. 5); as misunderstanding (e.g. *PI*, 90); misinterpreting (e.g. *PI*, 111); or putting a false

[10] This is not a claim that can be proved for all cases at once; it requires piecemeal examination of philosophical views: 'Problems are solved (difficulties eliminated), not a *single* problem' (*PI*, 133).

[11] See M. Lazerowitz's full discussion of this point in A. Ambrose and M. Lazerowitz, 'Ludwig Wittgenstein: Philosophy, Experiment and Proof', *British Philosophy in the Mid-Century: A Cambridge Symposium*, ed. C. A. Mace (2nd edn. London, 1966), pp. 155–74. What follows is indebted to this essay.

interpretation on words (e.g. *PI*, 194). This is perhaps because he is unclear about the grammar of certain words (e.g. *BB*, p. 35); or is 'misled by a form of expression' (*BB*, p. 28), or because his intelligence is bewitched by means of language (*PI*, 109). All of this forcefully suggests (although it is capable of other interpretations) that the metaphysician is making false or mistaken implicitly grammatical assertions – claims about the uses of words that the descriptive grammarian is supposed to set straight. In short, this view of traditional philosophy or 'metaphysics' represents it as just *false* descriptive grammar put in the verbal dress of an empirical claim. If a philosopher says, 'in a typically metaphysical way, namely without an antithesis' (*BB*, p. 46), 'I can only *believe* that someone else is in pain, but I know it if I am' (perhaps because he is impressed by the ever-present, because logical, possibility of undetected malingering on the part of others) then, on this view of what he is up to, the philosophical grammarian puts him right by pointing out to him that 'I know someone else is in pain' does really make sense, that 'believe' is ordinarily used in contrast to 'know' whereas here it is not, and so on. (cf. *BB*, pp. 53–4 – which, again, is amenable to a different reading from that suggested here.) The philosophical grammarian's reminders would in this case serve much the same purpose as G. E. Moore's famous 'translations into the concrete' – and probably to as much effect.

But alongside this view of philosophy, which depicts the philosopher as grammatically muddled, confused, or wrong-headed, there is another, and to my mind more powerful, view which comes out in Wittgenstein's *Investigations* comment on the example given above :

> 'I can only *believe* that someone else is in pain, but I *know* it if I am.' – Yes : one can make the decision to say 'I believe he is in pain' instead of 'He is in pain'. But that is all – What looks like an explanation here, or like a statement about a mental process, is in truth an exchange of one expression for another which, while we are doing philosophy, seems the more appropriate one.

Just try – in a real case – to doubt someone else's fear or pain'
(*PI*, 303).

Here the philosopher is not represented as making the *mistake* of
saying, in effect, 'The verb "to know" has no use in connexion
with other people's fears or pains', but rather, for some reason or
other, again perhaps because he is impressed by the logical possibility of undetected malingering in every case of another's
apparent fear or pain, of having *decided*, and then only while he
is doing philosophy, to substitute one expression for another. In
any actual case of another's fear or pain, the philosopher behaves,
linguistically and otherwise, in much the same way as other men.
('Does a realist pity me more than an idealist or a solipsist?' *BB*,
p. 48.) Again, a philosopher might say that propositions about the
future are not real propositions, perhaps 'because he has been
struck by the asymmetry in the grammar of temporal expressions'. His saying this 'is all right as long as it isn't meant to be
more than a decision about the use of the term "proposition"; a
decision which, though not agreeing with the common usage of
the word "proposition", may come naturally to human beings
under certain circumstances. . . . The danger is, however, that he
imagines he has made a kind of scientific statement about "the
nature of the future" ' (*BB*, p. 109). In these and other cases the
philosopher is depicted not as making a mistake about how certain
expressions are used, not as misunderstanding or misinterpreting
or being misled by forms of expression, but rather as objecting to
the way in which certain expressions are actually used (the
reasons he gives for his view express the objection) and deciding,
if only while he is doing philosophy, to use them in a new way;
or recommending a new notation, 'in the sense in which a notation can be recommended' (*BB*, p. 60), his implicitly grammatical statement recording a rule governing his linguistic innovation. And of all of this he does with the air of a scientist
announcing a discovery.

The man who says 'only my pain is real', doesn't mean to say
that he has found out by the common criteria – the criteria,
i.e. which give our words their common meanings – that the

others who said they had pains were cheating. But what he rebels against is the use of *this* expression in connexion with *these* criteria. That is, he objects to using this word in the particular way in which it is commonly used. On the other hand, he is not aware that he is objecting to a convention. He sees a way of dividing the country different from the one used on the ordinary map. He feels tempted, say, to use the name 'Devonshire' not for the county with its conventional boundary, but for a region differently bounded. He could express this by saying: 'Isn't it absurd to make *this* a county, to draw the boundaries *here*?' But what he says is: 'The *real* Devonshire is this.' We could answer: 'What you want is only a new notation, and by a new notation no facts of geography are changed.' It is true, however, that we may be irresistibly attracted or repelled by a notation. (We easily forget how much a notation, a form of expression, may mean to us, and that changing it isn't always as easy as it often is in mathematics or in the sciences. A change of clothes or of names may mean very little or it may mean a great deal.) (*BB*, p. 57.)

The suggestion that emerges here is that doing philosophy – or metaphysics – is playing a special kind of language-game: of objecting to a linguistic convention, substituting 'a new notation', and then perhaps objecting to the innovation.

> For *this* is what disputes between Idealists, Solipsists and Realists look like. The one party attack the normal form of expression as if they were attacking a statement [i.e. an empirical statement]; the others defend it, as if they were stating facts recognized by every reasonable human being (*PI*, 402).

What makes this appropriately called a 'language-game' (though *not* in the sense in which Wittgenstein usually uses this expression) is that, however much a linguistic innovation may mean to a philosopher, his metaphysical 'theory' is what P. Hallie calls 'a rootless grammatical claim disguised as an empirical one'[12] – root-

---

[12] Philip P. Hallie, 'Wittgenstein's Grammatical-Empirical Distinction', *The Journal of Philosophy*, LX (1963), p. 569. Hallie claims that Wittgenstein draws the distinction between the empirical and the grammatical too

less, not only because it is unsupported by convention or common practice, but also because it is in a way idle; it is not taken seriously, actually put into practice, by the philosopher himself, *except* when he is doing philosophy; which means that it is disengaged from the workaday world in which language is used to perform a host of vital and practical functions. 'For philosophical problems arise when language *goes on holiday*' (*PI*, 38); and 'The confusions which occupy us arise when language is like an engine idling, not when it is doing work' (*PI*, 132).

This view alone seems to make sense not only of Wittgenstein's claim that philosophical propositions are grammatical – the linguistic-mistake view is consonant with that – but especially of his characterization of his own work as 'purely descriptive' and of his saying that the terms 'problem' and 'solution' are in a way misapplied when used in reference to philosophical difficulties. For 'descriptive' serves to *contrast* what Wittgenstein does with what the traditional philosopher or metaphysician does, and hence to make his work aptly described as 'one of the heirs of the subject which used to be called "philosophy" '. Were his grammatical remarks offered merely as true ones, as against the false ones of the metaphysician, metaphysics would be no less 'descriptive' than Wittgenstein's philosophical grammar. But if what the metaphysician is engaged in is notational innovation, the artificial but often dramatic redrawing of terminological boundaries, which might be called 'innovative grammar', then 'descriptive' has a point. Then also the 'reminders' which the descriptive grammarian assembles and his bringing words back from their metaphysical to their everyday use (*PI*, 116) serve not to *correct* linguistic mistakes, but simply to make clear the nature of the game that is being played with words. His battle is not against

---

sharply, and he sets out to show that 'a grammatical recommendation or proposition can be both a grammatical proposition and an empirical one' (p. 567). But all Hallie succeeds in showing is that a philosopher may give reasons for introducing a new notation, among which may be some straightforward empirical propositions. That an empirical proposition may serve as a reason for making a grammatical innovation, however, does not make that proposition evidence for the truth of the grammatical proposition in which the innovation is expressed, which it would have to do were the proposition empirical *as well as* grammatical.

151

'the bewitchment of our intelligence by means of language' (*PI*, 109) but against the bewitching possibilities, of which language is a fertile source, of idle terminological innovations that have the air of important truths. On this view of philosophy, this is all his 'solution' of a philosophical 'problem' can consist in. For no important philosophical problem has ever been *solved* to the satisfaction of all competent philosophers, and if Wittgenstein is right this is precisely what we should expect.

In the balance of this paper I shall try to bring this rough sketch (for it is no more than that) of Wittgenstein's view of philosophy as grammar into connexion with the persistent controversy between realists and nominalists in an effort to shed some light on the nature of that notorious dispute.[13]

In Ch. XVII of *An Examination of Sir William Hamilton's Philosophy* Mill wrote metaphysical realism's obituary : this doctrine, he says, 'is now universally abandoned'; it 'could not . . . permanently resist philosophical criticism, and it perished'; it is 'no longer extant, nor likely to be revived'. Like many similar announcements in the history of philosophy, Mill's obituary was premature : the doctrine was not dead, only dormant; or if dead, then like the phoenix it arose renewed from its ashes. For, as is commonly known, the view reappeared, vigorous and full of life, in the early years of the present century in the philosophies of Russell and Moore, to name but two of its adherents. Again it may have seemed to some 'to have aged more rapidly than its authors, and to have died, or fallen into oblivion', in recent years, but upon examining 'Moore's and Russell's principal argument for the reality of universals, in order to determine whether any spark of life remains in it' – 'Is it truly dead, or only neglected?' – A. Donagan concludes that it is still very much alive.[14] And surely this is what the history of philosophy would lead one to expect : philosophical positions – except for scientific theories

---

[13] I ignore the views of a third party to the debate, those of the conceptualist, not because they are less interesting but simply for reasons of economy. I also largely ignore the differences between 'Platonic' and 'Aristotelian' realism.

[14] Alan Donagan, 'Universals and Metaphysical Realism', *The Monist*, vol. 47 (1963), pp. 211–46. Quoted remarks are from pp. 211–12.

classified as philosophical, e.g. Aristotle's theory of the ethereal spheres – rarely, if ever, perish. Being criticism-resistant, as it were, they remain to be taken up by anyone attracted to them; which is one of the great enigmas of philosophy.

The opposition between realism and nominalism is sometimes put this way : a realist asserts that there are universals as well as particulars; a nominalist denies this – there are no universals. Although this is misleading, as we shall see at once, put this way the opposition clearly appears to be a dispute over 'what there is', over the truth-value of an existential proposition – 'There are universals' – which has all the earmarks of an hypothesis such as 'There is life on Mars'. Whether it is of this nature, however, is precisely what is to be seen.

To clear the ground a little, we may begin with the trivial grammatical point that 'universal' has a use. Consider the 'existential' statement 'Red (redness, the colour red) exists' or 'There is such a colour as greenish-blue'.[15] As Wittgenstein says (*PI*, 58), this might simply mean that something is red, or greenish-blue; in which case it is straightforwardly empirical. But there are contexts (consider 'There is such a colour as greenish-blue but no such colour as greenish-red') in which 'what we really *want* is simply to take "Red exists" as the statement : the word "red" has a meaning. Or perhaps better : "Red does not exist" as " 'Red' has no meaning".' Here what may appear to be an empirical claim about what there is, is in fact implicitly grammatical, and its truth-value is independent of the actual existence of red things : 'If "X exists" is meant simply to say : "X" has a meaning – then it is not a proposition that treats of X, but a proposition about our use of language, that is, about the use of the word "X" ' (ibid.). Leaving aside for the time being the question of a possible analogy between 'There are universals' and 'There are red things', suppose that 'There are universals' is implicitly grammatical. In that case, it amounts to no more than the claim that the noun 'universal' has a meaning

---

[15] Moore reports that Wittgenstein held that ' "There is such a colour as greenish-blue" is "grammar".' G. E. Moore, *Philosophical Papers* (London, 1959), p. 276.

or use. Although it is quite possible that a philosopher might deny this (I know of none who has), *this* denial is not what nominalism amounts to. If it did, then the dispute between realists and nominalists should have been settled before it began, namely, as soon as Aristotle introduced the substantive – or its Greek equivalent – into the parlance of philosophy. But ' "Universal" has a meaning or use' obviously does not describe its use, but only – as Wittgenstein says in another connexion – gives us a paper draft on such a description (*PI*, 383).

We can get a little cash for our draft if, still taking 'There are universals' as implicitly grammatical, we give it a further interpretation : 'The phrase ". . . is a universal" is applicable to or predicable of something'; which is not the same as saying ' ". . . is a universal" is applicable to some thing', for the nominalist does not deny that 'universal' is applicable to something, whereas he does deny that it is applicable to some thing. To what is 'universal' applicable? The nominalist answers : to words or signs and to them alone. This is sometimes taken as definitive of nominalism. Mill, for example, defines nominalism as the view that 'There is nothing general [i.e. universal] except names'.[16] And Hobbes, whom Leibniz referred to as 'a super-nominalist', declared 'The word *universal* is never the name of anything existent in nature . . . but always the name of some word or name', and 'there [is] nothing in the world universal but names; for the things named are every one of them individual and singular'.[17] This dictum is often confused with (i.e. taken as equivalent to or as entailing) another statement often attributed to nominalists :

[16] loc. cit. cf. A. D. Woozley, 'Universals', *The Encyclopedia of Philosophy,* ed. Paul Edwards (New York, 1967), vol. 8, p. 199 : a nominalist holds that 'only words are general' – as opposed, presumably, to things.

[17] The first remark is from Thomas Hobbes, *Elements of Philosophy,* ed. Molesworth (London, 1839), i, 20; the second from *Leviathan*, I, iv. That all existent, or possibly existent, things are individual, particular, or singular is said to be definitive of 'ontological nominalism', e.g. by G. Küng, 'Nominalism', *The New Catholic Encyclopedia* (New York, 1967), vol. 10, p. 483. cf. David Hume : 'It is a principle generally received in philosophy that everything in nature is individual' (*A Treatise of Human Nature*, Bk. I, Pt. I, Sec. VII); and George Berkeley : 'it is a universally received maxim that every thing which exists is particular' (*Three Dialogues Between Hylas and Philonous*, I).

'There is nothing common to a group of things called by the same name other than that they are called by the same name.'[18] But as far as I can see the two statements are quite independent of one another : to be universal – or a universal – and to be common to two or more things are not necessarily the same, nor does being the first necessarily imply being the second – at least not as the nominalist uses the words in question.

Abelard held that 'things (*res*) can not be called universals, taken either singly or collectively, because they are not predicted of many', hence 'it remains to ascribe universality of this sort to words alone'.[19] Here Abelard was adopting Aristotle's definition – or at least what he took to be Aristotle's definition – of 'universal' : 'By the term "universal" I mean that which is of such a nature as to be predicated of many subjects, by "individual" that which is not thus predicated. Thus "man" is a universal, "Callias" an individual.'[20] Since a predicate is a word, and a

---

[18] This is usually taken as a definitive of 'extreme nominalism', but I know of no nominalist who ever said it; and authors who define extreme nominalism in this way go on to say that no one – except Humpty Dumpty – has ever been an extreme nominalist. Extreme nominalism appears to be a straw man. Hobbes, to be sure, is sometimes said to have been an extreme nominalist, but I question below whether he was. In any case, the maxim is capable of several interpretations, some of which a nominalist would accept; e.g. 'There is no *thing* common to a group of particulars called by the same name'. See also note 38 below.

[19] 'The Glosses of Peter Abelard on Porphyry' (from the so-called *Logica Ingredientibus*), *Selections from Medieval Philosophers*, ed. and trans. Richard McKeon (New York, 1929), vol. I, p. 232. Note that in all these remarks words and things – or 'word' and 'thing' – are contrasted.

[20] *On Interpretation*, 17ᵃ39. This is the Oxford translation. Note that it puts quotation marks around the words 'man' and 'Callias', making it appear that what is predicable of many subjects is the word 'man'. And this seems to be the way Abelard read it, even though neither medieval Latin nor ancient Greek employed quotation marks. Compare with this J. L. Ackrill's translation : 'I call universal that which is by its nature predicated of a number of things, and particular that which is not; man, for instance, is a universal, Callias a particular'. *Aristotle's Categories and De Interpretatione* (Oxford, 1963). According to Ackrill (Notes, p. 75), although Aristotle sometimes speaks of 'saying' or 'predicating' a name of a subject, his basic view is that 'what is "said of" something as subject is itself a thing (a species or a genus) and not a name.' Whether 'predicate' signifies a linguistic expression or something non-linguistic, e.g. an attribute, quality, or property is an issue (grammatical) which has divided philosophers to this day. It has been a source of some confusion and, as we see, is implicated in the realist-nominalist controversy.

universal is a predicate, a universal is obviously a word – a general word as opposed to an individual word, e.g. a proper name.

> Just as, therefore, certain nouns are called appellative by grammarians and certain nouns proper, so certain simple words are called by dialecticians *universals*, certain words *particulars*, that is, individuals. A *universal* word, however, is one which is apt by its invention to be predicated singly of many, as this noun *man* which is conjoinable with the particular names of men according to the nature of the subject things on which it is imposed. A *particular* word is one which is predicable of only one, as *Socrates* when it is taken as the name of only one (loc cit.).

That 'universal' is applicable to no thing (but not 'to nothing'), that it is applicable only to words or names, does not prevent Abelard's saying that two or more things may have something in common, viz. what he elsewhere calls a 'common status':

> Individual men, discrete from each other . . . are united nevertheless in that they are men. I do not say that they are united [*conveniunt*] in man [*in homine*], since no thing is man except a discrete thing, but in being man [*in esse hominem*]. But *to be a man* is not the same as a man nor any thing. . . .[21]

A man is a thing, but being a man is not.

Whatever the historical connexion between Hobbes and the medieval nominalists may have been, his position strikes me as very like theirs. According to J. W. N. Watkins's excellent book on Hobbes,[22] Hobbes's 'nominalist ontology' consists in the claim that 'there is nothing universal in the world but names, every thing named being individual and singular' (p. 144). Names

[21] Abelard, op cit., p. 237. In the last sentence I have added the indefinite articles, which are lacking, of course, in the Latin.
[22] *Hobbes's System of Ideas* (London, 1965), Ch. VIII.

Hobbes thinks of as 'the bricks out of which language is built', and, like many philosophers before and after him, 'he divides names into proper names, and common or universal names' (pp. 140, 143). But, according to Watkins, 'Hobbes did not consistently abide by his nominalist ontology', for 'he sometimes allowed that a common name may stand for something which is *not* individual or singular – for a characteristic or a property or (as he called it) an *accident* which may be shared by many individual things' (p. 144); 'his statement that some names are names of accidents is inconsistent with his statement that there is nothing universal in the world but names, every thing named being individual and singular. For Hobbes goes out of his way to contrast accidents with individual things. . . .' (p. 148). But just where is the inconsistency? Consider : (1) 'Every thing named is individual and singular'; (2) 'There is nothing universal but names'; (3) 'Some universal (common, general) names are names of (stand for) accidents'; (4) 'The same accident may accompany (belong to, characterize) or be shared by many things'; and (4) 'Accidents are not (individual) things'. So far, I detect no inconsistency among these propositions. (1), which is not the same as 'Everything named is individual and singular', does not imply 'Every name is the name of one or more things'. If it did, then it would be inconsistent with the conjunction of (3) and (5). Again, if Hobbes held (6) : 'Something is a universal name if and only if it is the name of many individual things', then (6) too would be inconsistent with the conjunction of (3) and (5). But did Hobbes hold (6)? I do not see that he did. He may have explained the difference between *some* universal or general names and proper names by saying that while a proper name, such as 'Socrates', names one thing only, such universal names as 'man' name many things, but this is not the same as defining a universal name as the name of many things. Watkins, it appears, would like us to think that (4), together with the assumption that there are accidents, implies the existence of universal things; but it does not. An accident, as we have seen in the case of Abelard's 'common status', may be said to be common to many without being said to be universal; and that a common or universal name may stand for something that is not individual does not imply that it may stand for or name some *thing* that is not individual.[23]

Although nominalists often put forward and argue for the truth of such claims as 'Only words are universal(s)', 'Every thing is individual or particular', 'An accident (quality, property, common status) is not a thing', and 'A predicate is a word (name, linguistic expression)', as if they expressed non-linguistic facts, it is noteworthy that no evidence derived from observation or experiment is ever offered in support of them; indeed, we cannot imagine what such evidence would look like. 'Only words are universals' is not logically equivalent to 'Only males have served as justices of the United States Supreme Court'; nor is 'Every thing is individual (singular, particular)' logically analogous to 'Every justice of the Court has been a male', or 'An accident is not a thing' to 'An owl is not a herbivore', or 'A predicate is a word' to 'An owl is a predator'. Each and every one of the nominalist's claims is implicitly grammatical. What his dicta amount to, as far as I can see, is no more than the following: 'The term "universal" is applicable to (predicable of) words alone'; 'The term "individual" or "particular" applies to whatever the term "thing" applies to – but not only to that, for it also applies to certain words, e.g. proper names' (and this together with the first statement adds up to the claim that 'universal thing'

[23] In connexion with the nominalist's claim that every thing is individual or particular, it is interesting to note that William of Ockham held that there is a sense in which everything, not merely every thing, is individual. *Unomodo hoc nomen singulare significat illud quod est unum et non plura.* As a 'transcendental' term 'individual' signifies whatever is one and not many, and in this sense there can be nothing that is not individual. Not only is Socrates individual, but wisdom too, or being a man, or being white is individual. For just as Socrates is one (man) and not many (men); so wisdom is one (virtue) and not many; being a man is one thing (though not one *res*), being a horse is another; white is one colour, red another; etc. This, however, is not 'ontological nominalism'. If it were, Plotinus would have been an ontological nominalist (see *Enneads*, VI, iv, 1). But 'individual' may also be a 'term of second intention', and as such it applies only to 'discrete terms', a discrete term being a sign of one thing (*res*) only, e.g. a proper name, a universal being a sign of many. See Ernest A. Moody, *The Logic of William of Ockham* (New York, 1935), pp. 81–2.

In short, as a transcendental term 'individual' contrasts with nothing; it is 'without antithesis'; only as a term of second intention does it have an antithesis, but there it serves to distinguish between signs alone, not things.

expresses an absurdity); 'The term "thing" does not apply to whatever the term "accident", "quality", or "property" applies to'; and 'Whatever the term "predicate" applies to the term "word" ("name", "linguistic expression") also applies to, but not conversely'. For consider 'Every thing is particular'. Here the word 'particular' is being used 'in a typically metaphysical way, namely without an antithesis'. 'Particular' as opposed to what? Not 'universal', for 'universal thing' is disallowed. Hence, 'Every thing is particular' does not describe, is not about, things, e.g. dogs and cats, trees and stones, but, if about anything, about 'thing'. As Wittgenstein says of those who hold that there can be no such thing as an unconscious thought :

> They state their case wrongly when they say : 'There can only be conscious thoughts and not unconscious ones'. For if they don't wish to talk of 'unconscious thought' they should not use the phrase 'conscious thought' either (*BB*, p. 58).

So here : if it is logically impossible for there to be universal things, then 'Every thing is particular' is otiose and amounts to no more than 'Every thing is a thing'.

In the nominalist's use of the statements adduced we can clearly see a number of linguistic boundaries being drawn, to use a metaphor often employed by Wittgenstein. Whether the boundaries drawn coincide with those of the standard map is hardly answerable; for, except perhaps for the word 'thing' there is no standard map. 'Universal', 'particular' (as used in philosophy), and 'predicate' are terms of art, technical or semi-technical expressions, which a philosopher is free to use more or less as he pleases. Seen as implicitly grammatical propositions, then, the nominalist's dicta are not reports on how these terms have been used, but expressions of his decision to use them in the ways indicated. And who is to say him nay? Even R. I. Aaron, an opponent of nominalism, admits that one of the faces of nominalism amounts to no more than the decision to use the substantive 'universal' as a synonym of 'general word' :

> In examining this theory [nominalism] it must first be admitted that the nominalist has the right to use the term 'universal' as

he chooses and may use it as a synonym for the general word, and only in this way. This is a matter of convention, and though it is true that normally the word has been used in other ways yet it may be thus used if the nominalist chooses.[24]

But if 'universal' means the same as 'general word', then 'Universals exist', taken now as non-grammatical, is equivalent to 'General words exist', and no realist, of course, denies this, for the existence of general words is basic to his case. At this level, then, no difference, other than a trivial verbal difference, can be discerned between realism and nominalism. Can this be all the debate has been about for over two millenia? Clearly not. But to see what else there is to it we must see the nominalist's claims in opposition to, as denials of, certain claims made by realists.

J. L. Austin once said, 'People (philosophers) speak of "universals" as though these were entities which they often stumbled across, in some familiar way which needs no explanation. But they are not so.'[25] He goes on to suggest that if we want to know what a universal, as a putatively non-linguistic entity, is, we must look at the arguments given for the existence or reality of universals, since ' "universal" *means* in each case, simply "the entity which this argument proves to exist" ' (p. 5). Now 'that celebrated argument which above all, seems suited to prove the existence of "universals" in the most ordinary sense of the word' (p. 2) – Plato's famous one-over-many argument was a version of it – takes two forms, what might be called an ontological and a linguistic form :

(A) 'If this is red and that is red, then this and that must have something in common. Call what they have in common a "universal".'

(B) 'If we apply the same name, e.g. "red", to two or more things, then they must have something in common, something of

[24] R. I. Aaron, *The Theory of Universals* (Oxford, 1952), p. 224. Is it true that 'universal' is *normally* used in other ways?

[25] J. L. Austin, *Philosophical Papers* (Oxford, 1961), p. 2.

which the name is the name. Call what they have in common, what is named, a "universal".'[26]

As Austin notes (p. 3) 'this is a *transcendental* argument' : it tries to show that without universals something that obviously is possible would be impossible. According to version (A), if two things – roses, fire engines – did not have something in common, then they could not both *be* red; while according to version (B), if they did not have something in common, they could not be *called* 'red' – or any other word that means the same as 'red'. So a universal is what different things have, or may have, in common and that we call by the same name.

In the light of these arguments we can understand why philosophers say what they do about the nature of universals : (1) 'A universal is a recurrent characteristic, either a property (quality,

---

[26] Argument (A) may involve an intermediate step: 'Call what they have in common a "property", "quality", "characteristic", or "predicate", and call properties, etc. "universals".' An analogous argument can be framed to introduce relations, as well as properties, as universals.

A. Donagan (op. cit., pp. 231–2) points out, in a Russellian rejoinder to Quine, that (A) can be symbolically generalized as follows: If $Fa$ and $Fb$ are both true, then it must be true that $(\exists f)fa$ and $fb$. Quine, of course, admits such facts as that more than one dog is white, but, as is well known, he disallows, rules out, quantification over predicate variables – and this, for the most part, is what his 'nominalism' amounts to. ('By treating predicate letters as variables of quantification we precipitate a torrent of universals. . . .' W. V. Quine, *From a Logical Point of View*, paperback ed., New York, 1963, p. 123.) To this Donagan replies, 'The device of quantification is not private property; and any logician may be called upon to answer whether the result of a particular quantification is or is not true. Prima facie, that Fido and Rover are both white is a sufficient condition of the truth of the proposition $(\exists f)f(\text{Fido})$ and $f(\text{Rover})$; and if any proposition expressed by means of quantification over predicates is true, then *some* quantification over predicates is ligitimate, and no considerations of elegance or convenience can justify prohibiting it.'

But does quantification over predicate variables 'commit' one to the existence of universals? Quine obviously thinks it does, but other philosophers think it does not. Well, does it?

As for (B), A. C. Lloyd claims that if one assumes he is using the *same* word, 'red', in 'This is red' and 'That is red', he is already assuming a real universal, viz. the name; in which case, the argument, he says, contains a *petitio*. ('On Arguments for Real Universals', *Analysis* II (1951), p. 102.) As if matters would be improved if we argued 'In saying "This and that are red" we are using the same name.'

predicate) or a relation';[27] (2) 'A universal is anything which may be shared by or be common to two or more things, something that has (or may have) instances';[28] (3) 'A universal is the meaning of an abstract or general word'.[29] (3) is clearly related to (B); (1) and (2) to (A). Also (1) and (2) appear to be equivalent, for that which may be shared by or common to two or more things, that which has instances is precisely a property or a relation or – to add what chiefly preoccupied ancient and medieval philosophers but which in modern times have been construed as properties or conjunctions of properties – a species or a genus. And (3) is related to (1) and (2) in that – according at least to some philosophers who hold (3) – the meaning of an abstract or general word is precisely a universal as it is defined or described by (1) or (2).

In the light of these arguments we can also see why D.F. Pears says, ' "Because universals exist" is the answer to at least two general questions: "Why are things what they are?" and "Why are we able to name things as we do?" '[30] For (A) apparently explains why things are as they are: if the colour red, a universal, did not exist, then it would be impossible for two or more things – or indeed for one thing – to be red.[31] And (B) apparently explains how it is that two or more things can be called 'red': had they nothing in common, here the colour red, then they could not rightly be called by the same name, here 'red' or 'red thing'. To be sure, some philosophers, Pears among them, hold that these so-called explanations are bogus explanations, not

[27] See, e.g. G. E. Moore, op. cit., p. 31; John Wisdom, *Problems of Mind and Matter* (Cambridge, paperback ed. 1963), p. 25; H. H. Price, *Thinking and Experience* (London, 1953), pp. 8–10; R. I. Aaron, op. cit., pp. 233–42.

[28] See, e.g. Bertrand Russell, *The Problems of Philosophy* (London, 1950 – originally 1912), p. 93; A. E. Duncan-Jones 'Universals and Particulars', *Proceedings of the Aristotelian Society*, XXIV (1933–4), p. 70.

[29] See e.g. A. J. Ayer, *Thinking and Meaning* (London, 1947), pp. 23–4; Arthur Pap, *Elements of Analytic Philosophy* (New York, 1949), p. 68; Bertrand Russell, op. cit., p. 93.

[30] D. F. Pears, 'Universals', *Logic and Language* (Second Series), ed. Antony Flew (Oxford, 1953), p. 52.

[31] For the great classic statement of this point, see Plato's *Phaedo*, 100 C-D: 'It is by beauty that beautiful things are beautiful.'

really explanations at all, for they are 'circular and uninformative'. A. J. Ayer, for example, says:

> Thus the word 'yellow' designates a universal, and since it is a fact that some things are yellow, we can say, if we like, that this universal exists. But we do not in any way explain the fact that some things are yellow by saying that they are instances of the universal 'yellow', or by saying that this universal exists. We merely re-state it in a more mystifying way. Nor do we explain that we use and understand class-symbols [general words] by saying . . . that we are familiar with universals: here again we do no more than re-state it (op. cit., p. 24).

But Donagan demurs. Replying to Pears, whose charge is at this point much the same as Ayer's, he says (i) that to be told that 'a necessary condition of the truth of propositions of the form "$x$ is red" is that the universal *red* is real' is 'informative'; and (ii) that although 'We are able to call things red because they are red' (Pears's formulation) is 'circular and uninformative', 'We are able to call things "red" because they are red' shows that the realist 'is looking to a fact about the world to explain a fact about language' (op. cit., p. 238).

Now (A) does amount to the claim that a necessary condition of the truth of '$x$ is red' is the 'reality' of the universal *red* (though not necessarily in the sense in which Donagan here understands 'the reality of a universal' – we shall consider that shortly). But is the explanation informative? Note that (A) is presented as an entailment – and, with minor alterations, it would become a logical equivalence. For it says that it is impossible that 'This is red and that is red' is true while 'This and that have something in common, viz. the colour red' is false. 'The universal *red* is real', unless it is implicitly grammatical in the way suggested above, is either entailed by or equivalent to 'Something is red' or 'The colour red is a universal (which is analytic in the realist's notation) and something is red'; in which case it is contingent. Hence, although both the antecedent (or explicandum) and the consequent (or explicans) of (A) are both contingent, (A) as a whole is *a priori* or necessary. It is thus 'explanatory' in much the same way as 'N is my father's mother' is explanatory of N's being my paternal grandmother. One is free to call this an 'explanation', I suppose, and to say that it is 'informative', but it is clearly different from 'If Caesar declined the crown, it must be because he lacked political ambition'.

The same is true of (B). It too is presented as an entailment or logical equivalence : 'It is not possible that we (univocally and correctly) call this and that "red" unless they are red'; where again both antecedent and consequent can be understood as contingent. But if this is an explanation which looks to a fact about the world to explain a fact about language, it is quite different from the following. Suppose a subject were shown a series of coloured cards and were given the instructions 'Whenever you come upon a red one, call it "blue" '. A casual observer watching the subject perform might say 'He calls it "blue" because it is red'. His remark is an hypothesis in a way in which 'We call this "red" because it is red' is not. As Wittgenstein observes (*BB*, p. 135), 'To say that we use the word "blue" to mean "what all these shades of colour have in common" by itself says nothing more than that we use the word "blue" in all these cases.'

Whether (A) and (B) are explanatory, however, is relatively unimportant compared to the question whether they entail the existence or reality of universals as entities in addition to or alongside or present in the things that are said to have something in common and to which general words are applied. For among philosophers (those cited in notes 27–9 being a case in point) who do not use 'universal' simply as a synonym of 'general word' – who use it in a realist, as opposed to a nominalist, manner, so to speak – some hold that these lines of argument do establish the reality of universals as entities other than particulars, while others deny that they do. Further, there is no dispute over the simple evidence cited for the reality of universals, either that general words have meaning, in the case of (B), or that, for example, some ripe tomatoes are red and some fire engines are red, in the case of (A). We are thus faced with an enigma, one which D. J. O'Connor puts this way : 'Now clearly there is something very strange about a debate in which a truism is offered as evidence for a controversial thesis in metaphysics. And although there are plenty of arguments which have been used against the realist position, they too are of the same curious kind. They adduce evidence which no one can controvert because everyone accepts it already.'[32] What appears to be at issue, then, is whether the antecedents of (A) and (B) entail their consequents. Even this, however, is not quite right. After offering as 'a provisional description' of a universal that 'it is what is common to all objects which we normally call by the same name', A. D. Woozley says he thinks that *all* philosophers would agree that there is something answering to this description and that therefore there are universals in the sense indicated. For not only do they agree that we use general words and that such words have meaning (what would it be like for them not to have meaning?), but also that 'there is something or other common to all objects to which we refer by the same general word'. (Woozley's confidence is perhaps excessive here, but never mind.) Where, then, is the disagreement? 'Where disagreement begins is at the next stage, at which we ask what *is* common to a group of particulars, or what is *meant* by the phrase "common to a group of particulars". The problem of universals is the problem of answering these questions.'[33] In other words, it is not the antecedents of (A) and (B) that are at issue, nor even whether the words of (A) and (B) express entailments; but what is at issue is the interpretation or 'analysis' of their consequents.

This strikes me as an apt description of at least a good part of the dispute. To appreciate its force we need only look at the difference between realism or 'the Philosophy of Universals' and what Price calls 'the Philosophy of Resemblances' (which is often identified as 'moderate nominalism'), i.e. see how a realist and how a resemblance-theorist construes, understands, or 'analyses' a statement of the form '. . . s, or . . . things, have some-

[32] D. J. O'Connor, 'Names and Universals', *Proceedings of the Aristotelian Society*, LIII (1952-3), p. 174.
[33] A. D. Woozley, *Theory of Knowledge* (New York, 1966), p. 74. Also H. H. Price, op. cit., p. 13. Price holds that we cannot dispute the facts on which the Philosophy of Universals is based, but we can doubt the realist's analysis of those facts.

thing in common'. First the realist, then the resemblance-theorist.

According to Austin (pp. 2–3) what (B) shows – or tries to show – is that there must be 'some single identical thing' common to two or more things called by the same name, in which case a universal *is* just 'that *x* which is present, one and identical, in the different [things] we call by the same name', that *x* which is named (denoted, designated) by the name. Worded in this way, (B) becomes an argument for realism. For, as Austin's words plainly suggest, the consequent of (A) now becomes 'This and that must have (share, partake of) some one thing, the same and identical in each case'; that of (B), 'They must have some one thing, the same in each case, something of which the name is the name'.

According to what we may call a 'strict resemblance-theory', to say that two or more things have something in common is not to say that they have or share some one identical thing which is named or denoted by the predicate-expression truly applied to them, but is rather to say that they resemble (are similar to, are like) one another in some specifiable or recognizable way. Thus H. H. Price (op. cit., p. 13) allows that if, say, 'Fire engines are red' is true, then it 'is admittedly in some sense true' that fire engines have something in common, viz. the colour red. 'But would it not be clearer and closer to the facts, if we said that all these objects resemble each other in a certain way?' To which Price's answer is, Yes.[34] Why? Because 'it is resemblance which is more fundamental than characterization [characters being universals], rather than the other way round' (p. 17), which means that '. . . have the same character' (or even '. . . instantiate the same universal') is to be defined in terms of '. . . resemble each other in a certain way', and not vice versa.[35] Thus, accord-

---

[34] Even though he later (p. 30) makes the revealing admission that both the Philosophy of Universals and the Philosophy of Resemblances 'cover the *same* facts', which 'strongly suggests' to Price that they are simply 'two different (systematically different) terminologies, two systematically different ways of saying the same thing.'

[35] A. D. Woozley, *Theory of Knowledge*, holds that this view is 'substantially correct'. After stating the Aristotelian theory of universals, according to which 'Two things have something in common' = 'Two things have or

ing to a strict resemblance-theory, the consequent of (A) finally becomes 'This and that resemble each other in colour and the colour is red'; that of (B), 'They resemble each other in a certain respect, the respect being specified by our calling them both "red" '. (Hobbes, it seems, was a resemblance-theorist. After saying, in *Leviathan*, that names alone are universal, he goes on : 'one universal name is imposed on many things, for their similitude in some quality, or other accident.')

There are two well-known objections to this view. The first is known as 'the "in some respect" argument' : A cannot be like B without being like B in some respect; but this implies that there must be something, i.e. some one thing, the same and identical, common to any pair of objects between which resemblance holds. (Apparently Locke, although he held a resemblance-theory of sorts, accepted this objection.)[36] To this objection two replies are given : (i) Not all resemblance is resemblance in some respect. In Hume's words, 'blue and green are different simple ideas, but are more resembling than blue and scarlet', and they resemble each other 'without having any circumstance the same', i.e. in no respect.[37] (ii) Even if all resemblance is resemblance in some respect, this does not entail the existence of universals *in rebus* as the following series of equivalences shows : 'A is red and B is red'='A and B have something in common, viz. the colour red'='A and B resemble each other in respect of being red'='A (which is red) is like B (which is red)'='The red of A is like the red of B'. So, 'what is meant by saying that there is something common to A and B in virtue of which they are alike is that the

share a common property', he cites various senses of 'sharing' and 'having in common', only one of which will apparently support the Aristotelian view, viz. the sense in which two varieties of apple are good keepers. But this, though 'unobjectionable', will not really support the Aristotelian view. Why? Because all we would (could?) mean is 'that a number of things were (to some degree or other) like each other' (p. 81; also p. 93). Woozley holds that the resemblance-theory 'does not abolish universals, unless "universal" is taken as the name of an entity.' It says there are universals, but it means by this only that 'objects can be classified according to degrees of likeness and unlikeness and according to our decision where and how to limit group membership.'

[36] See A. D. Woozley, 'Universals', p. 203.
[37] *A Treatise of Human Nature*, ed. Selby-Bigge, p. 637. cf. Woozley's 'Universals', p. 203.

red of A is like (maybe exactly like) the red of B'; and the latter likeness is 'a fundamental and not further analysable relation.'[38] Again, in Price's words, it is resemblance that is fundamental.

The second, and perhaps more important, objection is that resemblance, likeness, or similarity must itself be a universal in the realist's sense. As Russell expressed the objection in *The Problems of Philosophy* (p. 96):

> If we wish to avoid the universals *whiteness* and *triangularity*, we shall choose some particular patch of white or some particular triangle, and say that anything is white or a triangle if it has the right sort of resemblance to our chosen particular. But then the resemblance required will have to be a universal. Since there are many white things, the resemblance must hold between many pairs of particular white things; and this is the characteristic of a universal. It will be useless to say that there is a different resemblance for each pair, for then we shall have to say that these resemblances resemble each other, and thus at last we shall be forced to admit resemblance as a universal. The relation of resemblance, therefore, must be a true universal. And having been forced to admit this universal, we find that it is no longer worth while to invent difficult and unplausible theories to avoid the admission of such universals as whiteness and triangularity.

In *An Inquiry into Meaning and Truth*[39] he holds that what forces us finally to admit resemblance as a true universal is that to appeal to a series of resemblances resembling each other is to commit oneself to 'an endless regress of the vicious kind'. To this objection there are again at least two replies: (i) The objection assumes that if A (which is blue) is similar to B (which is blue) and B is similar to C (which is blue), then both similarities are the same and are therefore instances of the universal *similarity*.

---

[38] Woozley, *Theory of Knowledge*, pp. 97–8. cf. also A. C. Lloyd, op. cit., pp. 102–4; and H. H. Price, op. cit., pp. 20–1. Woozley's view provides us with another interpretation of the extreme nominalist's maxim: 'There is no property or accident common to a group of particulars called by the same name; there are really only likenesses among the individual accidents of each'.

[39] Penguin Books (Baltimore, 1962). p. 327.

But, apart from the fact that there are similarities which are not the same but only similar, to say that the similarities are the same is simply to say 'that A and B and C are like each other in being blue'. So 'The similarities are the same' does not entail 'The similarities are instances of the universal similarity'.[40] (ii) 'If there is an infinite regress, it is not a vicious one'.[41]

Between realism and the strict resemblance-view there are, as one might expect, intermediate positions. For instance, there are those who, apparently impressed by Russell's argument, are willing to admit at least one universal, *similarity*; but 'having been forced to admit this universal' they do not feel compelled to go on and admit others. Rather they set out to explain the nature of other universals – or apparent universals – 'in terms of the relation of resemblance, which is itself a universal'.[42] Then there is R. I. Aaron. By 'universals' he means basically 'recurrences found in the natural world'. But recurrences, as he sees it, 'are of two sorts, identities and resemblances'.

> The colour of this postage stamp does not resemble the colour of the second postage stamp but is identical with it; to speak of resemblance here would be to speak falsely. We do observe identical qualities and there are *universalia in rebus* . . . one and the same shade of red is here *and* there, in two places at one and the same time.

But 'qualities are not the only discoverable identities, there are also relations' : if A is to the left of B and B is to the left of C, then the *same* relation obtains between A and B as obtains between B and C. Not all recurrent qualities and relations, however, are identities; some are merely similarities : 'Behind the use of "ultramarine" lies the observation of the identical shade, but behind that of "blue" there lies the observation of identical

---

[40] Woozley, *Theory of Knowledge*, pp. 100–1. cf. A. J. Ayer, 'On particulars and Universals', *Proceedings of the Aristotelian Society*, XXXIV (1933–4), p. 58.
[41] A. C. Lloyd, op. cit., p. 104. Also H. H. Price, op. cit., pp. 23–5.
[42] A. J. Ayer, 'On Particulars and Universals', p. 57. See also H. H. Price, 'Thinking and Representation', *Proceedings of the British Academy*, LXXXII (1946), pp. 83–122.

shades together with the observation of likeness between them.'
That is, if A is ultramarine and B is ultramarine, and C is indigo
and D is indigo, then A and B, and C and D, are the same in
colour, but A and B are merely similar in colour to C and D. In
so far as he recognizes identities in quality or relation, Aaron
thinks of himself as a realist, but he takes his recognition of
recurrent similarities that are not identities as a departure from
realism : 'Thus in asserting that universals are recurring similarities as well as recurring identities our theory is shown to be different from both realism and nominalism' – and, he might have
added, from a strict resemblance-view.[43]

It is now time to consider the nature of the opposition between
realism and the alternatives to it that we have blocked out. The
first and most important thing to notice is that the various
analyses offered of the consequents of (A) and (B) are all *a priori*.
Despite occasional talk about observing recurrences, being closer
to the facts, and the like, the claims of the realist and his opponents are obviously not empirical. The only *facts* at issue, other
than perhaps linguistic facts, facts amenable to confirmation by
observation, are such simple facts as that fire engines are red,
and *these* facts, as we have noted, are not in dispute. The disagreement is solely over the 'interpretation' or 'analysis' of such
facts, or rather of the propositions that express them; and as such
it is grammatical. According to the realist 'A and B have something in common' is logically equivalent to 'A and B have (share,
partake of) something, one and the same in each case'; while
according to the strict resemblance-theorist, it is equivalent to 'A
and B resemble each other (in some way)'; and according to
Aaron it may be equivalent to either, depending on what A and
B are said to have in common.

In *The Blue Book* (p. 55) Wittgenstein says :

> We use the phrase 'two books have the same colour', but we
> could perfectly well say : 'They can't have the same colour,
> because, after all, this book has its own colour, and the other
> book has its own colour too'. This would be stating a gram-

[43] All quotations are from Aaron's *The Theory of Universals*, pp. 232-6.

170

matical rule – a rule, incidentally, not in accordance with our ordinary usage.

It would also be stating a grammatical rule to say 'They can't have the same colour, only similar colours' or 'We say they have the same colour, but really their colours are only similar'. Now if what were at issue between the realist and his opponents were how the words 'same' and 'similar' are actually used, then Aaron would seem to be closer to the truth than either the realist or the resemblance-theorist : for it is sometimes quite proper to say that two things have the same colour, and not *just* exactly resembling colours, e.g. when they are both ultramarine. At other times it is quite proper to say that they are not the same, but merely similar, in colour, e.g. when one is scarlet, the other magenta – though even here there just might be occasion to say they have the same colour.[44] But Aaron too is led to misrepresent the facts (still assuming that what he says is descriptively grammatical); for is it *always* wrong to say of two blue things, one of which is indigo, the other ultramarine, that they are the same in colour? Clearly not. As Wittgenstein reminds us (*BB*, p. 133), 'We use the word "similar" [and, he might have added, the word "same"] in a huge family of cases.' As for whether resemblance or sameness is really fundamental, when I say 'the same' do I always really mean similar? or when I say 'similar' do I always really mean the same in some respect? Clearly neither; and yet the realist, it seems, would have me believe the latter, the resemblance-theorist the former.

The way in which the issue is debated between these parties, however, would suggest that they are not concerned about how words are in fact used; hence, that their 'theories' are not descriptively grammatical; and hence, that they are not making *false* claims about how words are used. But since their 'theories'

---

[44] cf. Wittgenstein's discussion of a case where red and green might be said to have something in common – other than that they are colours; and another where light ('Cambridge') and dark ('Oxford') blue might be said to have nothing in common. *BB*, pp. 134–5.

The argument, of course, has nothing special to do with colours. The same considerations apply to 'same shape', 'same size', 'same nature', 'same essence', and so on.

are implicitly grammatical, we can only suspect that they are involved in a game of re-drawing the boundaries around the use of 'same' and 'similar'. What each is stating is a grammatical rule – 'and a rule, incidentally, not in accordance with ordinary usage.' Their use of 'same' and 'similar' is a metaphysical use of words; their 'theories', grammatical innovations in 'the sheep's clothing of a metaphysical formulation', to borrow D. J. O'Connor's phrase.

Still, granted that it is even sometimes correct to say ' . . . are the same', e.g. ' . . . have the same colour', does this imply the reality of universals as entities, entities denoted (named, designated) by the predicate-expressions of true propositions? Before considering this question, which goes to the heart of the matter, I pause to examine a passage from Wittgenstein which, it has been claimed, finally *solves* the problem of universals.

Probably the most frequently quoted passage of *Philosophical Investigations* is 66–7, the famous 'family resemblances' passage :

> Consider for example the proceedings that we call 'games'. I mean board-games, card-games, ball-games, Olympic games, and so on. What is common to them all? – Don't say : 'There *must* be something common, or they would not be called "games" – but *look and see* whether there is anything common to all . . .

> And the result of this examination is : we see a complicated network of similarities overlapping and criss-crossing : sometimes overall similarities, sometimes similarities in detail.

> I can think of no better expression to characterize these similarities than 'family resemblances' . . .

This would appear to connect with argument (B) and therefore to be a contribution to, or a variant of, the resemblance-theory,[45] and therefore to be anti-realist. And after quoting this passage, together with *BB*, pp. 17–18, R. Bambrough says, 'The passages I have quoted contain the essence of Wittgenstein's solution of the

---

[45] It seems to be taken in this way by Woozley, 'Universals', p. 205.

problem of universals'.[46] I question whether these passages have any direct bearing on the problem of universals at all, or at least whether they have the bearing they are thought to have.

Before producing Wittgenstein's putative solution of the problem of universals, Bambrough asks what the range of application of the example of games is meant to be. With what kinds of concepts is Wittgenstein *contrasting* that of games? Ayer says he is contrasting complicated concepts, such as 'game', 'reading', etc., with simple concepts, such as 'red'. To which Bambrough replies, after citing *BB*, p. 131 and *PI*, 73 – evidence which strikes me as insufficient to the conclusion drawn : 'Wittgenstein could as easily have used the example of red things as the example of games to illustrate "the tendency to look for something in common to all the entities which we commonly subsume under a general term" ' (p. 193). But could he? Not if Bambrough's own exposition (p. 189) of the concept of family resemblance is correct – which it seems to be. Further, 'Now what should we answer to the question "What do light blue and dark blue have in common"? At first sight the answer seems obvious : "They are both shades of blue". But this is really a tautology' (*BB*, p. 134). That this is really a tautology does not seem to bother Bambrough, although it should. Strawson, on the other hand, says that Wittgenstein is contrasting two kinds of complex concepts, 'those which are definable by the statement of necessary and sufficient conditions and those which are not' (p. 194). To which Bambrough now replies that this misses the point Wittgenstein is concerned with :

> In the sense in which, according to Wittgenstein, games have nothing in common except that they are games, and red things have nothing in common except that they are red, *brothers have nothing in common except that they are brothers.* It is true that brothers have in common that they are male siblings, but their having in common that they are male siblings is their having in common that they are *brothers*, and not their having

[46] Renford Bambrough, 'Universals and Family Resemblances', *Wittgenstein: The Philosophical Investigations: A Collection of Essays*, ed. George Pitcher (Garden City, N.Y., 1966), p. 191.

in common something in addition to their being brothers (ibid.).

'What then *is* the contrast Wittgenstein meant to draw?' None at all. Wittgenstein is calling our attention to, reminding us of, something that is 'trivially and platitudinously true', namely, that what all games have in common is that they are games. Although platitudinous, this is 'an important philosophical truth' (p. 197). 'For of course games *do* have something in common. They *must* have something in common . . . The simple truth is that what games have in common is that they are games' (ibid.). The reason why this is an important philosophical truth is that the nominalist, by saying that games have nothing in common except that they are *called* 'games', denies it (which depicts the nominalist as denying a manifest tautology!), while the realist misunderstands its central importance and 'feels that he must look for something that games have in common apart from their *being* games' (pp. 195–6). (That is, the realist apparently takes the platitude in question to entail that games have something in common *in addition to* their being games.) By uttering a tautology, then, Wittgenstein is represented as passing between the horns of the realist-nominalist dilemma: he is 'neither a realist nor a nominalist' (p. 199).

Apart from the prima facie implausibility of this reading of *PI*, 66–7, there is, first, evidence in the texts that runs counter to it: e.g. *PI*, 75, 77, 156–64 (the long discussion of the concept of reading); *BB*, pp. 25, 27–8, 44, 117, 130–3. Even in the 'family resemblances' passage itself there are clear signs that it is not to be read this way. For how does Wittgenstein come to introduce the notion of family resemblances? In response to those who accuse him of taking the easy way out: ' "You talk about all sorts of language-games, but you have nowhere said what the *essence* of a language-game, and hence of language, is: what is common to all these activities, and what makes them into language or parts of language" ' (*PI*, 65, italics mine). What Wittgenstein is resisting, then, is the demand that he give a *definition* of 'language'. Again, at the end of *PI*, 67, he says:

But if someone wished to say: 'There is something common to all these constructions – namely the disjunction of all their common properties' – I should reply: Now you are only playing with words. One might as well say: 'Something runs through the whole thread – namely the continuous overlapping of those fibres'.

Why does he mention disjunction here except to contrast it with conjunction, the sort of conjunction involved in ' " . . . is a brother" = " . . . is a male and is a sibling" '? Second, there is the additional evidence, for what it is worth, that those who look for what is common try to produce a definition of 'game' analogous to that of 'brother'.[47] But, finally, the overriding consideration is that, in *PI*, 66 itself Wittgenstein says 'Look and see'. You do not have to – indeed you cannot – look and see whether all games are games. If 'Look and see' is to be taken seriously as a directive, then there are only two things you could see if you looked. (1) You might see, as a matter of *empirical* fact, that all games have some common feature, e.g. that they are all amusing; but any feature so discovered would obviously not be a 'defining feature' of games, a feature in virtue of which we call something a 'game'. Here looking and seeing calls for *comparing* things; it is like looking to see if all the books on a certain shelf have red covers. (2) You might see, as a matter of *linguistic* fact, that all games have something in common in the way that all bachelors have something in common, viz. being marriageable but unmarried males. But this would be to see simply that a word is defined in a certain way.

I conclude from all this that R. K. Richman is right:[48] the

---

[47] e.g. 'Play is any deliberate activity whose main end does not lie outside itself; a game is an organized, rule-governed form of play'. Anthony Quinton, 'Locker Room Metaphysics', *The New York Review of Books,* August 21, 1969, p. 22. cf. G. E. Moore, op. cit., p. 313: 'He [Wittgenstein] said both (1) that, even if there *is* something common to all games, it doesn't follow that this is what we mean by calling a particular game a "game", and (2) that the reason why we call so many different activities "games" *need* not be that there is anything common to them all'. (my italics).

[48] Robert K. Richman, 'Something Common', *The Journal of Philosophy,* LIX (1962), pp. 821–30. Richman rightly notes that essentialism does not entail realism.

'family resemblances' passage is not directed at realism or nominalism, but at *essentialism*, particularly at that classical brand of essentialism that holds that every general term or predicate-expression must be definable in terms of a conjunction of properties, and that this conjunction of properties is what everything univocally called by the same general name must have in common. Although some essentialists, such as Plato, were also realists, others, such as Socrates (if we accept Aristotle's testimony) were not; hence, essentialism does not imply realism and should not be confused with it.[49] What no doubt leads to the confusion is that there is an essentialist, as well as a realist, interpretation of (B), namely, where 'If two or more things are univocally called by the same name, they must have something in common' is offered as an implicit definition of 'univocity' – a definition which both Wittgenstein and Austin resisted – and not as an argument for universals. As a definition of 'univocity' it can be resisted by claiming that a word *is* univocally applicable to things – actually sorts of things – that merely resemble one another in various ways; which *looks* of course like an assertion of the resemblance-theory as an alternative to realism. To see (B) as an argument for the reality of universals, however, we must see it in conjunction with the realist analysis of the consequent of (B), an analysis which an essentialist need not accept, since it holds that a general name, univocally applied (we are not concerned here with cases of homonymy or ambiguity, obviously), names, denotes, stands for, or designates one thing, the same and identical in each case, which is other than the thing of which it is predicated. What this game and that game have in common is simply their being games, nothing else? Fine; then their being games is something, one and the same in each case, which is denoted by the word 'game'. Bambrough gives the realist all he needs, for realism is simply not the view that all $\phi$'s have something in common in addition to their being $\phi$'s; it is the view that being $\phi$ is some thing named by '$\phi$' other than the things that are said to be $\phi$.

[49] Austin, I think, confuses the two, as his reply to the realist's argument shows; he attacks it as if it were an argument for essentialism. op. cit., pp. 6–8, and 37–42.

In analysing Russell's argument for the reality of universals as entities, Donagan points out that it requires as a premiss what he calls 'the Realist Principle', viz. that 'the primitive predicates occurring non-redundantly in true propositions denote real things';[50] not the things of which the predicate is truly predicated, but something else; not the things that are rightly said to have something in common, but *what* they have in common. (The connexion of this Principle with the realist analysis of the consequents of (A) and (B) is obvious.) Donagan goes on to argue that although Russell at times tried to restrict the application of this Principle to affirmative propositions alone, it cannot be so restricted. For 'since "in" is as much a constituent of the negative proposition "Russell is not in his room", as of the affirmative one, "Russell is in his room", the reality of the relation *in* would seem to follow from the truth of either one' (p. 217). 'Whether universals are real or have being . . . is a question altogether distinct from the question whether they are or are not exemplified' (pp. 241–2). Thus not only does the truth of 'Something is red' imply that there is a universal *red*, but, to borrow an example from Aristotle (*Post. An.*, 92$^b$7), the truth of 'Nothing is a goat-stag' implies the reality of the universal *goat-stag*. And this, it would seem, is the difference between 'Platonists' and 'Aristotelians': the former employ the Realist Principle in an unrestricted manner, while the latter confine its application to true affirmative propositions alone. Thus for the former there are unexemplified universals, while for the latter there are not. As Aristotle puts it (ibid.), 'One can know the meaning of the phrase or name "goat-stag" but not what the essential nature of a goat-stag is.' Since there are no goat-stags, there is no essential nature to be known, no real universal to be acquainted with or to be denoted. Still, the name 'goat-stag' is meaningful – which would seem to imply that a universal is not the meaning of a, or every, general term.

Now the Realist Principle, as well as the realist's analysis of the consequent of (B), embodies what Wittgenstein calls a certain

---

[50] By a 'primitive predicate' Donagan means a predicate expression that is 'neither a logical connective nor signifies a formal concept, and is predicable of many particulars.' op. cit., pp. 216–7.

'picture' of the way general words (must) work: they are names and stand to what they name as a proper name, e.g. 'Ludwig Wittgenstein', stands to its bearer, Ludwig Wittgenstein:

> You say: the point isn't the word, but its meaning, and you think of the meaning as a thing of the same kind as the word, though also different from the word. Here the word, there the meaning. The money, and the cow you can buy with it (*PI*, 120).

What is involved, in short, is an assimilation of general words to proper names; an assimilation that some philosophers, e.g. D. J. O'Connor (op. cit.), hold is based on a false analogy. To show that the analogy is false, O'Connor embarks on 'a comparative investigation of the ways in which proper names and general words do their work' (p. 177). He finds only superficial similarities between the two, but important differences. For example, proper names, like signposts, function as 'indicators', general words, at least when they are used predicatively, never do (pp. 179–80); 'proper names, strictly so-called, never have any semantic function as classifiers and . . . conversely, general words never have any semantic use as indicators' (p. 182); although both proper names and predicative expressions denote, they do so in different ways, for general words do, while proper names do not, 'determine a propositional function' (p. 185) – ' "blueness" cannot be a value of the propositional function "$x$ is blue" ' (p. 188).

The realist's answer to this is relatively easy to devise: Of course proper names and general words function in different ways. Proper names, for instance, cannot, while general words can, function as the predicate-expressions of propositions; though either can serve as subject-expressions. If 'blueness' or 'the colour blue' cannot determine the function '$x$ is blue' because 'Blueness is blue' is nonsense, that does not mean that it cannot determine the value of any propositional function, e.g. of '$\phi$ is a (the one) property that A possesses but B lacks'. It will do no good to say that this is merely equivalent to (reducible to, translatable as) 'A is $\phi$ but B is not $\phi$'. For if the first is equivalent to (reducible to) the second, the second is equivalent to (reducible to) the first. Moreover, it is undoubtedly true that proper names normally function as indicators, while general words do not, and that general words serve a descriptive and a classificatory function which proper names lack. But in order to serve a descriptive or classificatory function, general words must name (stand for, designate) a class or a property. You have overlooked the real basis of the analogy between proper names and general words: just as the name 'Bertrand Russell', if used univocally on different occasions, must refer to or 'indicate' one and the same person, so a general word, if predicated univocally here and there, must mean the same thing here and there, i.e. must designate or stand for the same thing here and there. Being the same at different places and times, what a general word stands for is as appropriate a bearer of a name as is a person or a horse.[51]

Wittgenstein's approach to the picture of language embodied in the Realist Principle is quite different from O'Connor's.[52] He reminds us that there is something very odd about the analogy by reminding us that the meaning of a word – what the realist says it stands for – is not, so to speak, detachable from the word in the way that the bearer of a proper name is detachable from his name. He does this in several ways. First, he denies that the bearer of a name – what the name may be said to denote, designate, stand for – is the same as the meaning of the name:

Let us first discuss *this* point of the argument: that a word has no meaning if nothing corresponds to it. It is important to note that the word 'meaning' is being used illicitly if it is used to signify the thing that 'corresponds' to the word. That

---

[51] To this Ayer ('On Particulars and Universals') replies that, although 'the same universal can be in different places at once' is 'an analytic truth' (p. 56), this rejoinder 'rests on the failure to see that the meaning of the word "same" as applied to qualities differs from the meaning of "same" as applied to things.' For 'to say that two objects have the same quality is simply equivalent to saying that they resemble one another in a certain respect' (p. 58). And we are back with the resemblance-theory again.

[52] But see *BB*, p. 82, where Wittgenstein does stress the difference in function between proper names and names of colours, etc.

is to confound the meaning of a name with the *bearer* of the name ... (*PI*, 40).

The meaning of a name, proper or general, is not the same as its bearer – if it has one. Hence the name can have meaning, and can have the same meaning on different occasions, without having a bearer, let alone the same bearer; and even if it has a bearer, that bearer is not what it means. (Cf. *PI*, 55; More, op. cit., pp. 260–1.)

Connected with this notion of meaning or naming is the picture of properties as ingredients :

The idea of a general concept [i.e. what a general concept means or names] being a common property of its particular instances connects up with other primitive, too simple, ideas of the structure of language. It is comparable to the idea that *properties* are *ingredients* of the things which have the properties; e.g. that beauty is an ingredient of all beautiful things as alcohol is of beer and wine, and that we therefore could have pure beauty, unadulterated by anything that is beautiful (*BB*, p. 17; cf. p. 144).

'Wine is alcoholic' means that wine contains alcohol, and 'alcohol' is the name of an isolable chemical substance; but 'Tennis balls are spherical' does not mean that tennis balls contain sphericity, and 'sphericity' is not the name of an isolable substance, even though it may properly be said to be the name of a distinguishable or discriminable shape.

Connected with the idea of properties as ingredients and with that of the meaning of a name as something corresponding to it is that of looking for a substance answering to every substantive :

The questions 'What is length?', 'What is meaning?', 'What is the number one?' etc., produce in us a mental cramp. We feel that we can't point to anything in reply to them and yet ought to point to something. (We are up against one of the great sources of philosophical bewilderment : we try to find a substance for a substantive.) (*BB*, p. 1.)

We have the substantives 'meaning', 'the meaning of *w*', 'the colour red', 'the relation north of', etc., and we are inclined to think that they must denote something, that is, some thing or entity. 'We are looking for the use of a sign, but we look for it as though it were an object *co-existing* with the sign. (One of the reasons for this mistake is again that we are looking for a "thing corresponding to a substantive.")' (*BB*, p. 5.) And the idea that there must be substances corresponding to substantives gives rise to the idea of etherial objects, abstract entities :

> But let me remind you here of the queer role which the gaseous and the aethereal play in philosophy,—when we perceive that a substantive is not used as what in general we should call the name of an object, and when therefore we can't help saying to ourselves that it is the name of an aethereal object. I mean, we already know the idea of 'aethereal objects' as a subterfuge, when we are embarrassed about the grammar of certain words, and when all we know is that they are not used as names for material objects (*BB*, p. 47).[53]

That a general term must stand for an object, coupled with the realization that not all general terms are used to refer to objects (that some would not normally be said to stand for or be names of objects at all), in the way that 'chair' would naturally be said to stand for objects, i.e. chairs, leads to the claim that they must stand for aethereal objects, objects visible to the mind's eye alone. And this in turn leads to the distinctively philosophical claim that

[53] cf. Wittgenstein's *Remarks on the Foundations of Mathematics*, G. H. von Wright, R. Rhees, and G. E. M. Anscombe eds., G. E. M. Anscombe trans. (Oxford, 1956), p. 136 : ' "Ideal object." "The symbol '*a*' stands for an ideal object" is evidently supposed to assert something about the meaning, and so about the use of "*a*". And it means of course that this use is in a certain respect similar to that of a sign that has an object, and that it does not stand for any object. But it is interesting what the expression "ideal object" makes of this fact.'

cf. J. S. Mill, loc. cit., where it is said that the realist doctrine has been universally abandoned, 'being one of the most striking examples of the tendency of the human mind to infer difference of things from difference of names, – to suppose that every different class of names implied a corresponding class of real entities to be denoted by them. . . . Man, being a name common to many, must be the name of a substance common to many, and in mystic union with the individual substances, Socrates and the rest.'

there are at least two kinds of objects or entities, material and abstract; which uses 'material' and 'abstract' as if, like 'blue' and 'green' or 'canine' and 'feline', they served to distinguish among objects. But this is to do no more than point to a difference of grammar between such words as 'meaning', 'property', and 'relation' and such words as 'dog', 'mountain', and 'chair'. To adapt a remark Wittgenstein makes about the expression 'sense datum' (*BB*, p. 70): 'Queerly enough, the introduction of this new phraseology has deluded people into thinking that they have discovered new entities, new elements of the structure of the world, as though to say "I believe that there are abstract entities" were similar to saying, "I believe there are monsters in the lakes of Scotland".'

Perhaps Wittgenstein's most important strategy in this connexion, however, is his injunction to speak of the use of a word, rather than of its meaning, wherever we can.

> For a *large* class of cases – though not for all – in which we employ the word 'meaning' it can be defined thus: the meaning of a word is its use in the language (*PI*, 43).

Of course, the meaning of a word can *sometimes* be explained by pointing to its bearer (ibid.), but not always. In either case, if we think of words as being like tools, their meanings as being like the uses of tools (*PI*, 11), or think of words as money, their meanings being like the uses of money and not like the things that can be bought with money (*PI*, 120), we may no longer be inclined to say that every general term (primitive predicate) must denote something. For we are not inclined to think of the use of a word as an entity corresponding to the word, any more than we are inclined to think of the use of a hammer as an entity corresponding to the hammer.

What, then, do Wittgenstein's reminders add up to? Apparently to the claim that being the meaning of a general word or primitive predicate is *not* being something corresponding to the word, something that can exist independent of the word, and hence something the word stands for or denotes in addition to the things to which it may be applied or of which it may be predicated.[54] To appreciate the force of this claim we must consider the logical status of the Realist Principle to which it is apparently opposed.

Although Donagan says (p. 239) that what realism asserts, viz. 'that something in the world corresponds to every primitive predicate', is not uninformative, it is surely questionable whether it is any more informative, or informative in any other way, than 'Every rod has a length'. For despite the fact that the Realist Principle appears to be about the world, it is clearly not empirical. For how is it to be verified? How is one meant to tell whether it is true? It will obviously do no good to look at dogs or compare the colours of postage stamps, or even to look at how words, e.g. colour words, are used. One's only recourse is obviously to further argument. Here, although he does not provide us with that argument, Donagan tells us (pp. 243–4) what a 'proof of' the Realist Principle would at least look like. It would rest on two premisses : (1) that not all predicative expressions are analysable into non-predicative ones; (2) that 'whether or not a proposition is true depends on how the world is, and not on how anybody, plain or scientific, chooses to think about it.' As for (1), this is meant to be supported by the claim that we cannot dispense with at least one predicative expression, namely, ' . . . is similar to . . . '; by which I take it that it means we cannot dispense with at least one predicative expression that stands for a universal; which is, of course, Russell's reply to the strict resemblance-theorist. As such, (1) is obviously philosophically moot, that is, forever debatable without hope of resolution; to say nothing of its begging the question. As for (2), it, I presume, means 'Whether an *empirical* or *contingent* proposition is true depends on how the world is'. If it does, then it would be widely regarded as analytic. If it does not, if it is meant to encompass *all* propositions, including such patent tautologies as 'If a rod has a length, then a rod has a length', it too is philosophically moot. In any case, (1) and (2) are themselves not empirical but *a priori*, and if the Realist

---

[54] Compare this summary statement with the nominalist's 'A common status, e.g. being a man, is not a thing named by "man" '; 'An accident is not a thing'; etc.

Principle does follow from (1) and (2), or any similar premisses, it too must be *a priori*.[55] The Realist Principle is obviously a putative entailment: 'If "φ" is a primitive predicate of a true proposition, then "φ" denotes something (an entity) other than that of which "φ" is truly predicated'. Against this we have Wittgenstein's seeming counter-entailment: To be a primitive predicate of a true proposition is not to denote an entity other than the entity of which the predicate is truly predicable. Is there a genuine issue here? If so, how is it to be resolved?

Taken as a descriptive grammatical proposition the Realist Principle amounts to the claim that ' "φ" is predicable of something' means the same as ' "φ" denotes or stands for a real thing other than the thing that is said to be φ', which readily becomes ' "φ" is the proper name of φ'. As an explanation of the use of the words in question, this is obviously something that only a philosopher would say – which may explain Russell's complaint (*Problems of Philosophy*, pp. 93–4) that although most words stand for universals hardly anyone but a philosopher realizes that there such entities as universals. According to one of Wittgenstein's views of philosophy, then, the Realist Principle is mistaken, and Wittgenstein's reminders serve to point out the mistake: ' "φ" is predicable of something' does *not* mean ' "φ" stands for an entity other than the entity that is said to be φ'; a general word is *not* the proper name of an entity. This assumes, however, that the Realist Principle *is descriptively* grammatical. But suppose it is not. Then, according to another of Wittgenstein's views of philosophy, it embodies a notational innovation: the Realist Principle is a proposition that would be necessarily true, 'true by definition', *if* its linguistic counterpart were contingently

---

[55] Russell's Realist Principle will obviously not be supported by (2) alone. For although (2) is consistent with Russell's principle, it is also consistent with an alternative principle, which Donagan states as follows (pp. 227–8): 'while something in the world must correspond to a true [contingent?] proposition, that correspondence need not be point for point . . . there need not be a constituent in the world for each constituent of the proposition.' (cf. *PI*, 449: 'We fail to get away from the idea that using a sentence involves imagining something for every word.') 'The correspondence *must* be point for point'; 'The correspondence need *not* be point for point.' Which is it?

true and described a convention of usage. Here Wittgenstein's reminder, his counter-entailment, can be taken in one of two ways: either as an *objection* to the innovation in question, a *defence* of conventional usage, in which case his position is tantamount to nominalism; or simply as a way of indicating that and how a notational innovation is all that is at issue, which is not tantamount to nominalism. Since it is implausible to credit realists with making mistakes about how words are actually used, one is left with the notational-innovation view of the matter. In that case, he may be inclined to say in answer to the persistent inquiry 'But *are* there real universals?' what Wittgenstein says in another connexion (*PI*, 79): 'Say what you choose, so long as it does not prevent you from seeing the facts [that is, the relevant grammatical facts]. (And when you see them there is a good deal you will not say.)'

185

# 8

# SAYING AND MEANING

FRANK EBERSOLE

Like many another I was once committed to a certain type of philosophical endeavour – a type which goes under the names of 'linguistic analysis' or 'conceptual analysis'. I thought that any of a large number of words such as 'cause', 'responsible', 'mind', 'implies', 'art', 'meaning', and so on needed 'clarification', and that the required clarification could be given by an 'analysis' of the word in question. Then I read Wittgenstein. My first reaction was to add footnotes to the things I had been writing. Then I added appendices. Finally I tore the things up; and I have been trying in various ways to overcome a state of paralysis ever since.

A lot of philosophical words have come over the dam and down the stream since Wittgenstein's *Investigations* became available in 1953. And I am surprised – but not really surprised – that the stream has not changed its course. My reactions and hence my expectations are obviously eccentric. Of course Wittgenstein did change the terrain. But the stream of analytic philosophy runs strong, and it quickly made a few changes and flowed over the new ground. It swirls in a few new eddies. One of the adjustments it has made to Wittgenstein's impact on the terrain is this: there is no reason why an analysis should give the 'essence' of a term, or the 'necessary and sufficient conditions' for a term's application. It may well be that the word or phrase in question refers to many different sorts of things with various 'family resemblances' to each other. Perhaps, then, one can find central or basic groups of things, groups of 'paradigm cases'. Perhaps not. At any rate a summary of the several kinds and their interrelations will do. The purpose of 'analysis' remains the same; only the form has changed. More accurately, the analytic philosopher now thinks that his goals can be achieved by analyses of different forms: the form will be determined by the case at hand.

Also, one of the historical developments from Wittgenstein's work has given the analysts new heart. Following Wittgenstein's lead many philosophers became interested in the 'uses' of words. And this led to an interest in 'speech-acts', which are presumably the simplest and most basic things we use words to do. The word 'promise' is the key word in the speech-act of promising; the word 'good' is a key-word in the speech act of commending. Philosophers quite naturally were led to characterize the meanings of words in terms of the contributions they make to speech-acts. This characterization of the meaning of words has been at best a programme, and analytic philosophers have generally felt there is an insuperable difficulty in the way of carrying out the programme. Although the word 'promise' in 'I promise' contributes to the making of a promise, it does not contribute to the making of a promise in 'He promises' or in 'If I promise, then . . .'. It has seemed clear to analytic philosophers that the meaning of a word must be the same in all its occurrences, and so the 'use' of a word in making speech-acts is no part of the meaning of the word. Hence many analytic philosophers feel that they now have good reason to conclude that a 'use' theory of meaning is doomed to failure. And so the meaning of a word is not to be explicated in terms of its contribution to speech-acts, but is rather to be explicated by 'analysis'.

With changes in style and interest, the analytic tradition continues. From Wittgenstein it has apparently learned a little, objected to most, and gone on. Now I find this a little surprising – but really not so. If analytic philosophers had simply ignored Wittgenstein I should not in this way be surprised at all. The form of their objections is the thing that surprises – but even it is not really surprising. They object mainly that Wittgenstein's conception of the 'use' of a word or phrase is so unclear as to be useless, and consequently that Wittgenstein cannot offer a coherent theory of meaning or semantics. Now I really find this is a bit surprising because I do not see how it is possible to read Wittgenstein as offering an alternative to analysis, or as proposing a semantical theory or a theory of meaning. Surely he must be taken as exploring the possibility of something else in philosophy – something other than analysis – something other than any form of analysis.

I should like somehow to examine these things : the analytic philosopher's concerns with words and concepts, his complaints against a 'Wittgensteinian' theory of meaning (or lack of it), the status of a Wittgensteinian theory of meaning (or lack of it), and some related questions. But I am not brave enough, nor do I have the talents or temperament to go head-long into all this, to examine all the texts and all the arguments. I have in mind something else – something more indirect and less risky. I shall try to imagine a dialogue between a new-day analytic philosopher and a young 'disciple' of Wittgenstein, wherein each can air his objections to the other. This means, of course, that my 'disciple' of Wittgenstein will have to be defective from the outset – in order to allow himself to object to my analyst. But at the end I shall want to offer some morals on the dialogue, and so at that point I may be able to discount my Wittgensteinian's defect, or make allowances for it, or perhaps even take it away. My new-day analytic philosopher I shall name *Willby*. I imagine him to be stolid and hard-working. When he finds something in his opponent's views which he can use, he graciously adopts it. When he does not understand what his opponent is saying, he tends to ignore it. He is not easily turned aside. My self-styled Wittengensteinian I shall name *Nelson*. Quite naturally, I imagine him to be uncertain about his role in the discussion. Sometimes he acts as though he thinks Willby has some deep problem with which, as a disinterested outsider, he is trying to help. Sometimes he acts as though he were trying very hard to understand Willby's thinking. He tries to put himself in Willby's place and tries to take on his problems for himself : he tries to heal another with his own stripes. (It has been suggested that he got this attitude from reading the essays of O. K. Bouwsma, but I am unable to confirm or disconfirm this suggestion.)

I want Willby and Nelson to talk about the nature of knowledge, and especially I want them to consider such things as whether a person knows he is in pain, whether G. E. Moore knows he has a hand, or whether G. E. Moore knows that *that* is a tree, and some others. But I shall provide my characters with somewhat fresher examples out of which they can get the same issues. So let them consider these two examples: (1) While on a camping trip Charlie became lost in the mountains and was missing for nearly two weeks. After days of fruitless searching, a rescue team found him and brought him back to town. That was yesterday. Charlie was weak from exposure and very sick because he had cut his right hand and the wound had become gangrenous. Of course the rescue team rushed him to the hospital, and a staff doctor, after giving him a brief examination, said that his hand would have to be amputated immediately. Soon afterwards Charlie lost consciousness, full of anxiety about the loss of his hand. He fell into a deep sleep, and while he was asleep several specialists re-examined his hand and came to the conclusion that amputation would not be necessary. This morning Charlie awoke suddenly, as from a nightmare, and the sickening thought came into his mind – that now he had no hand. He immediately held up his hand and looked carefully at it while moving it all about. As one would expect, he seemed relieved and pleased to find his hand still there in the midst of the bandages. Through an observation window one of Charlie's best friends was watching him as he awoke and examined his hand.

(2) Harry spent the afternoon working on his antique car and afterwards spent a long time washing-up. He had a hard time scrubbing his hands clean, even with pumice-soap. His right hand was especially greasy and resisted cleaning, so he spent a long time over it, scrubbing it, holding it up and looking at it carefully. Finally he smiled with apparent satisfaction. During the time Harry was scrubbing his hands, his friend stood watching him from the next room.

For the philosophical discussion I have in mind, the important thing about these examples is this. Charlie's friend may later tell the story of Charlie's accident and rescue and all that followed. He may tell how he watched Charlie's wakening, and tell of the change in Charlie's face from painful uneasiness to pleasure. He might well say, 'Charlie saw that there was no cause to be con-

189

cerned. He knew then that his hand was not amputated.' Charlie, too, might later tell the whole story, and as he tells about his wakening he might say, 'I was relieved. I knew that my hand was not amputated.' On the other hand, if Harry's friend told about Harry washing his hands, he will not say, 'Harry knew that his hand was not amputated.' If Harry himself were to tell how hard it was to wash his hands clean, he would not say, 'I knew my hand was not amputated.'

*Willby:* As you know, I am interested in the philosophical analysis of certain concepts; or what I think is the same thing, I am interested in giving a philosophical account of the meanings of certain words and phrases. Recently I've been concerned with the concept of knowledge, that is, with the meaning of the word 'know'.

*Nelson:* And how is your work going? Have you arrived at any results?

*Wil.:* I long ago came to the conclusion that the concept of knowledge is not a unitary one: that not all the things called knowledge have any features in common. Rather, there are many groups of different things, related in different ways to each other. There is knowing a person, knowing a subject, knowing how to do something, knowing that something is the case, and many more.

*Nel.:* Is that the end of the matter?

*Wil.:* Far from it. It's just the beginning. When a concept stretches over different kinds of things there is generally one root or basic kind. Usually there is some linguistic mark to indicate the basic kind. One needs to see how the concept became extended from the basic kind to other kinds, and one needs to examine each type, but essentially the basic one. *Knowing that* seems to me clearly the basic type of knowledge, and I am currently trying to determine whether all cases of that one type have common and peculiar characteristics.

*Nel.:* And how do you go about making that determination?

*Wil.:* I put before my mind all sorts of examples. I try to think what features they share. If I can think of features they share, then I try to think of another example which may not have those features, and so on. I'm sure you understand the procedure.

*Nel.:* Have you thought of the example where Charlie knows that his hand is not amputated?

*Wil.:* I shall make a note of it, although I do not think it's a particularly important example.

*Nel.:* What do you say about the example of Harry washing his hands?

*Wil.:* As it stands, and all by itself, I suppose it can be treated as an example of almost anything – or of nothing. But, being presented alongside the example of Charlie, and compared with it, then it too can be treated as an example of a man who knows that his hand has not been amputated. Harry, too, knows that his hand has not been amputated.

*Nel.:* I thought you would say that. If a comparison with the case of Charlie were presented to them, many philosophers would say that the Harry case is an example of someone knowing something. But it differs from the Charlie case in what I should think is a most important way for your inquiry. One does not say of Harry that he knows his hand has not been amputated. In fact, one could not say so and be understood.

*Wil.:* But surely it *is* a very simple and clear case of knowledge. Harry certainly knows that his hand has not been amputated. Of course if I were on the scene, I should not say that Harry knows his hand has not been amputated, but what I should say does not affect the facts of the matter. One must not confuse what people say of things on certain occasions with what the things are. It is a simple fact that he knows his hand has not been amputated, just as it is a fact that his name is 'Harry', and his hands are wet. If he doesn't know that his hand has not been amputated, what on earth does he know? There would be no reason for my saying that he knows it, no point in saying it. But these considerations do not affect the fact that he does know it.

*Nel.:* You seem to agree to this: that if one were to say that Harry knows, he would not be understood. Surely that's right. If someone were to say to me that Harry knows I should not

191

know what to make of it. I should think at the least that he had some wildly mistaken ideas. Maybe he believes that some fiendish surgeon has been amputating people's hands while they are asleep. And he believes that after amputation the surgeon grafts a very realistic plastic hand in place of the real one. He thinks that Harry suspects he has been a victim of this fiendish surgeon and that he is now worrying over whether his hand is the real one or not. So now, when he says 'Harry knows that his hand has not been amputated', he means that Harry, while washing his hand and inspecting it, has found out that he has his regular hand and not one of those plastic ones. In truth, it is so unbelievable that anyone should think anything of that kind that I should not know what to think.

*Wil.:* I agree, of course, that one would not be understood.

*Nel.:* But *you* are now saying to me that Harry knew that his hand had not been amputated. How am I to understand you?

*Wil.:* That is completely different. We're talking of an example.

*Nel.:* Help me to see in what way I am to understand you when we talk of the example. Suppose you had been eating a piece of dry bread and were mumbling through a mouthful of it. 'I can't understand you', I say. Then you swallow the bread, clear your throat, and repeat, 'Harry knows . . .'. Now I can understand you. That can't be the sort of thing you mean.

*Wil.:* You know perfectly well it isn't. I don't mean that you can make out the words I say. I could be reciting a nonsense rhyme and you could understand me in this way. I don't mean 'understand me', I mean 'understand *what I said*'.

*Nel.:* But, after clearing your throat of bread and speaking, you could have asked, 'Do you understand what I said?' I should have replied, 'Yes, I understand what you said.'

*Wil.:* Perhaps 'what I said' is not the phrase I want, but the words aren't important.

*Nel.:* One can understand a Mynah bird, or what a Mynah bird says – if he speaks in your native language, otherwise perhaps not.

*Wil.:* You know I don't mean anything like that. I don't mean any of these things. I mean you can understand what I say because it's true that Harry knows his hand has not been amputated. That's not quite a complete and accurate reason because you could also understand what I said if it were false. But what I said is either true or false, and in seeing that it is either true or false you can understand perfectly what I said.

*Nel.:* If understanding what someone said is like that, then presumably anyone at all could have understood Harry's friend saying 'Harry knows . . .'. But that could not be understood. You agreed that it could not.

*Wil.:* I see I shall have to refine my terminology. There are clearly two kinds of 'understanding what is said' : understanding what is said in *that* situation, and understanding what is said. In place of 'understandable in *that* particular situation', I shall say 'intelligible'. Let me say that what Harry's friend said when he said 'Harry knows . . .' is understandable then, but not intelligible. What I say to you when I say that Harry knew is both understandable and intelligible.

*Nel.:* I do not understand why you think it understandable. But let that pass now. Tell me : why do you think I should find it intelligible? Intelligibility requires the right situation.

*Wil.:* You are thinking there is only one kind of situation, or rather you are thinking of only one kind. There are two : let me call them 'on the scene' and 'over the scene' situations. Now someone on the scene at Harry's hand-washing could not intelligibly say 'Harry knows . . .', but I am not on the scene. The Harry incident is a story, an example. I am not a character in the story : I have no speaking part in it. I am removed entirely from the scene of Harry's hand-washing. I am commenting on the example as an example. That's what I mean by an 'over the scene' situation. Surely one can say something *about* a story which he could not say *in* the story. I'll try to illustrate. Suppose I tell you a story, say about a man named Burke. He goes for a drive in the country with a friend. They pass a field of green grass with a cow grazing on it. Burke will not say 'That's a cow'. But I who am inventing the story say that they passed a cow. I now say of the example I have created, 'It would not be intelligible for either Burke or his friend to have said that the animal in the field is a cow, but I in creating the example say the animal is a cow.'

*Nel.:* But the story of Harry washing his hands is not like that. If I were to create or recreate the example of Harry washing his hands, I should not find it necessary to say that he knows his hand has not been amputated. In fact if I talked in that way I should not – to use your term – be intelligible. I should just as soon say that I should not be understood, or say that what I said would not be understood. That is, I should not be understood unless there were some question about my enunciation, my odd use of words, my strange grammar, or something like that. Then perhaps I should be understood in one of the ways you do not want.

*Wil.:* I think you are trying to confuse me with sophistical objections. Surely it is as plain to you as it is to me that Harry knows his hand has not been amputated. He knows that he has a normal hand on his arm as well as he knows his own name. He also knows that he is awake, has a nose on his face, and much more. Of course these are things he knows. If someone on the scene at Harry's scrub-up were to say any of these things you would understand what he said; but of course you would find them unintelligible. That means you would not, in that situation, know what to make of them. You would not understand why the person said these things. But you would understand what he said, and that's all I need to insist upon. If you understand what someone says who says 'Harry knows . . .' then surely you will agree that it is true.

*Nel.:* I'm sorry to say that I do not understand any of this very well. But I wish you would show me how I, here and now, am to understand or find intelligible your insistence that Harry knows his hand has not been amputated.

*Wil.:* Sometimes I think your philosophical position makes you dishonest. You say you do not understand when you understand prefectly well. What do you really expect me to do? If you like, I can remind you of the situation I am now in – as I talk to you.

*Nel.:* Perhaps I do not understand the situation as you do. It might help if you would tell me how you think of it.

*Wil.:* I am not a character in the example. I am commenting on the example. I am not creating it now, or retelling it, I am commenting on it; and I am commenting on it from a very special point of view. I'm sure that if I explain that point of view then my remark will become intelligible (but really, you already know what that point of view is). From that same point of view I might comment on the cow example. I want to say that sometimes an animal can be a cow without its being intelligible for anyone to say that it's a cow. This is a philosophical comment on words and on the nature of things words refer to. It is a comment on the word 'cow', on the nature of cows. It says something about the concept of a cow or of *cowness* or *cowhood*. My comment on Harry's hand-washing is intended to bring out something about the concept of knowledge, namely that knowledge can exist where it is not intelligible for anyone to speak of it. It is intelligible for me to tell you that Harry knows . . ., because I tell you in this particular situation, one where we are engaged in a certain sort of philosophical inquiry; and you understand that situation as well as I do.

*Nel.:* My uneasiness may be just that I do *not* very clearly understand that situation. I am trying to get a feel for your project and your methods.

*Wil.:* Well, I might try to collect before my mind all the sorts of animals called 'cows' in order to help me formulate comments on cowhood. I am trying to collect all the cases of knowledge I can think of in order to formulate comments on the nature of knowledge. I am reminding myself that I must not omit an animal from the class of cows simply because it would not be appropriate for someone to call it a cow. Similarly I am reminding myself not to ignore a case of knowledge just because it is not appropriate to speak – on the scene – of the person in question as knowing something.

*Nel.:* Perhaps I am hopeless, but maybe I can understand the inquiry better if I let you go on with it. Let that part stand so we can get on. When you come upon a case where we should

195

not say that somebody knows, then how can you be sure that it is a case of knowledge? How do you recognize it?

*Wil.:* You seem always to want me to explain the things which are so simple and obvious that they are hard to explain. They are hard to explain just because they are so very simple and obvious. This recognition was involved in our learning words as children. We heard someone speak of this cow and that cow, and very quickly we could recognize a cow in a situation where no one spoke of it at all. Although we have forgotten this, it is easy to see that we must have learned words in that way. In surveying examples to help with philosophical analysis one merely recapitulates the procedure of childhood. One begins with animals in situations where they are called 'cows', and then sees that in other situations where they are not called 'cows' the animals are the same. And the same with knowledge. One begins with cases where we speak of somebody knowing something, and then we see that other cases are the same, even though we do not say of them that somebody knows something. Many other cases are the same, even when it is unintelligible for someone on the scene to speak of somebody knowing something.

*Nel.:* You might be suggesting several different things here. Let me mention two of them because I hope they are *not* what you have in mind. First, we can imagine many animals which we should not know what to call in any circumstances. That is, they are not clearly 'cows', and they are not definitely 'not cows' either. Do you mean that when you arrive at an analysis of the concept *cowhood*, you can then see that some of these animals are the same as cows, and hence are really cows?

*Wil.:* I don't want to rule that out as the outcome of an analysis of a concept. But I agree with what you are suggesting, I think. In the beginning, in order to fasten attention on the concept, I certainly do not want to consider anything other than clear-cut definite cases of cows – or of knowledge.

*Nel.:* You are prepared to discover that 'concepts' are not 'neat' and unitary. (I shall use your word 'concept', but I should rather talk of the meanings of words.) You said that the 'concept' of knowledge was not unitary. This leads me to wonder whether you are suggesting the second thing that came to mind. Perhaps you will see that some animals which are never, under any circumstances, called 'cows' are the same as cows, and hence they are really cows. You might discover that our 'concept' is defective or inconsistent or something, and replace it – or try to replace it – with another.

*Wil.:* I don't want to rule that out either as a possible result of a philosophical analysis and a valuable one, too, sometimes. But that discovery, if it comes, cannot affect the way I proceed. I have no way to proceed other than to consider those cases where our ordinary concept applies, that is, to consider those animals in some situation where we call them 'cows' and those people in some situation where we say that they know something. What I am saying is this: it is easy to see that animals in other situations where they are not called 'cows' are exactly the same as these. And the same with cases where it is unintelligible to say 'He knows . . .'. In fact it is so easy to see, that we are scarcely aware that a recognition of sameness is called for. It has become incorporated in our understanding of words. The situation determines what we can and cannot intelligibly say, but the animals or the facts of the matter are exactly the same.

*Nel.:* The way you lean on the cow analogy suggests that you are pleased with it: you must think that giving the meaning of a word is always very like telling what are the distinguishing marks or characteristics of some animal.

*Wil.:* Not for every word; but for the kind of word with which we are concerned, the two strike me as being very similar. And incidentally, I think the words with which we are concerned, general referring words, or concrete general words, are the ones which give the dimension of meaning to our language. Yes, the two strike me as being very similar.

*Nel.:* Good. Then perhaps that gives me a way of coming to understand your enterprise better. Perhaps you can explain your concern to me in terms of something I think both of us understand pretty well, namely recognizing and identifying birds and talking about their distinguishing marks. Maybe it will be all right to think of that as a model in terms of which to understand what you are doing.

*Wil.:* It seems a good model, if you think you need one.

*Nel.:* So, I shall try to think that finding and stating the meaning of a general word is like writing a certain part of a field guide to birds, specifically, that part which tells the distinguishing features of each species. For each bird it gives the things to look for, and tells how to distinguish that bird from others with which it might be confused.

Sometimes there is another part of the bird book. It tells something about a bird's habits or life history. It tells what is interesting or remarkable about the bird. This part will discuss features or characteristics of the bird which make it worth talking or writing about. So these features correspond to the conditions under which we use a word – as opposed to the word's meaning.

*Wil.:* I've never before thought about this, but it seems to be a very good analogy.

*Nel.:* It helps me a little. At least it helps me give some form to my incomprehension. My first difficulty is this. I really need something like this model to guide me, but when I have it I don't know how to use it. When thinking about knowledge, I don't know quite what to look for under the heading of 'feature' or 'characteristic'. When using the bird book I know what sort of thing is going to be mentioned as a feature of a bird, even though not just anything we can think of counts as a 'feature'. The book may say immature Myrtle and Audubon's warblers are indistinguishable. This does not mystify me. The author of the book must have distinguished them, but if I were to ask him, 'By what feature can you make the distinction?' I expect he would say, 'None at all. I have observed specimens whose parentage I know.' I realize that you, unlike the author of the bird-book, want parentage to be a feature and – I can only say – 'almost anything else', but I don't know how to understand the 'almost anything else'. It is like 'and so on'. I could understand an ornithologist explaining a bird-book if he said 'colour of nape, rump, wing-tips, shape and length of tail, shape of beak, and so on.' But I have only the bird-book analogy with which to understand your enterprise. Your 'and so on' and the ornithologists' are not the same at all.

*Wil.:* Yes, of course I count parentage as a feature. Here is another good example of the kind of thing we are talking about. Parentage is something which is a feature, but in that particular situation is not called a feature.

*Nel.:* This difficulty of mine in seeing what is to be a feature is not my only problem. I also have trouble understanding how you can so clearly see what is a feature of the thing as opposed to a feature of the speech-context. In the case of birds I have no trouble in seeing what goes under the heading of distinguishing or identifying features as opposed to remarkable things such as the magnificent flight of the albatross, the odd song of the chat, or the unusual nest of the ovenbird. This is because I know a great deal about birds and how they are classified. I know which features are apt to be significant and which ones not. I should never for a moment think that the magnificence of the magnificent frigatebird was an identifying feature, nor the unusual fidelity of the Cardinal to its mate.

But I don't for the life of me see how I can be expected to see that same unimpeachable distinction in the case of knowledge. In fact I am troubled by the regular shift in our discussion from 'the meaning of "know" ' to 'the nature of knowledge'. The word 'knowledge' suggests something I can find in a situation like a bird in its habitat. We can *have* knowledge and we can *have* a crow in a cage. Of course this analogy is misleading and I have to fight it. We are not concerned with the features of 'knowledge'. We are not concerned with the meaning of the word 'knowledge', but with the meaning of the word 'know'. Maybe this is the way I should put the right question to myself: 'What features must I have to correctly say "I know" (even though it might not be intelligible for me to say so)?' I am trying to get in the spirit of the thing, but right away I want to blurt out, 'to correctly say I

199

know I've got to be ready to stick my neck out, willing to let people count on *me*.'

*Wil.:* And, as you suspect, that is the wrong kind of feature. You have given one of the conditions for saying or asserting that someone knows, not one of the features of knowledge. One who knows is willing to stick his neck out – but he is willing to stick his neck out only because he knows.

*Nel.:* Then what of this as a likely feature? I can correctly say 'I know' if I can give good reasons.

*Wil.:* That is the right kind of feature, and a very plausible candidate for an essential mark of knowledge. Again, I think you understand better than you pretend to.

*Nel.:* Your ability to make this distinction astounds me. I suspect the ability comes from some secret you are holding back.

*Wil.:* I don't know what it could be, except perhaps this. I look for features which make the thing what it is, as distinguished from features which provoke talk about it. So in helping to isolate the meaning of the word I look for what is common to occurrences of the word in assertions, questions, commands, negations, conditionals, disjunctions, and so on.

*Nel.:* I realize that whatever the meaning is going to be, say of the word 'know', it will be the same for all occurrences of the word : it will be the same in 'He knows', 'He ought to know', 'He does not know', 'If he knows, he can tell us', 'Does he know?' and so on. But only situations where we say 'He knows' or 'I know' give us instances of someone who knows. So when we turn to examples, as your procedure requires, only a 'categorical assertion' will give us an instance of knowledge – as you say – or the thing itself whose features we want to survey.

*Wil.:* Still, I must think of being able to move or transport it into the other contexts.

*Nel.:* I realize that most of my problems come from trying to use the bird-book model. But I need it; without it I seem to have nothing. Let me tell you one more difficulty I have with the model, and then I'll be done with it. Sometimes you say you want to find out what knowledge is. Sometimes you say you want to find out what the word 'know' means. And you say these are the very same. I am unable to think of 'What is knowledge?' and 'What is the meaning of "know"?' as the same *question*. I do not know what to make of the question 'What is knowledge?' so I have to think about the meaning of the word 'know'. But the bird-book model does not help me to think about the meanings of words.

Suppose that I am leafing through my field guide to birds and casually read what it says under 'limpkin'. I might say that I learned what a limpkin is, but I should not say that I learned the meaning of the word 'limpkin'. If I do not know how to recognize a limpkin, I might ask a bird-expert 'What are the distinguishing features of a limpkin?' I should not ask him, 'What is the meaning of the word "limpkin"?' What do you say about this?

*Wil.:* Quite honestly, I have never thought about it. I am inclined to say that you have produced more examples of the very thing we have been talking about. In each case you are concerned with the meaning of the word 'limpkin', it's just that you do not *say* that you are concerned with the meaning of the word 'limpkin'.

*Nel.:* I was afraid you would say that. I cannot offhand think of any example where one is concerned with distinguishing features or characteristics, and where his concern is with the meaning of words. I was about to accuse you of misrepresenting your inquiry, but you have blocked me.

There is another thing which I find confusing about the way you conduct your inquiry. Sometimes you talk about the 'concept of knowledge', and sometimes about the meaning of the word 'know'. You think of these – or at least you say you think of these – as coming to the same thing. But this talk of 'concepts' in connexion with an inquiry into the meaning of a word disturbs me. I think it throws me off.

*Wil.:* Why is that?

*Nel.:* We do think sometimes and talk sometimes about the meaning of familiar words: words like 'chair', or 'egg'. But we do not think or speak of the concepts of egg or chair – at least not *just* of the concepts. We might say of a furniture designer that he has a new or exciting concept of a chair. We might say of a biologist that he has a new concept of an egg – meaning that he has a new theory about the role of the egg in the life-history of animals. He sees the egg in a new way. But we do not mean to contrast these new concepts with some 'ordinary concept' which all of us have. We do not say that everyone has a concept of a chair or of an egg.

*Wil.:* Again – this should not surprise you – I think we do all have an 'ordinary' concept of a chair or an egg, although, of course, we do not say so. As before, the fact that we do not say something does not mean that it is not so.

*Nel.:* I'll never cease to be surprised at the way that one doctrine of yours takes care of so many things I think of as real objections. In this case, however, my misgiving comes from something more than the fact that we do not speak of having ordinary concepts of eggs and chairs and toads. The idea you have of an ordinary concept gets its force from contrast with 'new concept', 'bold concept', 'interesting concept' and others. When we speak of someone having a novel or exciting concept of a chair, we do not mean that he has a new meaning or an exciting meaning for the word 'chair'. And when we speak of someone having a new or interesting concept of an egg we do not mean that he has given the word 'egg' a new meaning or an interesting meaning. Talk of new concepts or exciting concepts is not talk about the meaning of words. So if talk about old or ordinary concepts gets its force from these idioms, then it is not talk about meaning either. When we want to express disapproval of a new concept or reject it, we do sometimes say such things as 'I prefer the ordinary concept' or 'I'll stick with the old concept'. In saying these things we are not saying anything about the meanings of words.

*Wil.:* I think perhaps you are right. When, ordinarily, we talk of concepts we are not talking of meanings. I shall have to say that I am using the word 'concept' in a new and technical sense. And I regard 'the concept of an X' to be equivalent to 'the meaning of the word "X" '. Since I do regard the two expressions as equivalent, I shall be glad to give up 'the concept of . . .' and always speak of 'the meaning of . . .'.

*Nel.:* 'The concept of a(n) X' and 'the meaning of the word "X" ' do not always work in the way you want. We cannot always substitute some one word for X in the two expressions and get meaningful results. It works for 'cow': 'The meaning of the word "cow" ' becomes 'The concept of a cow'. It does not work for 'know': 'The meaning of the word "know" ' becomes 'The concept of a know'. I suspect the word 'knowledge' came in to rectify this. What you really want for 'The concept of . . .' is an abstract noun : the concept of bovinity or cowhood, the concept of knowledge. But one cannot in general say the same things using 'cow' and 'cowhood' or 'know' and 'knowledge'. 'I know that the man is a spy' and 'I have knowledge that the man is a spy' come to quite different things. I suspect we lose sight of something important in uses of 'know' if we think of 'I have knowledge' in its place.

*Wil.:* If this has caused any confusion, I am willing to talk always of the meaning of 'know' or of the verb 'to know'.

*Nel.:* I am glad, because I have always had to try to translate in my own mind your 'concept of knowledge' and even your 'knowledge' into 'meaning of the word "know" '. But the fact that you have used this word 'concept' seems to me symptomatic. It carries the suggestion that there is something besides the use of a word to which we can look for its meaning. I believe you think of a 'concept' as something like a picture in the bird-book, as something which shows the identifying features. You think that general concrete words refer to things only because of the features of the things. You seem to have nothing to go on but this bird-book picture of words and meaning, and I think the picture misleads you.

*Wil.:* And you act like a doctor who has gone mad and has lost most of his medical memory : he can remember the symptoms and cure for only one disease. He now thinks that everybody has that one disease, and cannot understand why they do not all come to see him.

*Nel.:* I don't want to obstruct the discussion further. I am willing to assume that you can use your picture to guide you through whatever complications you meet. So let us return to your judgment that the Charlie and Harry cases are the same. It is essential to your procedure that you judge these and many other cases to be the same, isn't that so?

*Wil.:* Yes. They are exactly the same in the way I am concerned with. They are quite clearly the same, and in being the same are both cases of someone who knows something. Charlie knows that his hand has not been amputated. Harry is in the same position. He is conscious, alert: he is carefully looking at his hand. Then surely he knows his hand is there on his arm, functioning as usual.

*Nel.:* You are getting ahead of me. I think you are also getting ahead of yourself. You seem to be mentioning the 'features' of one who knows, and then finding the cases the same because they share these 'features'. You are supposed to see that they are the same, and *then* reflect on what makes them the same.

*Wil.:* I agree. I was only trying to be emphatic in my judgment that the two are the same.

*Nel.:* Two things about this bother me. The first is this. I simply cannot put myself in a position where I can see that the two cases are the same. In fact, I feel inclined to say exactly the opposite: the two are not the same at all. They strike me as quite different. I am supposed to be inquiring into the meaning of the word 'know'. In one case there is something which makes the use of the word 'know' understandable: I think it is the presence of doubt or anxiety. In the other case, use of the word 'know' is not understandable: in that example there is no need for the resolution of doubt, no need for assurance. If I am to be concerned with the meaning of the verb 'to know' I had best be concerned with just such things, those things which determine our use of the verb.

*Wil.:* In expressing your feeling that the two differ, you too have put the cart before the horse: you have pointed out in what respects they are different.

*Nel.:* Yes. And that is my second misgiving about this business of 'same'. Neither of us feels secure in his judgment of 'same' or 'different' without trying to mention features and explain what makes the two cases same or different. It is not supposed to be that way. You are supposed to see that they are the same, and hence both cases of knowledge. And you are supposed to see that they are cases of knowledge before you can tell what features every case of knowledge must have. And even if each of us could explain what features determine whether the cases are same or different, we should still feel insecure in our judgments because they do not agree with each other. Yet they are supposed to be direct and simple judgments on a matter we are quite familiar with.

*Wil.:* But I am sure, all the same, that I am right about this, and that you are simply wrong.

*Nel.:* I believe we need to think some more about judgments of sameness or difference. We are supposed to be in the position of one who makes a reliable judgment that two things are the same or different and who cannot tell how he made the judgment. After careful reflection, then – but only then – can he tell which things were relevant, which irrelevant, and so on. Let me try to think of an example.

Suppose that a dancer is teaching a student how to do a scene in a ballet – one which he has often done. 'Watch me,' he says, 'and then try at first to do the same things.' He dances; and then the student dances. He says, 'That's fine. You did exactly the same : you can start from there.'

*Wil.:* I don't find the example helpful.

*Nel.:* Maybe it isn't. I think it is very incomplete. But let's try to consider a few things we need in order to fill it out. The teacher may be old and no longer agile – also perhaps out of practice. The student was not expected to duplicate the teacher's stiffness, or his slips. The teacher may try very hard to bring out originality in his students. If the student had a style of his own, he was not expected to give it up. He would be expected to dance as *he* dances, not as the teacher does. On the other hand, the teacher might be a strict classical task-master. Then he would not tolerate stylistic originalities, and in that case even an elegant original performance would not be 'the same'.

*Wil.:* All these things are pretty clear, but why are you going over them?

*Nel.:* In this case one can't appreciate the basis on which a judgment of sameness or difference is made without an intimate understanding of the dance, the attitudes of the teacher, the abilities of the student, how the teacher views these abilities, the student's style and how it relates to the teacher's and so on. If the teacher made his judgment in my presence, I should simply have to accept it. He could try to explain it to me, but I could not understand until I learned all those many things about the dance which I do not know. Without all that, I could not discuss his judgment with him; I could not agree or disagree with him.

I realize this is hasty, but I want to draw a tentative conclusion. If one tells a story to illustrate all the factors lying behind a judgment of sameness or difference, it will have to be an unusually complete and detailed story . . . I'm sorry, I should not indulge myself in sarcastic understatement. . . . Such a 'complete and detailed story' is, of course, unimaginable. The story-teller has to count on his listener's knowing all the relevant things. His audience must be *in* on it: they must 'belong to the club'.

At long last I'll draw a conclusion from this. You and I do not have an audience of the right sort to which to direct our judgments. Clearly I am not a member of your audience, and you are not a member of mine. We do not belong to the same club. In fact, we do not even know what club we could join in order to get the comprehension we need.

*Wil.:* I don't see why one can't just *say* in what respects he wants two things to be compared. Why not just say in what respects two things are to be the same?

*Nel.:* I hoped that my example would show this to be impossible. Perhaps if someone had a minor or very specific misunderstanding of some kind, then the ballet teacher could point out to him some respect in which the performances were to be compared. But the teacher could not effectively point it out unless the other already understood that a certain likeness or similarity in that respect – and others unmentioned – makes the performance, here and now, the *same*. Such an explanation or justification can be given only against the background of a general understanding.

*Wil.:* Well, at least I'm glad you have put us in the same position : although we are not in the same club we are in the same boat, and it seems to be sinking. The conclusion clearly seems to follow that our judgments are baseless.

*Nel.:* I don't think we're quite ready for that conclusion. All we can learn from the example is something we already know. Philosophy is not an art like the dance. It does not have one following, one community of teachers, learners, admirers, and critics. It does not provide the proper setting for judgments of same or different.

But we knew that. Why should we forever behave as though philosophy were expected to be something which it is not? The talk of philosophers is lighter and more vaporous than the talk of people in the dance community. The words of philosophers support themselves, or at least they are expected to support themselves. Philosophy is all a story, and philosophers are story-tellers who are themselves characters in their own stories. When they make judgments of sameness or of difference, the judgments are backed by nothing but the stories out of which they arise.

While we are philosophizing together, you make a judgment that the Harry and Charlie cases are the same. I make a judgment that they are different. The least we can do is to tell the stories which might back these judgments in any way they can. Suppose I tell the story for you; and then you tell my story.

*Wil.:* I should certainly like to hear what you have to say for me.

*Nel.:* Don't expect anything very elaborate : I have already told part of it, I believe. What could the story be besides this? You have the idea that the general words which are basic to our language refer to things, actions, attitudes or whatever because of some characteristics of the things or actions or attitudes.

Whether a word applies to a thing depends solely on the nature of the thing, and in no way on features of the situation which determine whether people will in fact use the word in speaking about the thing. You judge that Charlie and Harry are the same in that both know something – because you think they have certain features in common. Of course they are different : Charlie has a question and he needs assurance. Harry has no question. This difference is part of the context or setting. Knowledge will give assurance if someone needs assurance, but one can know something quite independently of anyone's need for assurance. This is the story you yourself alluded to when you said that in childhood we learn to extend the application of our words from cases where it is appropriate for someone to say something to cases where it is not appropriate because we see that the two kinds of cases have the same features in themselves.

You have the idea that philosophers have some special, peculiar interest in determining what things are, or in determining what the concepts of things are, or in giving the meanings of certain words or phrases. You think of these as different ways of describing the same enterprise because listing the distinctive characteristics of a thing tells what it is; it unfolds the concept of the thing, and it gives the meaning of the word or phrase which refers to the thing.

In judging the Charlie and Harry cases to be the same you must have found that Charlie and Harry shared the required determining features. Therefore, from the beginning, you must have had a pretty good idea what these features were. You must have been pretty well prepared from the outset to say what the word 'know' means. I suspect it would have gone about like this : 'To know something is to be certain of that something, and to have the right to be certain of it (and in addition the something must be correct).'

*Wil.:* You have oversimplified, but I find the main outlines of the story recognizable. I shall not disown it, although I should like to add a few qualifiers.

*Nel.:* Now suppose you give my story.

*Wil.:* I don't believe you have revealed enough of yourself for me to do that. You have only said that the two cases, Charlie and Harry, are different because only one involves question and assurance. You said that this determined whether one said 'He knows' or 'I know', and that in characterizing the meaning of a word you would consider the factors which determine the use of the word, those factors which determine what one says.

*Nel.:* You have made an excellent start. But I suppose you are right : I had best continue the story myself since so much of my story depends on my – so far unexpressed – opposition to yours. Your story is a philosophical theory of meaning, a 'Platonistic' one, if I may give it a name. And I am most suspicious of it. When we are trying to give the meaning of a word, I want to say it's not what we see when under the influence of your Platonistic theory that counts. It's what we say, or would say. It's what we say when not under the influence of any philosophical theory; what we should say in all the many situations we can imagine. A statement of the meaning of a word must take into account those things which determine when and where the word is used. We do not say of Harry that he knows his hand has not been amputated. We could not say it and be understood. Therefore it is not a case where the word 'know' applies, and this must be considered in any account of the meaning of the word 'know'.

Since I am prepared to say what does and does not count in giving the meaning of a word, I too must be prepared to say what I think 'know' means. A person knows something when we say, or could say, that he knows something. Much more is required than what you think of as 'features' of the person said to know. There is also the speaker (or thinker) who may be the same person or another. The word 'know' is used by one who has or has had doubts or uncertainties, and it is applied to someone in proclaiming him to have the authority or credentials necessary to resolve the doubts or uncertainties. To say that a person knows something is to say, among other things, that by reason of his position, training, experience, he can be held responsible for its correctness. In the very act of saying that he knows we put a person in a new position; we change his status. All these things must enter into an account of what the verb 'to know' means.

Your Platonistic theory, I believe, grows out of a certain picture of words and meaning. It depends upon one's thinking of words and the things of the world and the features of these things as three clearly distinct types of entities. The speakers of language use words to refer to certain groups of things because of some features of the things upon which they have fastened their attention. Your theory, I say, misrepresents and oversimplifies. Words are not related to things as labels are to the specimens on which they are fixed. At the risk of being overly metaphorical, I shall say that words and things are intermixed more completely than are earth, air, fire, and water at the beginning of the long year. The basic unit is not the word. Words are but parts of sentences, which are parts of discourses involving speakers and listeners, the world they live in, their activities, their way of life. Of course when we speak of the meaning of a word we must isolate a little and relegate much to the background. Even so, when we speak about the meaning of a word we cannot ignore the way it is used. We must not lose track of the way the word functions in the whole of language and life. As a reminder we can say that the meaning of a word is its use. The meaning of a word is the contribution it makes to sentences, to paragraphs – and in turn to speeches, prayers, poems, pleas – the contribution it makes to teaching, reprimanding, apologizing, getting the job done.

A definition of a word must be a happy spotlighting of the word without completely losing the background. It must condense and summarize its use. The best way to keep this in mind, I believe, is not to think of a word as a tag or label, but to think of it as a tool or instrument which is used by human beings. Any definition of a word is like the explanation of a tool. A complete account of what a hoe is must tell what it is used for, say to dig weeds and chop dirt clods. It must also explain why it is used when it is; and why for other purposes, say for breaking larger or harder clods or for digging holes, we use a mattock or a pick. Of course words are sometimes used as tags or labels, to name, to classify, and so on; so my theory encompasses yours in a way.

Your theory and mine seem designed to explain different things. You take it for granted that words and their meanings are elementary units, and you seem to be concerned with explaining how 'speech-acts' like asserting and promising, and more complex 'activities' like telling dreams and praying, could grow out of them. You are interested in going on to explain the more complex aspects of language once you have taken care of the simple business of meaning. Whereas I seem to begin with the things you think of as complex, and wonder how we could ever isolate anything as 'simple' as the meaning of a single word.

Since I have given your theory a name, I suppose mine deserves a name, too. I shall call it the 'instrumentalist theory'. Just as from the first you interpreted the examples in terms of your theory of meaning, so I interpreted them in terms of mine. I too must have had in mind from the outset some account of the word 'know' which would make only Charlie know that his hand had not been amputated. I suppose my account would go something like this: a speaker says of a person that he knows when there is a question for which the person has an answer, when the person is in a position to guarantee the answer, and he will stake his position on the answer and the answer is correct.

*Wil.:* I hope you understand that I have no disagreement with your formula as a kind of slap-dash summary of the 'use' of the word 'know'. When taken in the proper way it doubtless gives the salient conditions in which we say that a person knows. I disagree with it because it professes to give the meaning of the word 'know'. And in a way it does give the meaning of the word; but it gives the meaning only as a part, and it gives far more than the meaning. You seem to be aware that you are giving the conditions in which we say that someone knows rather than the meaning of 'know' because you begin

211

your formula with the words 'a speaker says of a person that he knows . . .'.

*Nel.:* This is exactly the difference between us. Whereas you count only part of what I include as giving the meaning of the word 'know', I count the whole thing. I am quite willing to rephrase my account, and have it begin 'To know is to be in a position to guarantee the answer to a question that the situation presents . . .'. I consider this change of no importance; the two accounts are equivalent. Either gives the meaning of the word 'know'.

*Wil.:* At least your story is considerably longer than mine; but I can already see that mine has the advantage of simplicity.

*Nel.:* I don't want to deny that either. I take it you are anxious to appraise the stories.

*Wil.:* I can think of many things to be said in favour of mine.

*Nel.:* No doubt you can. But before you begin, I should like to note one thing. Your theory and your definition of knowledge form one impenetrable whole. And I must reject it all together. You expect the word 'know' and your definition of it to have 'the same meaning'. Indeed this seems to be the main aim in your search for an 'analysis'. Since you have wrong ideas about the meaning of the word 'know', I should expect your definition to incorporate those wrong ideas. You say that Harry knows because, among other things, he is certain that his hand had not been amputated. I say he is not to be counted as an example of someone who knows because we should not say he does. Of course, we should not say he is certain any more than we should say that he knows. Even if you used words other than 'certain' in your definition the result would be the same. You might say that he knows because he 'is convinced' or 'has no doubt'. But we do not say that Harry is convinced of anything or that he has no doubt. All of the same differences between us will come back for the words in your definition as have arisen for the word to be defined.

And again. It still remains a mystery to me how you decide what is a feature of the thing or person to which a word applies as distinguished from what is a feature of the context in which the word is applied to the thing or person. Assuming that you agree with my summary account of what you call the situation in which we apply the word 'know', you could include most of it in your definition as a feature of the person who knows, that is he has the feature of being in a doubt-resolving position. But you do not. You count being able to give good reasons as a feature of a person; but being able to answer a question, presumably, is not. I do not know what you have to go on here except something like the bird-book picture, and I do not see how it can guide your decisions on such details.

Closely related to this point is another. Your theory ought to work best with those simplest of words, such as the word 'red'. Such a word, I take it, would be simplest according to your account, for surely it refers to things because these things have just one feature, namely the feature of being red. Yet it is harder to make your theory work for these words than it is for more complex ones. 'What feature do these (red) things have in common?' is surely never a question which has to do with the meaning of the word 'red'.

At this point, where an appraisal of the theories seems forthcoming, I shall interrupt the dialogue and attempt the appraisal myself. Perhaps I can get a briefer account in that way.

Both Wileby and Nelson are of the opinion that as philosophers they have some special, important concern with meaning. They offer their theories, the Platonistic and the instrumentalist, as explanations of what the meaning of a word is. These two theories, of course, are different and opposed.

What kind of appraisal is called for? Is one right, one wrong? What reasons can be given for or against either of them? Against what can I measure them? I do not know where to turn except to examples of how we talk about meaning. In the Sunday paper Ralph has found a list of words under the caption, 'Do you know these words?' He brings the list to me, saying, 'I know them all except these. What does "latitudinarian" mean?' I say, 'A latitudinarian is a person who is liberal in his standards of belief and conduct, especially on matters of religious doctrine and practice.' 'And here's another,' Ralph says. 'What does "grapnel" mean?' 'A grapnel is a kind of anchor. It's small, and has four or five claws or hooks. It's often called a *grappling hook*.' In telling someone what these words mean we give the characteristics or features of the persons or things to which the words apply. This is a common pattern in the way we explain the meanings of many words: we give the characteristics of animals, vegetables, minerals, artifacts, people, institutions, and so on. This seems to accord with the Platonistic theory. But then we also talk of the meanings of words in a way which seems to accord with the instrumentalist theory. An American visiting a small Mexican village sees a sign reading 'Go Gringo'. He asks me, 'Is that English or Spanish?' I say, 'It's English: it's expected to be understood by American tourists. Don't you know the word "gringo"?' 'No. What does it mean?' 'The word is used by Mexicans and other Spanish Americans. It is applied to Americans (i.e. Uniter Statesers) and used to express contempt.' Suppose a foreign visitor on a tour of America attends a political meeting with me. After the meeting he asks, 'What was that word or phrase the man at the back kept shouting?' I must think for a moment. 'Oh, you mean "at-a-boy"?' Yes, that's it. What does it mean?' 'It's an expression used to shout support for what someone is doing or saying, and to urge him on.'

Sometimes in explaining a word we explain who uses it and under what circumstances he uses it. Of course the Platonist will say that in cases like 'gringo' we are giving more than the meaning of the word, and in cases like 'at-a-boy' we are not giving the meaning at all. The Platonist may have to say that phrases like 'at-a-boy' have no meaning. As philosophers not so long ago used to say: his use of the word 'meaning' departs from our ordinary use of the word. But he is prepared for this observation. He is in fact speaking in a 'strict' and perhaps new sense. He undoubtedly thinks that our old sense creates philosophical confusions.

Or maybe the Platonist will say that he has discovered 'meaning' to have a 'family of uses', and he is concerned with only one member of the family. Then he will have to distinguish and characterize the various members of the family. I have no inkling as to how he could do this. It will not do for him to say that he is concerned only with that meaning of 'meaning' which comes to 'distinguishing features'. The instrumentalist thinks that is never a correct characterization of meaning.

How can the instrumentalist accommodate the Platonistic-sounding explanations of meaning? He will say that in explaining a meaning of a word we *always* give a condensed and pointed delineation of its use. But sometimes the main features of its use are so well understood that it would be tedious and unnecessary to mention them. Of course the word 'grapnel' is used to refer, point out, designate an object or objects which we describe or ask questions about, and so on, and so on. To explain the meaning of the word, all that is needed is to say that a grapnel is an anchor and to give the main features of the anchor; even so, the rest – the way the word is used – is always understood. In fact we could not explain the meaning of any word unless many things about its use could be taken for granted.

There is another obvious feature of our talk about the meaning of words and phrases. In most circumstances we do not say what words or phrases mean at all. If I were to ask at breakfast, 'What is the meaning of the word "egg"?' I should draw a complete blank. Or what if I should pause in the middle of a lecture and say, 'The word "blackboard" refers to a dark smooth surface upon which one can draw or write with chalk?' No one could make head or tail of that. In Willby's terminology it would be unintelligible. For certain other words there does not seem to be any question of meaning, or any talk of meaning in any circumstances at all. When does one ask, 'What is the meaning of the word "good"?' What, after all, is the question about the verb 'to know'? There does not seem to be any context in which we talk of the meanings of words like 'good' and 'know' except one in which a translation is wanted or given. Such a context can shed no light on Willby's and Nelson's concerns with meaning: they were not interested in what the English verb 'know' means in German or Swahili.

The Platonist is quite prepared to take care of this. The fact that we do not *say* that a word has a certain meaning does not affect the fact that it does have the meaning that it has. He will say that words, always and everywhere, have the meanings that they have: it makes no difference whether we talk about their meanings or not. And that does seem a mysterious thing for him to say. Nelson would think that Willby was, as usual, blinded by the model of the word 'cow': he was thinking that words have meanings as farmers have cows. If Willby were more alert than he is to the role of models and metaphors in philosophy, he would see that Nelson's model gave him the same conclusion as his own. Surely a tool has the use that it has, whether or not anyone finds it fitting to speak of it.

Nelson had many misgivings about the Platonist's enterprise of analysis which seem to me well founded. He found it hard to understand inquiry into 'concepts' or 'natures', especially when this inquiry leads one into thinking that knowledge and meaning, cows and birds, are items or beings or things marked out by their features or characteristics. He found it hard to understand how any such thinking could be construed as thinking about the meaning of words. He was, I think, quite properly suspicious of that picture of words and the world which seems to be the principal sponsor of this kind of thinking. When it came to giving a definition of 'knowledge' he quite wisely, I think, refused to engage in the Platonistic enterprise. He does not try to 'tell what knowledge is', or try to give 'an analysis of the concept of knowledge'. Rather, he tries to give a pertinent characterization of what is involved in saying 'I know' or 'He knows' in those cases where one knows *that*.

But even this is too much, and from this point onward, I think that Nelson is lost. In a way he realizes this himself and half acknowledges it by saying that he is telling a philosophical story in which he is one of the characters. How seriously, I wonder, are we expected to take that? On the question of knowledge he is drawn only part way into the Platonistic enterprise, but on the question of meaning he is drawn into it completely. Whatever it is that Willby says about meaning, Nelson seems to say the same sort of thing. Against all of his own objections he tells us what meaning is; he seems to be discoursing on the 'concept of meaning'.

The instrumentalist ought at least to be as wary of meaning as he is of knowledge. He ought to have occupied himself with the way the word 'meaning' is used. Sometimes he still seems to be following his own advice, because much of what he says is concerned with the use of the word as it occurs in phrases like 'explain the meaning', and 'give the meaning'. But if he had really examined the situations in which these phrases are used, he could hardly have discovered there his 'theory of meaning'.

The instrumentalist theory tells us that the meaning of a word includes the conditions of its use. But the instrumentalist theory as it came out in the dialogue told us nothing of the kind. The theory does not follow itself. Nelson, at one point, began a line of questions which if pursued would have shown him that his theory was self-stultifying. When I idly read the bird-book about the limpkin, I may say that I have learned what a limpkin is. I do not say that I have learned the meaning of the word 'limpkin'. When would I talk about the meaning of the word 'limpkin'? Except in making translations – which are not relevant here – I do not think we ever say 'The meaning of "limpkin" is . . .' or 'The meaning of the word "limpkin" is . . .'. Although we do not speak of the meaning of the word in this direct way, perhaps we can ask 'What does "limpkin" mean?' and get a satisfactory answer. Ev n though the answer did not use the words 'mean' or 'meaning', certainly it would give an explanation of the meaning of the word. Then when do we ask about the meaning of the word? On an ornithological field trip I might ask the instructor 'How do you identify (or recognize) a limpkin?' – not 'What does the word "limpkin" mean?' Suppose I get a postcard from a friend who is on holiday in Florida and he writes 'I saw a limpkin today'. Even though the word 'limpkin' is unfamiliar to me, I ask someone 'What is a limpkin?' Surely I do not ask, 'What is the meaning of the word "limpkin"?' Suppose instead that my friend writes that he has learned many new words in Florida and he sends a list on which the word 'limpkin' appears. Now, if the word is unfamiliar to me, I might take the card to someone asking, 'Can you tell me what this word "limpkin" means?' He may answer my question about its meaning: he may say, ' "Limpkin" is the name of a large, long-billed, rail-like bird.'

For common nouns like 'limpkin' it appears we do not ask about – and hence speak about – the meaning of the word unless we are so unfamiliar with the word that we are not even sure that it is a common noun. The same degree of ignorance is not required for other kinds of words. 'It says here on my report that I am taciturn. What does "taciturn" mean?' 'It means "silent – not given to conversation".' Talk of meaning may begin from misunderstanding or misuse. 'My English instructor says that I *vitiated* my own theory. Why does he think that a criticism? I should think that making my theory stronger would be a good thing.' 'You must not know what "vitiate" means: you seem to think it means "make stronger". It means "invalidate" or "make ineffective".'

According to Nelson an explanation of the meaning of a word must consider the circumstances in which the word is used. So, Nelson's definition of the word "meaning" should have taken these things into account. He should have noted that we do not speak of 'giving the meaning' or 'explaining the meaning' of a word except in certain circumstances. We give the meaning of a word only when there is some real question about the word – because it is unfamiliar, or because the meaning of the word has been confused with that of some other word. However, when Nelson explained the meaning of the word 'meaning', he was well aware that Willby was perfectly familiar with the word and that he had not confused it with some other word. Of course, Willby also gave his explanation of meaning when there was no proper occasion for it. He knew that there was no real question about the word 'meaning', but as a Platonist he does not care. He does not need to care because his theory allows him to speak of meaning when the word 'meaning' cannot intelligibly be used. Nelson, the instrumentalist, also knew there was no real question about the word 'meaning', but – at the risk of self-invalidation – he has to care.

Is this too strong? Is there no way that Nelson's theory can be kept standing on its feet? I can think of no way. His discourse on the meaning of 'meaning' causes his trouble. So can I not construe his theory as a discussion of the *concept* of meaning rather than as a discussion of the *meaning* of meaning? But how is he to think of the concept of meaning? He has not been able to understand Willby's talk of concepts except as a confused way of talking of meaning. He has always had to translate Willby's 'concept' into 'meaning'. Give him the 'concept of meaning' and he quickly converts it back into the 'meaning of "meaning"'. He suspects that Willby attaches some other significance to 'concept': he suspects that Willby thinks of a concept as something like a bird-book illustration. In some mysterious way the concept gives the identifying features of whatever it is a concept of: chickadee, game, anger, or knowledge. But he thinks this is a confused and wrong-headed idea. I can hardly give these ideas to Nelson in order to save him. He would then become indistinguishable from Willby.

Can I not take him at his word when he says that his theory is a 'story', and when he says that he is a character in his story making the judgment that Charlie and Harry are not the same? As a story, then, can his theory not stand? This is a strange move for Nelson to have taken. First he shows by appealing to an example that judgments of sameness and difference can only grow out of a living community of understanding and mastery. (I happen to know that he was prepared with many examples.) Then he makes philosophy an exception: it can provide a 'story' in place of the living thing. Maybe this is an apt way to characterize philosophy, but it does not make it any the less puzzling. This manœuvre gives Willby everything he needs: his 'story' is self-enclosed and impervious. Of course it gives Nelson the authorization he wants for his story as well. But his story, unlike Willby's, is not self-enclosed: it is intended to accord with the way words are used. Nelson says that an account of the meaning of a word must explain when and where it is used. He is committed to the idea that he is talking about the meaning of the word 'meaning'. So it follows that if he is concerned about when the word 'meaning' is used, he cannot be giving its meaning. He cannot be

219

giving its meaning because there is no occasion for giving its meaning. I think there is no way to save Nelson's theory from self-destruction.

Nelson was to be my defective disciple of Wittgenstein. And so he is. By being a character in a dialogue, he is an anomaly from the start: he violates Wittgenstein's warning against disagreeing with philosophers. He does not realize that in order to deny a Platonist one must be a Platonist. He goes against all of Wittgenstein's admonitions by eloborating a philosophical theory. He has Wittgenstein's words all right, but he does not have the spirit. He has clearly mulled long and hard over the passages in *The Blue Book* and *Philosophical Investigations* on meaning as use, and on words as tools. He even senses a puzzle in his discussion with Willby, but it does not become a real puzzle for him. He does not go off in solitude and wonder why he should be torn to and fro, why he should be able to think that Harry does know – and also think that Harry does not know.

Is there no way to save anything of poor Nelson? I shall venture this: that of the two theories, his is better than the Platonistic because it contains the seeds of its own destruction. His theory can, in a simple step or two, bring about its own annihilation. 'Why is that a merit?' I hoped that question would not arise, but if it does I can think in quick succession of four answers – each better than the one before:

(1) We can look at the instrumentalist theory as a machine with a built-in self-destructive mechanism. The machine is designed to help us rid ourselves of Platonism, and it does its job. But like every machine, it develops problems of its own. At the point where its troubles outweigh its usefulness, it activates its own self-destructive mechanism.

(2) Take away the polemics and we can look at the dialogue between Willby and Nelson as a philosophical investigation. In turn we can look at a philosophical investigation as a trip into strange country, full of hostile natives and dangerous animals. This trip like every trip must end somewhere; and after such a frightful trip as this, nothing could be better than to end up at home – to come back finally to the comfort and security of home.

220

The same too with philosophical investigation. ('What *we* do is to bring words back from their metaphysical to their everyday use.)' We were lost in our thoughts about meaning, and by reflecting on the instrumentalist theory we can be brought back – to see 'meaning', 'given the meaning', as the familiar landmarks they are. In the beginning I disparaged Nelson for his attitude: but maybe, in the end, as he is brought to grief we can be healed by his stripes.

(3) I have been reviewing and reminding myself of the circumstances in which we speak of giving the meaning, and of what we say in giving the meaning. As opposed to Nelson, I have been talking about what 'giving the meaning' *really* is, have I not? And there has been no misunderstanding or lack of understanding of the phrase. One might have a bad dream in which the familiar hardware and dry-goods of his life were distorted into fearful shapes. And upon awakening he might say to himself, 'This is my good old chair', 'This is my curved pipe, and this is my straight one'. There are reasons for memorializing the familiar. If there are no reasons, then it is harmless nonsense. If it is not familiar, then it is not time to memorialize.

(4) If you have to ask, you cannot get an answer.

# 9

# THE NOTION OF ERKLÄRUNG

TAKASHI FUJIMOTO

The family resemblance of some German words like *Klärung,
Erklärung, Klarlegung, Klarwerden, Klarmachen, Erläuterung,*
etc. seems often overlooked by those who usually read Wittgenstein's works in English translation. In the following I shall
attempt to show that the notion of *Erklärung* (clarification) or,
rather, a cluster of those notions mentioned above, is one of the
most important keynotes to illuminate the nature and the scope
of his philosophical inquiries as a whole.

I

Any person who read the *Tractatus Logico-philosophicus* (1918–
21) and the *Philosophical Investigations* (1936?–49) for the first
time would be surprised to find that both are remarkably different with respect to their literary styles and philosophical contents. As is well known among professional philosophers, the
realms of ontology, epistemology, logic and axiology (i.e. approxi-
mately the whole field of traditional philosophy) are fairly systematically developed in this order in the *Tractatus*, with that
monological tone which gives the work simple and crisp read-
ability. But in the *Investigations* and other works written after
the *Tractatus*, miscellaneous problems and their remarks appear
one by one without any definite logical order, while their styles
are mostly conversational. As to the more important contents in
the former : the logical atomism; the picture theory of language;
theory of truth functions; and the critique of ethics and esthetics
seem all to be refuted in the latter, in which mere descriptions of
various uses of ordinary language appear to replace them.
Historically, the *Tractatus* was a Bible for logical positivists in

the 1930s, whereas Wittgenstein's lectures and the *Investigations* were main sources of stimuli for the activities of the so-called linguistic analysts since about 1945. And Wittgenstein himself in the *Investigations* openly 'recognized grave mistakes' in the *Tractatus*. Thus, it has become a natural tendency that professional philosophers emphasize the difference, rather than the coherence, between these two works, dividing his philosophy into two different parts and naming them early and later Wittgenstein, respectively.

If we scrutinize *what* Wittgenstein was aiming at (not how he has dealt with it), however, this tendency is questionable. For instance, he says in the *Tractatus* (note the original German words inserted in parentheses):

> Philosophy aims at the logical clarification (Klärung) of thoughts. A philosophical work consists essentially of elucidations (Erläuterungen). Philosophy does not result in 'philosophical propositions', but in the clarification (Klarwerden) of propositions (4.112).

> Everything that can be thought at all can be thought clearly (klar gedacht). Everything that can be put into words can be put clearly (klar aussprechen) (4.116).

This goal of his philosophy is seen in complete agreement with what is sought in the *Investigations*, e.g.

> It is not our aim to refine or complete the system of rules for the use of our words in unheard-of ways. For the clarity (Klarheit) that we are aiming at is indeed *complete* clarity (I-133).[1]

> A main source of our failure to understand is that we do not *command a clear view* (übersehen) of the use of our words (I-122).

---

[1] (I-133) means that the quotation is taken from the Part I, section 133. Other numerical notations follow this example. I shall use hereafter, unless otherwise specified, the abbreviations *TLP.*, *PI.*, *RFM.*, for the *Tractatus Logico-philosophicus*, the *Philosophical Investigations*, and the *Remarks on the Foundations of Mathematics*, respectively, to refer to the sources of quotations.

For a large class of cases – though not for all – in which we employ the word 'meaning' it can be defined (erklären kann) thus : the meaning of word is its use in the language (I-43).

Isn't there a deeper explanation (Erklärung); or musn't at least the *understanding* of the explanation (Erklärung) be deeper? – Well, have I myself a deeper understanding? Have I *got* more than I give in the explanation (Erklärung)? – But then, whence the feeling that I have got more? (I-209).

I would assume, therefore, that Wittgenstein's concern throughout various stages of his philosophical development was always with this kind of clarification (Er-klärung).

Unfortunately, however, this concept of *Erklärung* is so frequently and deliberately used in all of Wittgenstein's works, especially in the *Tractatus* and the *Investigations*, that their translators cannot help translating it ambiguously into such different terms as 'explanation', 'definition', 'clarification', etc. depending on what context it is used in. The result is the disappearance of the common meaning of 'making clear' (klaren) from the translations. I would further illustrate this circumstance :

Examples A :

(1) It is as if someone were to say (erklärte) : 'A game consists in moving objects about on a surface according to certain rules . . .' – and we replied : You seem to be thinking of board games, but there are others. You can make your definition (Erklärung) correct by expressly restricting it to those games (*PI.*, I-3).

(2) And how he 'takes' the definition (Erklärung) is seen in the use that he makes of the word defined (erklärten Wort) (ibid., I-29).

(3) I do not want to call this 'ostensive definition' (hinweisende Erklärung), because the child cannot as yet *ask* what the name is. I will call it 'ostensive teaching of words' (ibid., I-6).

These sentences reveal some of Wittgenstein's major theses in what is called his later philosophy. But the word 'Erklärung' here is translated as 'definition', whereas it is translated as 'explanation', its most common meaning in modern German, in the following

Examples B :

(4) But how does he know where and how he is to look up the word 'red' and what he is to do with the word 'five'? – Well, I assume that he *acts* as I have described. Explanations (Erklärungen) come to an end somewhere. – But what is the meaning of the word 'five'? – No such thing was in question here, only how the word 'five' is used (PI., I-1).

(5) So one might say: the ostensive definition explains (erklärt) the use – the meaning – of the word when the overall role of the word in language is clear (schon klar ist) (ibid., I-30).

(6) ' "Red" means the colour that occurs to me when I hear the word "red" ' – would be a *definition* (Definition). Not an explanation (Erklärung) of what it is to use a word as a name (ibid., I-239).

(7) The correct explanation (Erklärung) of the propositions of logic must assign to them a unique status among all propositions (TLP., 6.112).

The notion of 'explanation', appearing, for example, in *Investigations* I-209 and I-239, is used in contrast to the notion of 'definition' (Definition). As is well known, however, definition and explanation are two different notions, just as explanation is different from 'description' in Wittgenstein's sense. And it is only in this latter case that Wittgenstein uses the word 'Erklärung' to mean exclusively 'explanation', when he wishes to distinguish it from mere descriptions (Beschreibungen). (See *PI.*, I-109; *RFM.*, II-78, II-85; etc.) Thus we may generally argue, on the basis of various uses of the word 'Erklärung' as discussed above, that the 'clarification' in question should be interpreted as a notion subsuming such concepts as 'definition' and 'explanation' and yet retaining the original sense of 'making clear'.[2]

[2] If this is the case, it is very misleading that, e.g. Professor Max Black cites only 'explanation' as the English translation of 'Erklärung' in the German Concordance of his *A Companion to Wittgenstein's 'Tractatus'*, Cornell University Press, 1964, p. 396.

If it should be this kind of 'clarification' that Wittgenstein was concerned about throughout his early and later philosophical activities, such an observation, for instance, that 'Wittgenstein's new philosophy is, so far as I can see, entirely outside of any philosophical tradition and without literary sources of influence',[3] could hardly be accepted without reservations. It is certainly true that Wittgenstein had an incomparably unique personality, was usually separated from any established academic circles, and sharply criticized traditional philosophies. It is also true that he has never attempted a systematic reading of traditional philosophy and even says as a logician that 'he had never read a single word of Aristotle',[4] so that he naturally appears to have been independent of any known systems of philosophy and to have opened up a completely new vista for a 'new' philosophy. But the clarification as such, as well as the criticism against previous systems of philosophy, has been and must always be the most basic concern of all 'genuine' philosophers. If so, we cannot regard Wittgenstein as being particularly singular in these regards. We should rather seek the originality of his philosophy not in his problems or concerns, but in his unique way of solving or dissolving philosophical problems, most of which have long attracted the concern of traditional philosophers since the time of Socrates and Plato. The difference between his early and later philosophies should perhaps be taken simply as the difference between his way (or method) of solving or dissolving unclarified issues in philosophy.

II

What, then, is the clarification? What is it to clarify anything? Well, to clarify something is to *understand* the thing in question. For 'understanding is effected by explanation (durch Erklärung

[3] Georg Henrik von Wright: 'Ludwig Wittgenstein, A Biographical Sketch', *The Philosophical Review*, vol. LXIV, No. 4 (Ocober, 1955), p. 539.

[4] Karl Britton: 'Portrait of a Philosopher', *The Listener* (June 10, 1955); Also reproduced in K. T. Fann: *Ludwig Wittgenstein: The Man and His Philosophy*, A Delta Book, 1967, p. 61.

bewirkt); but also by training' (*Zettel*, I-186). To understand the thing in question is to understand the 'meaning' *for us* of the thing in question. And to understand the meaning of the thing in question is to understand the meaning of the sign, especially the symbol, the typical species of which is the language of the situation in which the thing in question is involved. Thus, in either the *Tractatus* or the *Investigations*, the theory of meaning, or the general treatise on the relation between the language and the world at large, becomes the central issue, though the author is not merely concerned with such things as the correspondence between the language and the facts of nature (See *PI.*, II-xii). Also of course, this issue of meaning should subsequently involve the problems of the structure of the world, the nature of symbolism, the psychology of understanding, and the nature of those philosophical doctrines which have so far dealt with these problems.

In the *Tractatus*, for instance, it seems that the question as to how language (or thought) is possible at all, is raised and solved by showing that only those languages which would fulfil such and such conditions as specified in the book are possible; and these conditions are specifications of the clarity he seeks, when he says, 'What can be said at all can be said clearly' (Preface). Thus it is far from the truth to say, as did Russell and others, that the early Wittgenstein was concerned with the construction of a logically perfect or ideal language, while the later Wittgenstein shifted his interests to mere analyses of ordinary language. We should rather say that the author of the *Tractatus*, with an overall knowledge of the logic of Frege and Russell and Whitehead's *Principia Mathematica*, attempted to clarify (not construct but, rather, describe) what should be the general structure of meaningful languages, if any. And, for this clarification, he must have developed and arranged, in the *Tractatus*, the idea of how the world is constituted – if it has any structure at all – and then described the nature of the language which reflects such structures and finally, excluded those traditional philosophies (and indeed his own philosophy) which have no such structures at all. However, what is important here in comparing the early and

227

later philosophies of Wittgenstein is that he had never excluded ordinary language as meaningless. For he clearly says,

> In fact, all the propositions of our everyday language, just as they stand, are in perfect logical order. (Our problems are not abstract, but perhaps the most concrete that there are.) (*TLP.*, 5.5563.)
>
> In philosophy the question, 'What do we actually use this word or this proposition for?' repeatedly leads to valuable insights (ibid., 6.211).
>
> The different nets correspond to different systems for describing the world (ibid., 6.341). Whatever we can describe at all could be other than it is (ibid., 5.634).

Or, he seems to have left room for further examination of ordinary language as a different system for describing the world.

Now it should not be very difficult to understand the historical process of Wittgenstein's philosophical development. After the publication of the *Tractatus* he went to Austria to live in seclusion; but, perhaps persuaded by F. P. Ramsey and later by P. Sraffa, he renewed his concern with what it is for linguistic symbols to be meaningful, asking how to deal with the richness of everyday language and examining concrete uses of ordinary expressions. He was eventually led to conclude that we could never use such a simple notion as that of one-to-one correspondence between a sign and a thing as the only criterion of meaning. We might then say that, if his intention or aim was to understand things just as they stand (not to impose certain dogmas or ideas upon our world), the author of the *Tractatus* must have tried to pave the way to such understanding through the new logic of Frege and Russell, whereas the author of the *Investigations* aimed at it through the actual uses of ordinary language.

Wittgenstein's philosophical clarification (or understanding) may tentatively be termed either logical, or mathematical, or linguistic. And his major works, the *Tractatus*, the *Investigations*, and the *Foundations of Mathematics* could respectively be called the logico-philosophical, the lingua-philosophical, and the mathematico-philosophical remarks for the clarification of the issues in each corresponding field of study. Here again his conception of philosophy as an activity or therapy coincides with the hierarchic scheme of traditional Platonic philosophy as *episteme*, which was placed above, and subsumed, logic and mathematics as *dianoia* and linguistics probably as *pistis*, although there is no strict correspondence; and his practice of philosophy does not deviate much in spirit and scheme from that of traditional philosophers. That is, there is philosophy on the one hand as an approach to clarification, and its objects to be clarified on the other; and both are ontologically to be distinguished. Philosophical activities could then in principle be applied to any unclarified issues in any field of study. This Wittgenstein expressed by saying that 'there is not *a* philosophical method, though there are indeed methods, like different therapies' (*PI.*, I-133).

### III

Wittgenstein's philosophical activities in the post-*Tractatus* period were directed towards the clarification of four different but related groups of issues : issues concerning the meaning of words, knowledge and understanding, and the nature of mathematical reasoning. I would briefly review his ways of clarifying these issues.

*A.  Theory of Meaning*  In the *Tractatus* a language is said to be a totality of propositions (4.001); a proposition is said to have meaning if and only it it is a picture of reality (4.01), or is a description of a state of affairs (4.023). A word or a name is said to mean an object and the object is its meaning (3.203). And this is the essence of what is called the 'picture theory' of language. He is said to have developed this theory merely from a logical point of view. But, when he faced the problem of what to do with the multiplicity of the uses of ordinary language, he must have become aware of the narrowness of the applicability of the theory, or the fact that the theory cannot clarify various uses of everyday language. For, criticizing Augustine, he says, 'Not everything that we call language is this system . . . it is appropriate but only for this narrowly circumscribed region, not for the whole

229

of what you are claiming to describe' (*PI.*, I-3). Thus he is led to the well-known thesis that 'the fact that sentences have the same sense consists in their having the same use' (ibid., I-20); or 'there isn't any doubt that we understand the word . . . and its meaning lies in its use' (*RFM.*, I-130); or 'the meaning of a word is its use in the language' (*PI.*, I-43); where the use is usually determined by training or a special purpose that the user has in mind. This does not mean, however, that Wittgenstein had never thought of the meaning as the use of a language in his early days, but he had already had room for developing this new pragmatic clarification in the *Tractatus* – say, in 3.328, where he says, 'if a sign is useless (nicht gebraucht), it is meaningless', which contra-positively implies that the meaning of a sign is its use.

*B. Criticism of Philosophy* Wittgenstein's ideas concerning the nature of philosophical assertions had never basically changed throughout his early and later periods. They were all strikingly negative. He could expect no clarification or understanding of his questions and their answers from traditional philosophy. For 'most of the propositions and questions of philosophers arise from our failure to understand the logic of our language' (*TLP.*, 4.003); or the 'main source of our failure to understand is that we do not *command a clear view* of the use of our words' (*PI.*, I-122); and 'philosophy may in no way interfere with the actual use of language; it can in the end only describe' (ibid., I-124). Philosophy is at most a 'critique' or 'therapy' of language and can never have a meaningful system of its own. He even says, 'When we do philosophy we are like savages, primitive people, who hear the expressions of civilized men, put a false interpretation on them, and then draw queer conclusion from it' (*RFM.*, I-125). Perhaps this is why he 'must throw away the ladder after he has climbed up it' (*TLP.*, 6.54) and commonly attempted to persuade his students to give up philosophy as a profession.[5]

*C. Theory of Knowledge* Wittgenstein's epistemological stance was basically solipsistic in the *Tractatus* : 'The world is my world :

[5] Norman Malcolm : *Ludwig Wittgenstein, A Memoir*, Oxford University Press, 1958, p. 30.

this is manifest in the fact that the limits of language (of that language which alone I understand) mean the limits of my world' (5.62). To understand the world is then to clarify my world, or the structure of my language. But, if this language of mine is to be applied to the solopsistic ego or the self, it suddenly becomes senseless. For 'the self of solipsism shrinks to a point without extension' (ibid., 5.64) and 'there is no such thing as the subject that thinks or entertains ideas' (ibid., 5.631). The implication of this Humeian solipsism is that there is no such thing as language that can describe the self. Such a language, if any, is nothing but the 'sounds which no one else understands but which I *"appear to understand"* ' (*PI.*, I-269). It has no use, or it does not lead us to the understanding or clarification of what it means. For there are no rules or criteria that would guarantee the empirical validity or applicability of a private language. But, of course, this does not mean that one can have no private experience (Erlebnis); one is instead full of it. But the essential thing about it is that 'nobody knows whether other people also have *this* or something else' (ibid., I–272). Thus the private experience is something that cannot be *said*. If we can say, however, that it shows itself, like the epistemological self, then it is the mystical (*TLP.*, 6.522).

D. *Theory of Mathematics*  In the *Tractatus* 'mathematics is a method of logic' (6.2, 6.234). The only difference is that 'the propositions of logic are tautologies' (6.1), whereas 'the propositions of mathematics are equations' (6.2), which are also other kinds of tautologies in the sense that they do not express any thought (6.21). This is naturally an expression of Frege-Russelian logicism beyond which Wittgenstein did not go much further despite his overall criticisms of their doctrines. He thought he had clarified the nature of mathematics in this way. But later in the *Foundations of Mathematics* he looked for further clarification of it, saying, 'What mathematical propositions do stand in need of is a clarification (Klarlegung) of their grammar, just as do those other propositions' (V-13), because ' "mathematical logic" has completely deformed the thinking of mathematicians and of

philosophers' (ibid., IV-48). And he was led to say, 'I should like
. . . to show that we can get away from logical proofs in mathematics' (ibid., II-44), since mathematics is not a pure system of
tautologies like logic but 'a motley (buntes Gemisch) of techniques
of proof' (ibid., II-46), and 'I want to give an account of (erklären) the motley of mathematics' (ibid., II-48). Then he dealt
critically with various types of proof theory and related topics,
and was led to the conclusion that the certainty of mathematical
proofs did not consist in their universal validity (there is no such
thing!) but in their following rules (Regelfolgen). Their apparent
validity and applicability are determined by 'convention, or use,
or perhaps our practical requirements' (ibid., I-9). Thus his later
philosophy of mathematics, as of other fields he examined, turned
out to be considerably conventionalistic, operationalistic, or pragmatic, despite his criticism of and divergence from, say, William
James (*PI.*, I-342).

In this way the general character of Wittgenstein's philosophy
after the *Tractatus* might be roughly summarized by saying that
it aimed at clarifying unclarified issues and, in so doing, dissolving
them eventually in the light of everyday language or life. Clarification or understanding is a personal event, unless we assume
the intersubjectivity of personal judgments, and must 'come to
an end somewhere', or to the point where the problem no longer
troubles us. Wittgenstein wanted a complete understanding for
himself, although such understanding might be utterly personal
or Wittgensteinian. And this complete understanding is usually
obtained by 'taking a wider look around' (*RFM.*, II-Appendix
II-1) and changing our ways of thinking and living. The ultimate
goal of his life-long philosophical activity is thus revealed in the
following statements of his: 'The sickness of a time is cured by
an alteration in the mode of life of human beings, and the sickness
of philosophical problems could get cured only through a changed
mode of thought and of life' (*RFM.*, II-4); 'The solution of the
problem of life is seen in the vanishing of the problem. (Is not
this the reason why those who have found after a long period of
doubt that the sense of life became clear to them have then been
unable to say what constituted that sense?)' (*TLP.*, 6.521).

# NECESSITY AND LANGUAGE

### MORRIS LAZEROWITZ

'Wann man sich vor der Wahrheit fürchtet (wie ich jetzt), so
ahnt man nie die *volle* Wahrheit.'

*– Wittgenstein*

Underlying much of Wittgenstein's later thinking was the wish
to reach a correct understanding of the nature of philosophical
utterances, and this wish is also discernible in his *Tractatus*.[1] His
later investigations led him to some iconoclastic ideas about what
a philosophical theory is and what a philosopher does who
supports his theory with an argument. Wittgenstein saw more
deeply into philosophy than anyone before him had seen into it;
but, for the most part, he seemed to prefer to express his perceptions in metaphorical language rather than in the language of
straightforward reporting. Part of the reason for this may have
been the wish to soften the hard things he saw. Remarks like 'a
philosophical problem arises when language goes on holiday',[2]
and philosophical language is 'like an engine idling, not when it
is doing work'[3] give expression to disturbing perceptions into the
nature of technical philosophy, but use a form of the mechanism
of *sotto voce* to deflect them. Where their translations into
prosaic language would tend to stir up anxiety, these words can
be accepted as colourful jibes which need not be taken
seriously.

It is important to notice that he stated in a number of places
that philosophical propositions are not empirical. This insight into
the nature of philosophical propositions (and into the modes of

---

[1] See for example 6.53.
[2] *Philosophical Investigations*, p. 19.
[3] ibid., p. 51.

investigation employed in philosophy) made it fundamentally important for him to become clear about the logical difference between empirical statements and statements which have *a priori* necessity – and especially to clarify the nature of necessity, to obtain, so to speak, an inside look into it. He appears to have come out with a conventionalist view, which on the surface at least he seems never to have given up. This is the view, generally speaking, that necessary propositions are about the literal use of terminology in a language. A number of writers have in fact described him as a conventionalist, and it must be allowed that there is considerable justification for this description. One of his frequently cited expressions, 'rule of grammar', which he used to characterize necessary propositions, unquestionably lends some substance to the claim that he took one of the traditional positions about logical necessitation. On one occasion G. E. Moore, who was puzzled by the term 'rule of grammar', remarked to me that he thought Wittgenstein meant by it what is meant by the more familiar term 'necessary proposition'. My impression at the time was that Moore thought Wittgenstein was so using 'rule of grammar' that in his use of the term a rule of grammar was not verbal. Moore's line of reasoning was perhaps the following : a rule of grammar in Wittgenstein's sense is a necessary proposition, and since a necessary proposition says nothing about usage, a rule of grammar says nothing about usage. There can be no doubt, however, that Wittgenstein wished by his special use of the word 'grammar' to say that *in some way* necessary propositions are verbal.

I

Conventionalism is open to a number of obvious objections which Wittgenstein could not have failed to know. It is worth remarking that conventionalists who are aware of these objections are not moved to give up their position. This is mystifying and certainly calls for an explanation; for if conventionalism is taken at face value as making a factual claim about the nature of necessary propositions, the objections are as conclusive as any objections could possibly be. One frequently repeated criticism is that to suppose a necessary proposition to be one which makes a declaration about verbal usage, or one which 'records usage', is to imply that a necessary proposition is not necessary. The negation of a true verbal proposition is a false verbal proposition, but not a proposition which could not, in principle, be true. To put it roughly, the negation of a true verbal proposition is not a self-contradiction, and precisely the same kind of investigation which establishes the truth of a verbal proposition, such as recourse to dictionaries and the like, could, theoretically, establish its denial. To use an expression of Wittgenstein's, we know what it would be like for a verbal proposition, which happens to be true, to be false, and for one which is false to be true. By contrast, we do not know what it would be like for a false arithmetical *proposition* to be true, for example, for $4+3$ to be less than 7. Taken literally, the *philosophical* claim that necessary propositions are about usage is refuted with complete finality by the objection that the view that they are implies that they are not necessary.

Another well-known objection is that a necessary proposition does not say anything about terminology, because it says nothing about what language it is expressed in or about any words occurring in it. The two sentences 'Red is a colour' and 'Rot ist eine Farbe' have the same meaning, which would not be the case if the proposition expressed by the English sentence made a declaration about words occurring in the sentence, and the proposition expressed by the German sentence made a declaration about words occurring in it. Wittgenstein certainly was aware of these objections, and there is reason to think that his conventionalism, which undoubtedly was the usual philosophical article at first, was transformed by his growing insight into the ways language works.

Verbal usage and logical necessity are in some way bound up with each other, and it is not too much to think that part of Wittgenstein's investigation into language and necessity was directed to bringing to the surface the way in which they are bound up. Thus, in more than one place Wittgenstein remarks that a philosopher rejects a notation under the illusion that he is upsetting a proposition about things.[4] This observation shows a recognition of the difference between an explicitly verbal statement and its semantic counterpart formulated in a different idiom, an idiom which easily gives rise to the illusion that the statement is about things. The difference between a verbal proposition and a necessary proposition may only be a difference in the form of speech in which they are expressed. But the difference in the form of speech may be of great importance, and seeing this difference can lead to an understanding of the way in which language and necessity are connected. To put the matter more concretely, seeing the unlikeness, without losing sight of the likeness, between, say, the proposition that being an uncle entails being male and the proposition that being male is part of the meaning of the word 'uncle' can lead to a correct understanding of how the *sentence* which expresses the entailment proposition is related to the proposition it expresses.

Consider for a moment the following sentences :

(1) A camel is a herbivore

(2) Ein Kamel ist ein Pflanzenfresser

(3) A camel is an animal

(4) Ein Kamel ist ein Tier

(5) The word 'animal' applies, as a matter of usage, to whatever 'camel' applies to

(6) The word 'Tier' applies, as a matter of usage, to whatever 'Kamel' applies to.

The attempt to get clear on the notion of necessity requires seeing how (3) and (5) are related to each other, i.e. in what way 'A camel is an animal' is like 'The word "animal" applies, as a matter of usage, to whatever "camel" applies to', and in what way they are unlike. However, to see this it is necessary to see also what (1), 'A camel is a herbivore', has in common with (3) and in what way it is different from (3). Furthermore, it is important to see

---

[4] This phrasing of the idea follows the phrasing in *The Yellow Book*, which consists of notes taken by A. Ambrose and M. Masterman in the intervals between dictation of *The Blue Book*, 1933–4.

how the fact that (1) and (2) have the same meaning is both like and unlike the fact that (3) and (4) have the same meaning. A clear grasp of these features of likeness and unlikeness requires seeing how (3) is related to (5), and (4) to (6). Getting a proper view of these matters will help us understand what it is about the *philosophical* view that necessary propositions are verbal, or that they state facts of usage, which makes it possible for a philosopher to hold it despite being aware of conclusive objections to it. Seeing what makes this possible will help dispel the mystery surrounding a long-standing dispute in which able philosophers with a well-preserved sense of reality can, to all appearances, debate the truth-value of a view which is known to be false without having strange ideas about each other's psychology.

Some philosophers, for one reason or another, have denied that there is a difference between logically necessary and empirical propositions, a direct consequence of which is that there is no difference in kind between the propositions expressed by 'A camel is a herbivore' and 'A camel is an animal'. Without going into the reasons for the philosophical claim that there is no difference, it can be seen that the mode of verification relevant to the proposition expressed by the first sentence is different from the mode of verification relevant to the proposition expressed by the second : observation is relevant to the first but not to the second.[5] Both sentences, equally, can be expressed as general statements of the form 'All A's are B's', i.e. as 'All camels are herbivores' and 'All camels are animals', which makes it tempting to think that both are generalizations. Their grammatical similarity appears to blind some philosophers to an important semantic difference between them. The proposition expressed by the first sentence, unlike the proposition expressed by the second, does not, to use Kant's

---

[5] Wittgenstein has brought out the same point with the help of his special use of the term 'grammar': 'The way you verify a proposition is part of its grammar. If I say all cardinal numbers have a certain property and all men in this room have hats, the grammar is seen to be different because the ways of verfication are so different.' (Lecture notes, 1934–5) Wittgenstein undoubtedly uses here his word 'grammar' to refer to the difference in the logic of the two statements, the difference in their 'logical grammar'.

phrase, have 'strict universality'. The first is an inductive generalization from observed instances and could in principle be upset
by future instances: no number of confirming cases, however
large, removes the theoretical possibility of there being a camel
that is not a herbivore. By contrast, the second proposition has
strict universality, which is to say that, unlike the first, it does
not carry with it the theoretical possibility of being upset by a
counter-instance. And this means that it is not an inductive
generalization. C. I. Lewis has stated that a logically necessary
proposition might, in addition to having an *a priori* demonstration, be established by 'generalization from observed instances',[6]
that is, be established in the way in which a law of nature is
established in science. Undoubtedly what Lewis was impressed
by, and perhaps wished to highlight, is the similarity between
the sentences expressing the two. But putting aside considerations
of this sort, it will be clear that taken at face value his claim
implies both that a logically necessary proposition of the form
'All A's are B's' has an associated theoretical disconfirming instance and that it does not have one. The difference between 'A
camel is an animal' and 'A camel is a herbivore' may be brought
into correct focus by noting that the first can be expressed as an
entailment, *'being a camel* entails *being an animal'*, and the
second can not – *being a camel* does *not* entail *being a herbivore.*
Nothing is more plain than that being a camel is logically consistent with being a herbivore and also with not being a herbivore,
and that experience alone, not penetration into the meanings of
the words 'camel' and 'herbivore', will show whether it is a herbivore or not.

To come back to the philosophical claim that a necessary
proposition is verbal, it can easily be seen that even though it is
expressible in the form 'All necessary propositions are verbal', it
is not put forward as a generalization `which issues from an
examination of instances. Instead, it is put forward as a statement to which there can in principle be no exceptions, or as one
whose universality is 'strict'. Construed in this way it can be
restated as an entailment: *being logically necessary* entails *being*

[6] *An Analysis of Knowledge and Valuation*, p. 91.

*about the use of terminology.* But looked on as making an entailment-claim we are puzzled to understand the continued disagreement which revolves around it. There is no debate over whether *being a camel* entails *being an animal*; and if philosophical conventionalism did actually come down to a straightforward, elementary entailment-claim, to the effect that *being logically necessary* entails *being verbal*, there is no question but that the debate over it would have been brought to an end long ago. But if the conventionalist thesis is not to be taken as an entailment-statement, correct or incorrect, then truly a familiar view is turned into an enigma; we do not know *what* the conventionalist is asserting nor do we know what we are disputing. There can, of course, be no doubt that in some way we do understand the view and the arguments for and against it; and the conclusion would thus seem to be that our understanding of the view, like our understanding of our dreams, is hidden from us. Anyone who lets himself become a curious observer of the philosophical scene must have the fleeting thought that philosophy is an activity which takes place in one of the less lighted parts of the mind. Conscious understanding of the apparent entailment-statement should put us on the way to getting clear about the nature of philosophical views in general. For if, as Wittgenstein has declared, philosophical propositions are not empirical, then it is natural to suppose them *a priori* and to be making entailment-claims. Again, as in the case of the conventionalist position, the thing that needs to be seen is what makes possible the continued disagreements centring on them. For example, if the philosophical statement, 'A sense datum is private', is an entailment-statement, it is one which is turned into a mystery by the continuing disputation over it. The only hope of dispelling the mystery and arriving at an undistorted perception of the philosophical theory lies in becoming clear about how a logically necessary proposition is related to the sentence which expresses it, to put it generally, how logical necessity is related to language.

In the *Tractatus* Wittgenstein makes a number of remarks about tautologies which throw light not only on tautologies but also on all statements having logical necessity, whether analytic or synthetic *a priori*. Proposition 6.1 states that 'The propositions of logic are tautologies', and 6.11 that 'Therefore the propositions of logic say nothing'. The view which comes out of these two propositions is that tautologies say nothing. Usually the idea that tautologies say nothing has been linked with the idea that they say nothing about things, that is, with the notion that they have no 'factual content'. Thus in 4.462 Wittgenstein states that tautologies are not 'pictures of reality', the implication being that they give no ontological information. The statement 'It is either raining or not raining' says nothing about the weather; 'A plant is either an oak or not an oak' says nothing about what a plant is; 'An object is either a plant or not a plant' says nothing about what an object is. This can perhaps be made more perspicuous by considering the negations of these statements. The expressions 'not both an oak tree and not an oak tree', 'not both a plant and not a plant', do not function as predicates which tell us what a plant or an object is not, unlike 'not both a camel and not herbivorous', which does function to deny what a creature is. To say with regard to anything that it is not both a camel and not a herbivore is to say what the thing is not, and this is because the predicate 'both a camel and not a herbivore' presents a possible 'picture' of the thing. But to say with regard to a plant that it is not both an oak tree and not an oak tree is not to say what the plant is not, inasmuch as 'both an oak and not an oak' does not have a use to describe any plant, actual or hypothetical. Tautologies say nothing about what there is and what things are like, and contradictions say nothing about what there is not and what things are not like. Predicates of the form 'ø or not ø' equally with 'ø and not ø' have no descriptive content.

These considerations apply to all analytic propositions, and to synthetic *a priori* propositions as well. Kant and many philosophers after him have held that synthetic *a priori* propositions, the predicates of which are connected by 'inner necessity' to their subjects but are not components of them, have factual content, that is, delineate features of the world. But it will be clear that a true proposition, and hence a logically necessary proposition of whatever kind, will tell us something about what there is only if its negation states something to be the case which in fact is not the case. Kant's claim that the proposition that every change has a cause is *a priori*, although not analytic, has, as is known, been challenged and debated over and over again with a vigour which promises the debate immortality. Without going into it in detail, we may say that if *being a change* entails (whether synthetically or otherwise) *having a cause*, then *being a change and not having a cause* will not be a predicate of any conceivable occurrence and thus will not have a function to describe what does not take place. The conclusion would seem to be that the proposition that a change must have a cause, like a tautology, says nothing about what does or does not take place. Consider for a moment the proposition 'A red thing is not green'. It is clearly an *a priori* truth and it could be argued, in the following way, that it is also synthetic. *Being red* entails *not being green*, but the concept *not green* is not discovered by a 'dissection' of the concept *red*: the consequent-concept is not a conjunctive part of the antecedent-concept. In other words, it could be argued that the consequent is synthetically entailed by the antecedent, and thus that the proposition, 'A red thing is not green', is synthetic *a priori*. But as in the case of a tautology, it says nothing about what things are, if its negation does not present a picture of a hypothetical reality. And since *being red and simultaneously green* is not a predicate of a conceivable object, *not being both red and green* will fail to function as a predicate which says what a thing is not.

It becomes clear now that Wittgenstein's claim that tautologies say nothing can be extended to all propositions which have *a priori* necessity. With regard to tautologies he said they are 'not, however, nonsensical. They are part of the symbolism, just as '0' is part of the symbolism of arithmetic' (4.4611). The implication of this would seem to be that a sentence which expresses a proposition that says nothing is not a nonsensical combination of words like 'Duplicity reclines on the first odd prime'. It would generally be maintained that an indicative sentence which is not nonsensical, that is, one which is literally intelligible, must say something. To put it equivalently, a sentence which says nothing whatever would be said to be nonsensical or to have no literal meaning.

The idea behind this claim is that an intelligible declarative sentence must be about something, actual or imaginable, that it must have a subject about which it makes a declaration. A sentence which expresses an empirical proposition puts forward a claim about the world; it says something about what in fact is the case, or is not the case, and has some sort of subject of discourse. A tautology, which says nothing, but nevertheless is not nonsensical, must therefore have some subject matter about which it makes a declaration.

Some philosophers have identified the subject of *a priori* statements as the structure of the world. In his *Notebooks* 1914–16 Wittgenstein wrote: 'The great problem about which everything I write turns is: Is there an order in the world *a priori*, and if so what does it consist in?'[7] And in the *Tractatus* there is the suggestion that the subject of tautologies is identified as the structure of the world. In his own words, 'The propositions of logic describe the scaffolding of the world, or rather they exhibit it. They have no "subject matter". . . . It is clear that something about the world must be indicated by the fact that certain combinations of symbols – whose essence involves the possession of a determinate character – are tautologies' (6.124). The implication of these words is not that tautologies have no subject matter but rather that their subject matter is not of a certain sort. They are 'about the world' in a particular respect, namely, about its basic structure, and this, not the specific contents of the world, is their subject matter.

This notion would seem to be in accord with Leibniz' view that necessary propositions are true for all possible worlds. Leibniz' distinction between necessary, or identical truths, and truths of fact is that the latter hold only for particular possible worlds, true for some and false for others, while identical truths hold for every world, for the existing world as well as for nonexisting possible worlds. The underlying idea is that an *a priori* truth has some sort of ontological import. It is about the world, just as an empirical proposition is, but it is not only about this world. We may gather that Leibniz had the idea, whether or not he was

[7] p. 53e.

fully aware of it, that an *a priori* necessity refers to that which is invariant in all possible worlds, to what might be called a cosmic content; and this is the structure to which all possible worlds conform.

Wittgenstein's way of putting this is summed up in 6.12 : 'The fact that the propositions of logic are tautologies shows the formal – logical – properties of language and the world.' Some philosophers have characterized the three Aristotelian laws of thought as laws not only to which thinking must conform but also as laws to which things must conform. The proposition that nothing can be both an oak tree and also not an oak tree is a different kind of law from a law of physics, e.g. the law that every particle of matter is attracted to every other particle with a force that varies directly as the product of their masses and inversely as the square of their distance apart. A law of logic may be said to apply to special laws of nature as well as to the specific characteristics of things. The idea behind the views of Wittgenstein and Leibniz is that any system of things together with the laws governing their behaviour, however different from any other system of things and their laws, will fall under the same laws of logic, and more generally, the principles embedded in all *a priori* propositions. The cosmic picture linked with this idea is that *a priori* statements give the structure to which all things and laws, actual and possible, must conform. Contingent truths refer to the contents of the present cosmos; the totality of *a priori* truths details its logical structure. Thus, equally with empirical propositions, tautologies have a subject : the invariant structure of all possible worlds. Wittgenstein's two statements, 'Tautologies say nothing' and 'They are not nonsensical', would seem to imply on his own accounting that tautologies say nothing about what there is in the world but nevertheless do have a subject : the structure of reality which they explicate, or in some way reveal.

A philosopher who perceives that a tautology says nothing, for example, that 'It is either raining or not raining' says nothing about the weather, but who does not deny that it is intelligible will, if his thinking is governed by the formula 'An intelligible statement cannot be about nothing', *find* something which it is about. For a time Wittgenstein identified the subject of *a priori* truths as the structure of the world, but this seems to have been only a transitional view. The insight that necessary propositions have no factual content may develop into the perception that they convey no sort of information whatever about the world; and this seems to have occurred in Wittgenstein's thinking. One consideration which shows that tautologies have no factual content also shows that they are not about the structure of the world either. The negation of a logically necessary truth presents us, in John Locke's words, with an 'impossibility of thought'. The negations of 'A red thing is not also green' and of 'A physical particle which is in one place is not at the same time in another place' result in combinations of terms which stand for impossibilities of thought, namely, the expressions, 'a red thing which is green' and 'a physical thing which is in two different places simultaneously'. So to speak, they present us with conceptual blanks. It will be clear that if these phrases denoted concepts instances of which we could imagine, then instead of denoting impossibilities of thought they would present us with conceivabilities, that is, with 'thinkable states of affairs'.[8]

To suppose, however, that they apply to hypothetical instances is to imply that it is possible to conceive of what would upset a necessary proposition. It would thus imply that a necessary proposition is in principle falsifiable. It would imply that we know what it would be like for there to be a red thing which is also green, for a plant to be both clearly an oak tree and also definitely not an oak tree, and for one and the same oak tree to be in a given place and also elsewhere, and hence that we can envisage circumstances which would make true a self-contradictory proposition and make false a logically unfalsifiable proposition. Wittgenstein has remarked (3.031): 'It used to be said that God could create anything except what would be contrary to the laws of logic. – The reason being that we could not *say* what an "illogical" world would look like.' To this we might add that to deny that God could create something contrary to the laws of logic, or a self-contradictory state of affairs, is not to imply that

[8] This phrase is taken from 3.001.

there is something which God cannot do. For a putative descriptive expression which involves a contradiction has no descriptive content, i.e. has no use to describe anything, actual or not. Hence, to say that God can create nothing which goes against the laws of logic, or that God cannot create a state of affairs which answers to a self-contradictory expression, is not to use language to state what cannot be done. Wittgenstein appears to have intended this in 3.032 when he says 'it is . . . impossible to represent in language anything that 'contradicts logic'' '.

The implied difference between a phrase which denotes a logical impossibility and an expression which denotes a physically impossible state of affairs, one which, if it existed, would cancel an immutability in nature, is that the second presents us with a thinkable state of affairs, to use Wittgenstein's word, a state of affairs we can *picture* to ourselves (3.001), and the first does not. Thus the negation of a necessary proposition neither shows nor represents nor exhibits nor depicts what the structure of the world cannot be. Hence a necessary proposition does not represent or exhibit or depict a structure that the world must have. If the one does not show *what* the structure of reality cannot be, or perhaps better, does not exhibit a structure to which reality could not conform, then the other does not depict a structure to which reality must conform. The statement, 'A thing can be in one place only at a given time', would tell us something about what must be with regard to things in space only if 'A given thing is in two separate places simultaneously' *described* what cannot occur in space. In this regard 'A thing must be in one place only at a given time' is completely different from 'A thing is gravitationally influenced by other things in space'. The second describes what happens in space, the first does not.

Giving up the idea that the subject matter of tautologies is the structure of the world does not mean giving up the idea that they must have some sort of subject matter. Parenthetically, it is not difficult to see that the expression 'the logical structure of the world' is a made-up expression to which no clear meaning has been assigned. Its apparent function is to serve as the 'name' of

the subject matter of tautologies, devised in the course of looking for the subject matter under what might be called the 'regulative' formula that a literally meaningful statement must be
about something. A philosopher who thinks that tautologies are
in no way whatever about reality and who rejects the metaphysical claim that the meanings of general words are abstract
entities might then fix on the use of terminology in a language as
the subject matter of tautologies, and in general of *a priori* statements. A philosopher like Wittgenstein, who later saw more
deeply into the workings of philosophy than anyone else and
eventually arrived at the idea that a philosopher rejects a notation under the delusive impression that he is upsetting a proposition about things, will in the course of his intellectual odyssey try
out various 'theories' regarding the subject matter of *a priori*
statements. Wittgenstein certainly tried out conventionalism,
which represents the use of terminology as what necessary statements are about.

Elsewhere I have tried to show that a philosophical theory is
a gerrymandered piece of terminology, which because it is presented in the ontological form of speech tends to create an illusion
that conceals what is being done with language. Without going
into this here, it needs to be pointed out that an ontologically
presented re-editing of terminology can have either of two purposes, which do not necessarily conflict with each other. It can
have the purpose of highlighting in a graphic way a point of
usage; it can also have the purpose, undoubtedly unconscious, of
creating an illusion that a theory about things is being advanced.
In Wittgenstein these two purposes do not stand out in clear
separation from each other. It is safe to say that the conventionalist position which he sometimes took is the usual variety,
which itself is a philosophical theory, that is, a 'theory' with a
built-in possibility of endless disputation. The insight which goes
beyond conventionalism, and does not issue in a philosophical
theory, is to be found in his later writings; but he never presented
it in clear articulation, unshadowed by metaphor.

Traditional conventionalism is one of the theories which
appears to be adopted in the *Tractatus*. Thus, he wrote (6.126):

'One can calculate whether a proposition belongs to logic by calculating the logical properties of the *symbol*. And this is what we do when we "prove" a logical proposition. For, without bothering about sense or meaning, we construct the logical proposition out of others using only *rules that deal with signs*.'[9] This position also makes its appearance in some of his later work. Moore, in discussing some things Wittgenstein said about tautologies in his lectures 1930–3, suggests that Wittgenstein identified a statement of the form 'it is logically impossible that $p$' with the statement 'the sentence "$p$" has no sense'.[10] Moore went on to remark, 'why he thought (if he did) that "It is logically impossible that $p$" means the same as "The sentence '$p$' has no sense.", I cannot explain.'[11] He also reports him as having stated that 'the proposition "red is a primary colour" was a proposition about the word "red"; and, if he had seriously held this, he might have held similarly that the proposition or rule "$3+3 = 6$" was merely a proposition or rule about the particular expressions "$3+3$" and "$6$" '. Moore observed that 'he cannot have held seriously either of these two views, because the *same* proposition which is expressed by the words "red is a primary colour" can be expressed in French or German by words which say nothing about the English word "red"; and similarly the *same* proposition or rule which is expressed by "$3+3 = 6$" was undoubtedly expressed in Attic Greek and in Latin by words which say nothing about the Arabic numerals "3" and "6". And this was a fact which he seemed to be admitting in the passage at the end of (I) [notes of lectures in the Lent and May terms of 1930].'[12]

It is certainly not a rare thing for a philosopher to hold a view while aware of 'fatal' objections to it. This blitheness of attitude towards refuting evidence is not encountered in the sciences, and its occurrence in philosophy stands in need of explanation. In this connection, Moore's paradox forces itself on

[9] Wittgenstein's italics bring out the point.
[10] *Philosophical Papers*, p. 275.
[11] ibid., p. 276.
[12] ibid., p. 291.

247

our attention : 'The strange thing is that philosophers have been able to hold sincerely, as part of their philosophical creed, propositions inconsistent with what they themselves *knew* to be true.'[13] It may be unkind, but it appears to be true, to say that philosophers have not sincerely faced up to this paradox. Instead of being made curious about the nature of their activity, about what it is they are doing with words, they push the paradox out of their mind and go on doing philosophy with what seems to be a determined lack of curiosity. Be this as it may, there is no question but that Wittgenstein at times adopted a conventionalist view about *a priori* necessity, though he did not remain irremovably attached to it. Conventionalism does represent insight into the nature of logically necessary propositions, but presented in the form of a *theory* about *a priori* necessitation it is an obstacle to the understanding of the nature of philosophical statements. Wittgenstein overcame this obstacle and arrived at an understanding of how philosophy works. The following report of the way he began to think about language and necessity shows clearly his growing perception into the special way a sentence which expresses a necessary proposition and the necessary proposition itself are bound up with each other :

... '4' has two different uses : in '2+2 = 4' and in 'there are 4 men here' ... We must understand the relation between a mathematical proposition about 4 and an ordinary one. The relation is that if the word '4' is a word in our language, then the mathematical proposition is a rule about the usage of the word '4'. The relation is between a rule of grammar and a sentence in which the word can be used. ... Now is '2+2 = 4' about 4 or not? If the sentence 'I have 4 apples' is about 4, then '2+2 = 4' is not about 4 in this sense. If you say it's about the *mark* '4', be careful ... When do I emphasize the word 'rule'? When I wish to distinguish between '2+2 = 4' and 'There are 4 apples on the table' ... If I use the word 'rule' it is because I wish to oppose it to something else ... If 'There are 2 men here' is about 2, then to say

[13] ibid., p. 41.

'$2+2 = 4$' is about 2 is misleading, for it's 'about' in a different sense. . . . $25 \times 24 = 600$ isn't used as a rule for handling signs, though it would stand in the relation of a rule to a *proposition* using this equation.[14]

The objections to conventionalism, construed as making a claim regarding what necessary propositions are about, that is, regarding what their 'subject matter' is, are conclusive. It is unrealistic to think that the theory, taken at face value, could be held by anyone who was aware of them : it would require our having to think that the conventionalist was suffering from an odd mental condition which enabled him in some way to seal off the objections to the view from the view itself. Looked at through the spectacles of Moore's Paradox, we should have to imagine that a philosopher believes a view to be true while aware of objections which he knows show it to be false. The conclusion forced upon us, however strong our resistance to it may be, is that despite its appearance of making a claim regarding what necessary propositions are about, it makes no such claim. To understand what the conventionalist is trying to bring to our attention, consider three of the six sentences given earlier :

(1) A camel is a herbivore

(3) A camel is an animal

(5) The word 'animal' applies, as a matter of usage, to whatever 'camel' applies to.

The difference between (1) and (5) is obvious. (5) is about the word 'camel' and (1) is about what the word 'camel' denotes. That is, to put it roughly, one is about a word and the other about a thing. (3) is neither about the word 'camel' nor about what in (1) is denoted by the word 'camel' : it is neither about a word nor a thing. What we know in knowing that what (1) says is true is something about camels. What we know in knowing that what (5) says is true is a fact of usage, and what is known in these two cases is something in addition to our understanding the sentences.

[14]Notes of lectures, 1934–5, taken by Alice Ambrose. Compare the last sentences with *Tractatus* 6.126.

In this regard (3) is different from both (1) and (5). Understanding it is equivalent to knowing a fact about verbal usage, although this fact is not expressed by the sentence. (3) shares its form of speech with (1), the ontological idiom in which words are not mentioned and are usually used to refer to things. Its content, however, what might be called its invisible subject matter, is shared with (5).

Perhaps this point is best brought out in the following way: The fact that the sentence 'A camel is an animal' expresses a necessary proposition is equivalent to the fact that the sentence 'The word "animal" applies, as a matter of usage, to whatever "camel" applies to' expresses a true verbal proposition. To put it somewhat metaphorically, the verbal content of (5) is explicit and visible, while the verbal content of (3) is hidden; it is made invisible by the mode of speech in which the sentence is formulated. (1) has factual content, (5) has verbal content, and (3) has hidden verbal content. (3) is a grammatical hybrid which is sired by (1) and (5) and differs markedly from both. As an aside, it may be observed that philosophical theories about the nature of necessity are nothing more than academic assimilations of the offspring to one or other of the parents, with the consequence that its relation to one parent is, to use Wittgenstein's expression, hushed up.

The objections to conventionalism can now be seen to call attention to respects in which (3) is different from (5), and there is a temptation to take them to be objections against identifying (3) with (5). But if we can resist retreating into philosophical fantasy, we can understand how the conventionalist is able to hold his position only by supposing that he has made no such identification, however much his words suggest that he has. Supposing that the conventionalist does not in fact make this identification requires our thinking that conventionalism is not a description of the subject matter of necessary statements. Instead, it is to be construed as a way of highlighting the likeness between (3) and (5), in disregard both of their difference and of the likeness between (3) and (1). With his pronouncement that necessary propositions are really verbal the philosopher heightens a similarity which seems important to him, while minimizing a dissimilarity which seems unimportant to him. This he does by artificially stretching the use of the word 'verbal' so as to cover, if only nominally, necessary propositions. We might say, for the purpose of bringing out the point, that the word 'verbal' has two uses which are made to appear as the same use : the original use to describe the nature of some propositions, and a new descriptively empty use with what might be called a grammatical point. By means of this stretched use he brings nearer to us a similarity, while keeping at a distance a dissimilarity. Being a philosopher he dramatizes what he does by presenting it in the guise of a theory, to which, it must be said in his defence, he himself falls dupe. Instead of saying *a camel is an animal* is like *the word 'animal' applies to whatever 'camel' applies to* but is unlike it in not mentioning words, and that it is unlike *a camel is a herbivore* in not being about camels, he says 'The proposition *a camel is an animal* is *really* verbal'. When a philosopher uses the word 'really' he appears to be reporting a discovery, whereas, as Wittgenstein remarked, 'what he wants is a new notation'.[15] A new use of 'verbal' is presented in a way which creates the impression that the true nature of necessary propositions is being revealed.

To return for a moment to Moore's objection against saying that the proposition that $3 + 3 = 6$ is about the expressions '$3 + 3$' and '6', the objection, namely, that the same proposition which is expressed by '$3 + 3 = 6$' is expressible in other languages by words which say nothing about the Arabic numerals '3' and '6'. It is a fact that the sentences '$3 + 3 = 6$' and 'drei und drei macht sechs' mean the same, or express the same proposition; and they would not if the first said something about the use of '3' and '6' and the second said something about the use of 'drei' and 'sechs'. For the first says nothing about the German words and the second says nothing about the Arabic numerals. Since the two sentences express the same proposition, neither sentence can say anything about the symbols which occur in it. As is known, some metaphysically inclined logicians have adopted a view according to which these sentences and others like them are

[15] *The Blue Book*, p. 57.

about abstract entities.[16] To revert to sentences (1) – (6), one difference between 'A camel is a herbivore' and 'a camel is an animal' is, on the Platonic theory, that the first is about camels and the second about abstract camelhood. Here no more can be said about the metaphysical difference of 'subject matter', in the one case things, and in the other case supersensible entities, than that the Platonic theory, like the cosmic structure theory, is the product of thinking which is governed by the formula that an intelligible indicative sentence must be about something.

To continue the explication of Moore's point by reference to the sentences (1) – (6), it is correct English to say that (1) and (2), that is, 'a camel is a herbivore' and 'Ein Kamel ist ein Pflanzenfresser', have the same meaning. It is correct English to say that (3), 'A camel is an animal' and (4), 'Ein Kamel ist ein Tier', mean the same; but it is not a correct use of English to apply the phrase 'mean the same' to the pair of sentences, (5), 'The word "animal" applies, as a matter of usage, to whatever "camel" applies to', and (6), 'The word "Tier" applies, as a matter of usage, to whatever "Kamel" applies to'. Sentences (1) and (2) have a subject matter, as also do sentences (5) and (6); but (3) and (4) have only a contrived subject matter, which is to say they are made to appear to have a subject matter. Neither (3) nor (4) says anything either about words or about things, and this fact has led some philosophers to hold that they say nothing. Sentences (1) and (2) say the same thing about the same subject. This feature of the pair of sentences gives us one condition for the correct application of the phrase 'mean the same'. Sentences (5) and (6) do not satisfy this condition : they say similar things about their subjects, but their subjects are different, which makes it incorrect to apply the phrase 'mean the same' to them. By contrast, (3) and (4) have no subjects; but it is correct English, nevertheless, to say that they mean the same. They have the same meaning, although they make no declaration about anything. We might, in order to bring out a point, say that 'mean the same'

[16] For discussions of the views that propositions and the meanings of general words are abstract entities see especially 'Understanding Philosophy' in *Studies in Metaphilosophy*, and 'The Existence of Universals' in *The Structure of Metaphysics*.

does not have the same meaning in its application to (1) and (2) that it has in its application to (3) and (4). Although (1) and (2) translate into each other, and (3) and (4) likewise, (1) and (2) are about the same subject, while (3) and (4) have no subject.

Nevertheless, it is not true that (3) and (4) say nothing or that they are literally meaningless. To put the matter briefly, understanding them comes down to knowing facts about the use of terminology, although terminology is not the subject of these assertions. The sentence 'A camel is an animal' is a grammatical crossbreed with one foot, so to speak, in the correlated verbal sentence in the same language and the other in related nonverbal fact-claiming sentences. (3) and (4) translate into each other, which is a feature that makes it correct to apply the term 'mean the same', or 'have the same meaning', to the sentences, despite their not being about anything.[17] But a person who understands both sentences will know facts of usage in different languages, while a person who understands only one of these sentences would not know the fact of usage exhibited by the other. The phrase 'mean the same' is used to refer to one feature when applied to sentences in the hybrid idiom and is used to refer to a further feature when applied to fact-claiming sentences. But by artificially equating 'mean the same' with 'say the same thing about the same subject' – under the rule that a literally meaningful indicative sentence *must* be about something – a philosopher creates the illusion that (3) and (4) have a special rarified subject matter, that they are about supersensible objects which can only be grasped by the pure intellect. A comment of Wittgenstein's is worth noting in this connection : ' "The symbol 'a' stands for an ideal object" is evidently supposed to assert something about the meaning, and so about the use, of "a". And it means of course that this use is in a certain respect similar to that for a sign that has an object, and that it does not stand for any object.'[18] When

[17] It should be noted that 'mean the same' does not apply to all sentences which translate into each other, for example, to equivalent non-sensical sentences in different languages. A person who insists that sentences which translate into each other *must* mean the same is stretching the expression 'sentences which mean the same' so as to give it the same range of application that 'sentences which translate into each other' has.

[18] *Remarks on the Foundations of Mathematics*, p. 136.

a philosopher like Moore points out that (3) and (4) mean the same and therefore that neither could mean the same as (5) or (6), he is calling attention to a grammatical similarity between sentences which express necessary propositions and those which make factual claims about the world, while pushing into the background the likeness between sentences which express necessary propositions and those which express propositions about usage.

Wittgenstein sometimes characterized necessary propositions as rules of grammar, with the idea in mind that he was stating a theory about the nature of logical necessity. He was able to see past this idea, however, and at other times he called them 'rules of grammar' in order to direct our attention to an important feature of sentences which express necessary propositions. Probably part of his reason for wishing to accent the verbal aspect of necessary propositions was to remove the idea that they are about mysterious things and thus to dispel the occult air which tends to settle over them. But more important than this, he undoubtedly felt that getting a clear understanding of the nature of necessary statements is required for getting clear about how philosophy works. Seeing what breed of theory conventionalism is, which comes to seeing what a conventionalist does with the word 'verbal', or equivalent expressions, is the final step towards understanding the theories of philosophy. The conventionalist theory is one of a large family of theories, and to get an inside look into it is to get an inside look into the other members of the family.

Wittgenstein has said that what the philosopher needs in order to solve, or to 'dissolve', his problems is to 'command a clear view of our use of words'.[19] We might add that what he needs is an improved understanding of sentences which express or are put forward as expressing necessary propositions, and to see how they both conceal their verbal content and also create the impression of being about phenomena. It will be recalled that Wittgenstein stated that philosophical theories are not empirical, and that he also said that a philosopher rejects an expression under the delusive impression that he is upsetting a proposition about

[19] *Philosophical Investigations*, p. 49

things. This idea about the nature of philosophical theories and philosophical refutations is deeply rooted and according to him 'pervades all philosophy'.[20] The conventionalist theory will be recognized now as falling under Wittgenstein's characterization. It is not empirical : it is restatable as making the entailment-claim that being a necessary proposition entails stating verbal facts. Reformulating it as an entailment-statement dissolves the notion that it is an inductive generalization, and it also changes our idea of what a philosopher is doing who, to all appearances, is demolishing by unanswerable arguments a widely held theory about what a necessary proposition is. It brings into clearer view what the theory is not and it also puts us on the way to a correct understanding of what it is.

It is easy now to see why the conventionalist can hold his position against all conclusive objections. He is presenting a stretched use of 'verbal', a use which artificially covers necessary propositions, and is not using the word 'verbal' in the normal way to make a false statement about them. Equally with the philosopher who satisfies himself that he has refuted the conventionalist theory, the conventionalist can survive refutation after refutation and remain satisfied that, all the same, his theory is not incorrect. Both the philosopher who holds the conventionalist theory and the philosopher who rejects it suffer from the fallacy which pervades all philosophy : namely, the false notion that the dispute centres on the truth-value of a theory rather than on the academic redistricting of a term.

## II

This understanding of what the conventionalist theory comes to has direct application to the philosophical problem of the privacy of experience. Consider the following words : 'When philosophers assert that experiences are private, they are referring to a necessary proposition. It would be a contradiction to speak of the feelings of two different people as being numerically identical : it is logically impossible that one person should literally

[20] *The Yellow Book.*

feel another's pain. But these points of logic are based on linguistic usages which have, as it were, the empirical facts in view.
If the facts were different, the usage might be changed.'[21] When
we consider these words with care, we discern in them three
claims. One, explicitly stated, is that the sentence 'experiences
are private' expresses a necessary proposition. Another is the conventionalist view that the necessary proposition is really verbal,
i.e. 'the points of logic' are 'based on linguistic usages'. And still
a further claim is that in some way a matter of fact about experience is involved. What comes through quite distinctly in the
words that the 'points of logic are based on linguistic usages
which have, as it were, the empirical facts in view', and that 'if
the facts were different, the usage might be changed', is the idea
that experience is private, as a matter of empirical fact.

It is by no means uncommon for a philosopher to hold explicitly that his utterance expresses an *a priori* truth and also to
imply that it refers to empirical fact; and in the present case the
implication stands out in bold relief. To put the matter shortly,
what is being held is that the proposition expressed by 'Experience
is private' both is logically necessary and also has 'factual content',
i.e. makes a factual claim about feelings, pains, and the like.
Wittgenstein's observation that philosophical problems are not
empirical carries with it the implication that philosophical
answers to philosophical questions are not empirical. But it should
no longer be necessary to remark that the philosophical statement
that experience is private has its absorbing and continued interest for philosophers because, for one thing, of the empirical
picture associated with it, the picture of our having experiences
which no one is privileged to share with us.

The contradiction implied by the conjunction of philosophical
claims is blatant, and it parallels the contradiction frequently
pointed out in the view that necessary propositions are really
verbal, or that they are 'based on linguistic usages'. Philosophers
are not overly troubled by contradictions like these; indeed, such
contradictions become permanent additions to the content of
philosophy. Anyone who is realistic about philosophy will find it

[21] A. J. Ayer, *The Problem of Knowledge*, p. 202.

hard not to think of it as a growing collection of contradictory theories which are not given up and of paradoxes which remain in permanent suspension. A further contradiction can now be added to the collection. This is the contradiction that is implied by the conventionalist view of logical necessity in combination with the tacit claim that at least some necessary propositions are about things, in the present instance, the contradiction which comes out of holding that the proposition that experience is private is 'based' on the use of terminology and that it also states a matter of fact. To put the matter in terms of the *sentence* 'Experience is private', holding that it expresses a necessary proposition amounts, on the conventionalist thesis, to stating that it is *about the use* of the terms 'experience' and 'private', and thus that the sentence *does not use the terms* to make a statement about what they are ordinarily used to refer to. The contradiction which emerges is that a sentence which is about words rather than things is nevertheless about things. Perhaps a more perspicuous way of making this contradiction explicit is the following. On the conventionalist view, to hold that the sentence 'Experience is private' expresses a necessary proposition comes to holding, in part at least, that the phrase 'non-private experience' has been given no application to anything, i.e. that it has no descriptive function in the language. And to hold, in immediate conjunction with this, that the sentence refers to an empirical fact about experience, is to embrace the contradiction that a phrase which has no descriptive use nevertheless has one. It is important to try to understand what makes it possible for a philosopher to accept this and related contradictions, and treat them as if they somehow do not go against their views. The insight reached into the nature of the conventionalist view helps us toward an understanding of why a contradiction in mathematics eliminates a proposition but does not do this in philosophy.

The cited passage on pp. 255–6 tacitly implies that the phrase 'feels another's pain' refers to what is logically impossible, and thus that it does not have a use to describe a conceivable occurrence. It states, also, that if the empirical facts were different usage might be changed, which is to say that the phrase might then be given a descriptive use. It is not clear what the empirical facts are which the linguistic usages keep in view. The only facts which, so to speak, *fit* the case are those which would be described by 'feels another's pain', and which, if they obtained, might make us *give* a descriptive use to this combination of words. The passage is labyrinthian in its ambiguity, but what makes itself evident is the idea, which probably all philosophers have, that an expression for a logical impossibility describes what never in fact happens. One philosophical logician has said: 'That which necessarily is the case is also as a matter of fact the case',[22] and it is fair to infer that he also has the idea that what is logically impossible never occurs as a matter of fact. It cannot be pointed out too often that a phrase which expresses what is logically impossible, e.g. the phrase 'soundless crash of thunder', does not have a use to *describe* what is not or what cannot be: it simply has no descriptive function in the language in which it occurs. It may be useful to point out that the proposition that an expression which denotes a logical impossibility has no descriptive content is not itself an experiential proposition, but rather declares an entailment, to the effect that being an expression for a logical impossibility entails being devoid of descriptive content. The assertion that an expression refers to what is logically impossible is incompatible with the assertion that it describes what in fact never occurs: if it describes what does not occur, it does not refer to a logical impossibility, and if it refers to a logical impossibility, it does not describe what does not happen.

If the sentence 'Experiences are private' does refer to a necessary truth, in virtue of the ordinary conventions governing the use of 'private' as well as of experience-denoting terminology,[23] then it makes no declaration about experiences. It exhibits, without expressing, what is stated by the sentence 'The word "private" correctly applies to whatever "experience" applies to, such that

---

[22] G. H. von Wright, 'Deontic Logic and the Theory of Conditions', *Critica*, vol. II, No. 6, p. 3.

[23] It is hardly necessary to call attention to the fact that the philosophical use of the word 'experience' does not correspond to its everyday use. We should not, for example, say of a person in pain that he is having an experience.

the phrase "an experience which is not private" has no descriptive use'. And if the phrase 'feels another's pain' does, in virtue of the rules governing the words occurring in it, refer to what is logically impossible, then it does not describe what one cannot feel, or feelings that one cannot have. Now, a philosopher who holds both that 'feels another's pain' has no descriptive use and also that it describes what never happens, and declares that if what does not happen were to happen we might then *give* a descriptive sense to 'feels another's pain', would seem to have lost his way. It is tempting to think that anyone who states that a term which lacks a descriptive use might be given one if situations answering to it came into existence is making a mere mistake, which for some odd reason he fails to see. The terms 'eternity bone' and 'phlogiston' fell into disuse when it was finally decided that nothing existed which answered to them, and, undoubtedly, if the facts had been different the terms would not have fallen into disuse. But these cases are not comparable to the philosophical case, which is like that of being told that the expression 'prime number between 13 and 17' might be given an application if such a number were discovered.

There is a strong temptation to think that our opponents in philosophy make mistakes which are plainly visible to us but which they do not have the wit to see. Hardly any philosopher fails to succumb to it, not only because it makes him feel superior but also because it sustains the truth-value façade which hides from him the real nature of philosophy. The importance for the correct understanding of philosophy of putting aside the truth-value spectacles through which philosophers look at their work will be realized by anyone who is not on the defensive about the unexplained difference between the chronic condition of philosophy and the condition of the experimental and mathematical sciences. To put the matter in terms of a probability evaluation, it has now become more probable that philosophical assertions have no truth-value than that they do have truth-values which philosophers have been unable to agree on.

If we keep separate the statement that it is logically impossible for one person to feel another's pain from the statement that no one as a matter of fact ever feels another's pain, and suspend the idea that a mistake is involved, we can see how the two statements work with respect to each other to produce the philosophical theory that experience is private. Consider first the claim that it is logically impossible to feel another's pain, which is linked with and in fact derives its importance from the empirical picture of contents which are not accessible to more than one person, comparable in some ways to the contents of a bank box to which only one person has the key. If the claim about the impossibility of feeling another's pain is an *a priori* truth, understanding a sentence which expresses it is equivalent to knowing that the descriptive part of the sentence (the phrase 'feels another's pain', in the English sentence) has been assigned no use to describe anything.

It will be clear thus that if the phrase 'feels another's pain' expresses what is logically impossible, the words 'another's pain' do not have a use in the language to distinguish between pains that a person is able to feel and pains he is prevented, for one reason or another, from feeling. It will also be clear that a philosopher who asserts the impossibility of feeling another's pain draws from his assertion the consequence that a person can feel only his own pains. The background picture linked with the consequence is that of someone who is *confined* to feeling certain pains. But the picture turns out to be inappropriate to the words 'A person can feel only his own pains'. For 'feels his own pain' is semantically connected with 'feels another's pain' in such a way that if the second expression has no use to describe anything, neither does the first. The terms 'another's pain' and 'his own pain' serve to make a contrast, such that if in a certain context 'another's pain' describes nothing, in the same context 'his own pain' will describe nothing. Thus, if in the sentence 'By contrast to another's pain, which I cannot feel, I can feel my own pain', the phrase 'another's pain' does not describe what I cannot feel, then the phrase 'my own pain' does not describe what I can feel. Put somewhat differently, 'his own pains' will have a use to set off pains a person can feel from pains he does not or cannot feel only if 'another's pains' also has a use to set off pains a person does not or is unable to feel from those he does or is able to feel.

To imitate Bishop Butler, the sentence 'A person can feel his own pain and not another's pain' says nothing about what a person can feel, if the required contrast is cancelled by the failure of one of the terms to have a descriptive function. Either both terms have a use or neither term has a use. Hence if the philosopher of the privacy of experience followed through on the consequences of his claim with regard to 'feels another's pain', he would have to allow that 'feels his own pain' has no use to describe what a person is limited to feeling. But this, quite obviously, he does not wish to do. If he did maintain, whether explicitly or indirectly, that both expressions lacked descriptive sense, his 'theory' would vanish, cancel itself out of existence.

Wittgenstein has characterized as a typically metaphysical mistake[24] the use of one of a pair of antithetical terms in what might be called linguistic dissociation from its antithesis, i.e. retaining one of the terms while deleting the other by the artful technique of 'showing' by an argument that the other stands for a logical impossibility. He described at least some of his later work as consisting of 'bringing words back from their metaphysical to their everyday use'.[25] The semantic fact about antithetical terms is that if one of a given pair is stripped of its use in the language, without being replaced by a term to do its work, the other also loses its use. By bringing back words from their metaphysical to their everyday use, which is to say, by restoring to them their former use, the words which normally function as their antitheses *recover* their use. Wittgenstein's language sometimes suggests the idea that the metaphysical use of a term, as against its everyday use, is an actual use which assigns to a word the role of describing occult realities or real as against merely apparent states of things. It is clear, however, that a metaphysical use is not given to a term *independently* of the semantic suppression of its antithesis. Instead, its metaphysical use is *the result of,* and thus is created by, the ontologically reported suppression of the word. Instead of speaking of the metaphysical use of a term it would

[24] *The Blue Book*, p. 46.
[25] *Philosophical Investigations*, p. 48. This is easily recognized as 'linguistic therapy' for avoiding metaphysics.

be less misleading to speak of the metaphysical job a term acquires when its antithesis is (academically) cast out of the language. When one of a pair of antithetical terms is suppressed the other loses its function to describe, and takes on metaphysical, illusion-creating work.

A term which is shorn of its descriptive use by making its antithesis stand for a logical impossibility **does** not spontaneously acquire a new descriptive use. Any new use it has it must be given, and if it is not in fact given a use, the use it appears to acquire is one in appearance only. The problem is to explain how the illusion is brought about of its having a use to describe reality, how, in the present connection, the appearance is created that a dramatic claim is being made by the words 'A person can feel only his own pains'. If we go back to our interpretation of the conventionalist position, we can get a behind-the-scenes look at the semantic props which are used to bring to life the scene at the front of the philosophical stage. The props which produce the delusive picture of everyone being enclosed by a wall over which no one else can look are not either the wrong use of 'feels another's pain' and 'feels only his own pain', nor are they mistaken descriptions of their actual use in the language. The props are academic, linguistically idle alterations, which when held up against everyday, unrevised language, give rise to the delusive impression that a fact about the nature of feelings and sensations is being disclosed.

The assertion that it is logically impossible to feel another's pain, which is linked with the declaration that a person is limited, by logical necessity, to feeling his own pain, embodies a piece of gerrymandered terminology. The result is to *deprive* an expression of its use, as part of a game that is being played with language. The fact that the game is conducted in the nonverbal mode of speech conceals its verbal nature. What is being done with words is hidden all the more effectively by the fact that the use they have in everyday language *remains intact* in everyday language, which thus serves as a backdrop and gives to the game the appearance of a discovery. Wittgenstein has said that a philosophical problem arises when language goes on holiday, and it seems that the philosophical view that experience is private is, as we might say, an image thrown on the language-screen by an ontologically presented, non-workaday revision of grammar.

It is unrealistic to think that the verbal game by itself is so entirely captivating as to make it worth the candle. Its ability to keep thinkers in permanent intellectual thralldom requires us to suppose that something else is involved, something which it is difficult to recognize consciously. A brief speculation is permissible at this point, and it may be enlightening. The suggestion that part of the mind is a dark area whose contents are inaccessible to us tends to be received not only with the expected rejection but also with a kind of grudging fascination. Philosophers perhaps more than other intellectuals resist the idea that the mind contains a submerged Atlantis; but there can be no doubt that they too, and perhaps even more than others, sense that something in their own mind is detached from them, something from which they feel estranged and to which, try as they may, they cannot find their way back. It is not to indulge in wholly remote speculation to think that the philosopher is disturbed by this state of affairs within himself. And it need not come as a complete surprise to discover that his ambivalence about the submerged part of his own mind, both his inner perception of its existence and his denial, finds expression in his philosophical work. In view of the fact that a sentence which expresses a philosophical theory does not, despite appearances, describe or assert the existence of a state of affairs, supposing that an unconscious thought finds expression in it helps us understand what holds the philosopher spellbound to his view and also keeps it at a comfortable distance from his curiosity.[26]

The philosophical view that a person's experiences are private to himself carries with it the idea of inaccessible mental contents, and this idea suggests a connection of the view with the inaccessible unconscious. The view itself says nothing about our pains

---

[26] It also helps us understand why philosophers experience so much hostility to the notion of an unconscious part of the mind. The suspicion, which they may very well harbour, that the sole ideational, nonverbal content of a philosophical theory is a cluster of unconscious thoughts would naturally provoke a strong reaction against the idea of an unconscious.

and feelings, but appears to be a veiled way of expressing the perception of the existence of the unconscious and also of mitigating its disturbing quality. By his theory the philosopher reports his perception of the noumenon[27] within himself in an inverted way, in the form of a projection. He deflects the perception away from himself and onto others, who thus become externalized surrogates for his own unconscious. In the fantasy which accompanies this projection he also represents to himself his unconscious (his own mind in relation to other people), and in this way denies the fact that it is alien territory which lies beyond his reach. The words 'The experiences a person has are private to himself' give rise to the false notion that they have descriptive content; and the spell they are able to cause can be explained only by supposing they *do* have unconscious content. One concealed thought which the words might very well express is that the unconscious is outside of us and also that the contents of the unconscious are really no different from the contents of the conscious part of the mind. The philosophical 'view' that experiences are private, or that no one's experiences are accessible to anyone else, seems to be a mask for stating that the unconscious exists but that its contents are conscious.[28] Several remarks Freud has made throw light on the way some people cope with the uneasy perception that part of their mind is a lost land that lies beyond the horizon of consciousness. They are especially revealing in the present connexion. What he said needs to be quoted at some length and deserves to be read with care.

> ... the study of pathogenic repressions and of other phenomena which have still to be mentioned compelled psychoanalysis to take the concept of the 'unconscious' seriously. Psychoanalysis regarded everything mental as being in the first instance unconscious; the further quality of 'consciousness' might also be present, or again it might be absent. This of course provoked a denial from the philosophers, for whom 'conscious' and

---

[27] Kant's notion of a noumenal mind behind the conscious self is easily recognized as referring to the unconscious.

[28] At a more superficial level the philosophical view would seem to express a self-revelation : a felt inability to empathize with others.

'mental' were identical, and who protested that they could not conceive of such a monstrosity as the 'unconscious mental'. There was no help for it, however, and this idiosyncrasy of the philosophers could only be disregarded with a shrug. Experience (gained from pathological material, of which the philosophers were ignorant) of the frequency and power of impulses of which one knew nothing directly and whose existence had to be inferred like some fact in the external world, left no alternative open. It could be pointed out, incidentally, that this was only treating one's own mental life as one had always treated other people's. One did not hesitate to ascribe mental processes to other people, although one had no immediate consciousness of them and could only infer them from their words and actions. But what held good for other people must be applicable to oneself. Anyone who tried to push the argument further and to conclude from it that one's own hidden processes belonged actually to a second *consciousness* would be faced with the concept of a consciousness of which one knew nothing, of an 'unconscious consciousness' – and this would scarcely be preferable to the assumption of an 'unconscious mental'.[29]

### III

It is of special interest to apply the later Wittgenstein, or rather that part of Wittgenstein's later work which some philosophers find hard to fit into the continuity of his thought, to several philosophical statements in the *Tractatus*. Although it has become almost a commonplace, it is worth noting that our mind works at several different levels simultaneously and that what we are aware of at one level we can obliterate from our mind at another. John Wisdom has described the case of a person who under hypnosis saw a blank space wherever the definite article occurred on a page of print. The explanation of this curious state of affairs is that part of his mind blotted out what he saw with another part. This suppressing, or blotting out, mechanism seems to be

[29] *An Autobiographical Study*, International Library, no. 26, pp. 55–6.

used by philosophers who read Wittgenstein's later writings with intellectual blindness to the revealing things he said about philosophy. It has to be granted that the iconoclastic perceptions to which he gave expression do not fit into the continuity of his *philosophical* thought. Instead, they are remarkable departures from conventional philosophy. This is, perhaps, one reason why philosophers have been able to read Wittgenstein with a Parmenidean eye that eliminates the unconventional things he said about conventional philosophy.

As is known, Wittgenstein rejected the *Tractatus*, even though some of his later thought is continuous with it; and this rejection can be best understood if we look at it through the metaphilosophical spectacles he has given us. Consider the following selection of statements.

What can be described can happen too, and what is excluded by the law of causality cannot even be described (6.362).

Belief in the causal nexus is a superstition (5.136).

A necessity for one thing to happen because another has happened does not exist. There is only *logical* necessity[30] (6.37).

Just as the only necessity that exists is logical necessity, so too the only impossibility that exists is logical impossibility (6.375).

The impression these pronouncements make on us is that they advance factual claims about what exists or does not exist and about the irrationality of a common belief about how changes are brought about in things. Read in conjunction with each other, the sentences, 'A necessity for one thing to happen because another has happened does not exist' and 'Belief in the causal nexus is a superstition', give rise to the idea that propositions like 'The light must go out when the current is turned off' and 'A hummingbird cannot carry off a hippopotamus' are all being declared false. They also suggest the notion that a person who believes any of them to be true is holding a prescientific belief, one which, like the belief that heavier bodies fall faster than

---

[30] C. K. Ogden translation. Remaining quotations are from the D. Pears and B. F. McGuiness translation.

lighter ones, has been shown false by science. It is factual claims like these that Wittgenstein seems to be giving expression to by his philosophical sentences. But if we pause to reflect on them and relate them to other of his statements, we will realize that what he seems to be saying here is, to use a favourite expression of F. H. Bradley, mere appearance.

If we dispel the mists generated by the empirical talk with which philosophical theories about causation are surrounded, we can see that they are not empirical. A philosopher who declares that causation is a logically necessary connection between classes of occurrences is, obviously, not holding an empirical view about causation. Logical connections are not discovered by observing the behaviour of things, in Wittgenstein's words in the *Notebooks*, 1914–16, '. . . none of our experience is *a priori*'.[31] But neither does a philosopher give expression to an empirical claim who says that here is no causal nexus or says that causation is nothing more than constant conjunction. For he has ruled himself out from being able to say what it would be like for there to be a causal nexus, i.e. what it would be like for a change to take place in a thing by another thing acting on it. He has also ruled himself out from being able to say what else might supplement mere constant conjunction. Wittgenstein said in his *Notebooks* that whatever can be described at all could also be otherwise.[32] The implication of this is clear. The sentence 'A causal nexus (or productive causation) does not exist' expresses an empirical proposition only if the term 'causal nexus' has a use to describe something which, if it did exist, would make false what the sentence asserts. The sentence would express an empirical proposition only if matters could be other than it declares them to be. Since it does not describe what could be otherwise, it does not express a proposition about what is or is not the case.

We come to the same conclusion, if we bring in statement 6.362 above, 'What can be described can happen too, and what is excluded by the law of causality cannot be described'. The implication of these words is that the law of causality has no describ-

[31] P. 80e.
[32] ibid.

able exception, which is to say that nothing can be described such that if it existed it would upset the law. It is clear that a philosopher who holds that the law of causality has no conceivable or describable exception implies that, as *he* construes the words which give expression to it, they do not state an empirical proposition. It may be useful to point out that to say that 'what is excluded by the law of causality cannot be described' is to imply that *nothing* is excluded by it; otherwise it would be possible to say what is excluded, i.e. it would be possible to say what exceptions to the law would be like. On this claim about the law of causality, taken at face value, it has the character of a tautology, which also excludes nothing. This in general is the character of an *a priori* true proposition : it excludes no describable state of affairs. Whether or not the words 'A necessity for one thing to happen because another has happened does not exist' are being used to express an *a priori* proposition, it is clear that they do not express one that is empirical, i.e. one that *excludes* a describable state of affairs. The sentence which is joined to these words makes this evident, namely, the sentence 'There is only *logical* necessity'.

A philosopher who states that 'the only necessity that exists is logical necessity', or that 'the only impossibility that exists is logical impossibility', has not arrived at his claim by an inductive procedure, or by anything comparable to an inductive procedure. The difference between his sentences and a sentence like 'The only horses that exist are wingless horses' stands out. One is empirical and excludes what *can* be described. The other is used by the philosopher in such a way as to preclude his describing possible exceptions. The term 'the only' does not function in his utterance in the way it functions in the nonphilosophical sentence. Its function in the philosophical sentence is more like the one it has in 'The only even prime number is two'.

Seeing this makes it natural to think that a philosopher who says, 'The only necessity that exists is logical necessity', has the idea that he is using terminology in the accepted way to express an *a priori* truth. It also makes it natural to think that he has the idea that the sentence, 'A necessity for one thing to happen because another has happened does not exist', expresses an *a priori* truth. Without again going into an explanation of the nature of logical necessity, it can be seen that if he had this idea he could be charged with being in error about actual usage, that is, with having the mistaken idea that the use of 'necessary' is no wider than the use of 'logically necessary'. Again without repeating reasons elaborated in similar connections elsewhere, the conclusion that he has this idea has to be rejected, and with it the notion that the philosopher labours under the idea that he is making *a priori* pronouncements.

The alternative conclusion, which invariably provokes emotional resistance but nevertheless has great explanatory power in its favour, is that instead of being stubbornly fixated to a mistaken idea about usage he is in some way retailoring usage, artificially contracting or even supressing terminology. Instead of supposing him to think that the use of 'necessary' coincides with that of the term 'logically necessary' and that the use of 'impossible' coincides with that of 'logically impossible', this alternative requires us to suppose him to be contracting 'necessary' and 'impossible' into part only of their actual use, which he announces in the ontological mode of speech. Philosophers like to show contradictions or vicious infinite regresses in each other's views, and they do succeed sometimes in momentarily embarrassing each other, which is the sum total of what is achieved. In philosophy, showing a contradiction of one sort or another in a view does not remove it from the collection of optional theories. The philosophical view that the only necessity which exists is logical necessity, or that only logical necessity is real necessity, construed as making a factual claim that equates the terms *necessary* and *logically necessary* is subject to the obvious objection that it implies an infinite regression, comparable to the regression G. E. Moore pointed out in the ethical view that an act's being right is identical with its being thought right.[33] The metaphilosophical[34] construction of the view, that represents it as

---

[33] *Ethics*, pp. 123–4.
[34] For an explanation of the term 'metaphilosophy' see my note in *Metaphilosophy*, vol. I, no. 1, p. 91.

belonging to the family of 'theories' of which conventionalism is a member, offers an explanation both of how an astute thinker can overlook an obvious difficulty, why he could be embarrassed by having it brought to his attention, and also why the difficulty does not remove it from the collection of optional philosophical theories.

Wittgenstein has said that a philosopher rejects a form of expression under the illusion that he is refuting a proposition about things. This remark applies to his philosophical theories about causation and necessity in the *Tractatus*. The artificial contraction of the use of 'necessity' and 'impossibility' and the suppression of causal verbs (there is no 'causal nexus') is conducted in the style of discourse which we use to talk about things and which we also use to express necessary propositions. Presented in this way the words create the false but vivid impression that indubitable theories about the existence or nature of phenomena are being stated. There can be no doubt that this illusion answers to an unrelinquished yearning in the depths of the minds of philosophers, who continue to think that they can obtain knowledge of things without taking the trouble to go to them. The recent words of an important metaphysical philosopher strengthen this idea : 'What philosophers have supposed they were doing was pursuing truth; they were thinking about the ultimate nature of things – more critically than the common man, more profoundly than the scientist, more disinterestedly and precisely than the theologian.'[35]

[35] Brand Blanshard, review of *Philosophy and Illusion*, *Metaphilosophy*, April 1970, p. 178.

# WITTGENSTEIN'S PHILOSOPHY OF MATHEMATICS

### R. L. GOODSTEIN

Wittgenstein's profound insight into the nature of mathematics, which even a brief conversation with him could not fail to reveal, found expression in his published work only in scattered remarks, often tantalizingly cryptic and incomplete. His lectures at Cambridge, which I was privileged to attend between 1931 and 1935, and the many discussions which I had with him during that time, influenced my own thinking about the nature of mathematics to an extent which I only subsequently grew to appreciate and understand fully. Nonetheless there were only occasional allusions to mathematics in his lectures and certainly nothing amounting to a systematic study of the foundations of mathematics comparable with his work on the philosophy of language.

In conversation the originality of this thought illuminated even the most commonplace topic, from the return of the axe in Nazi Germany to the organization of society in war, the genius of Charlie Chaplin or the duty of the better educated party to a quarrel to take on himself the blame. One was conscious afterwards of the difference in one's thinking which the conversation had wrought but not of any specific new point of view that one could readily put into words.

Wittgenstein's thinking about mathematics was undoubtedly influenced by Gotlob Frege – he says as much in his introduction to the *Tractatus* – and perhaps also, but to a much lesser extent by L. E. J. Brouwer. The story of his meetings with Frege, as he told it to me, reveals as much of Wittgenstein as it does of Frege. Wittgenstein came to England before the First World War to experiment with rocket propulsion. His experiments were, I believe, conducted on a stretch of railway track just south of Manchester,

271

and brought him into contact with the philosopher Samuel Alexander who was in Manchester at the time. Wittgenstein became convinced that he was destined to be a philosopher and he sought Alexander's advice. Alexander told him that in his opinion Frege was the greatest living philosopher and so Wittgenstein wrote to Frege to arrange a meeting. Frege invited him to tea, and after tea they had a discussion in which (in Wittgenstein's own words) Frege wiped the floor with him. Wittgenstein returned to England very disheartened, but a year later he sought another interview with Frege and this time 'he wiped the floor with Frege, and though they met for tea many times after they never discussed philosophy again'. I have no reason to believe that Wittgenstein ever met Brouwer but he was clearly familiar with some of Brouwer's writings, as both the Cambridge lectures and the posthumously published *Remarks on the Foundations of Mathematics* show.

I had read Bertrand Russell's *Introduction to Mathematical Philosophy*, which he wrote in prison at the end of the First World War, before I went up to Cambridge in 1931, and found there a reference to a young man called Wittgenstein who had been working on the problem of tautology before the war. The Lecture List in October 1931 included a course of lectures by a certain Dr. L. Wittgenstein whom I rightly took to be the Wittgenstein referred to by Russell, and so I decided to attend the course. The first lecture was one of the most significant experiences of my life and I remember much of it more clearly than anything else I heard, before or since. The lecture was held in a room in Trinity Great Court, and I arrived a little late because I had some difficulty in finding the room. A remarkably good-looking young man was standing beside a blackboard and a white haired much older man (whom I first supposed to be Wittgenstein) was seated on a deck chair in front of the class. In fact, as I learnt afterwards, the lecturer was Wittgenstein and the older man G. E. Moore. The speaker was talking about a rope that we were to imagine had one end in the room, and stretched out of the window and across Great Court with its other end out of sight. Someone was measuring the rope, following it foot by foot from its end in the room.

Suppose that no matter how far the rope was followed the end was not found, could we ever say that the rope was infinitely long? Did it make any sense to say that rope was infinitely long? Could we devise a test to find if it was *infinitely* long? Of course, so long as the criterion was that of following the rope it made no sense to say that the rope was infinitely long; we could decide if it is was or was not longer than any chosen length, but there was no outcome to the attempt to measure the rope which would lead us to say that the rope was infinitely long. Was there then no sense in talking about an infinitely long rope? Imagine that we devised a machine which when applied to one end of the rope indicated the length of the rope by means of the angle through which a pointer on a dial turned, the length being proportional to the tangent of the angle turned through. Suppose we now applied the machine to a particular piece of rope and the pointer turned through an angle of ninety degrees, would we not now say that the rope was infinitely long?

This simple illustration has many important applications in the foundations of mathematics. It takes one, for instance, straight to the heart of the finitist controversy. Instead of measuring a rope let us seek for some particular run of digits in the decimal expansion of $\pi$. In his original discussion of this problem Brouwer chose to search for three consecutive sevens in the expansion, presumably because the digit seven occurred with less than average frequency in Shanks' famous nineteenth-century expansion of $\pi$. In fact Shanks' calculation was erroneous and recent determinations of $\pi$ to several thousand decimal figures show that the digit four rather than seven occurs relatively infrequently, but this is of only indirect significance. Let us however continue to discuss the problem of finding three consecutive sevens in the decimal expansion of $\pi$ – this is the form in which Wittgenstein considers the problem in *Remarks*, IV, 27. If we chance to find a sequence of three consecutive sevens then of course the question whether such a sequence occurs is answered in the affirmative, but is there any way of deciding that this sequence does *not* occur? However far we develop the expansion of $\pi$, if we do not find three consecutive sevens then we cannot say whether this sequence will occur or not. Does it then make any sense to ask whether the sequence occurs? If you now say that, whether you find the sequence or not, surely it is the case that this sequence either occurs in the expansion or it does not, then Wittgenstein points out that you are being misled by a false analogy with a finite decimal. The further expansion of $\pi$, he says, is the further expansion of mathematics. Can one say of the hero of a poem that is yet unwritten that he either has a sister, or has none? And suppose we argue that even if no man knows the infinite expansion of $\pi$, then surely it is known to God and so it is determined whether the sequence of three sevens occurs or not. Then Wittgenstein retorts in effect that God's knowing is of no more help to us here than the prophecy of a Sibyl, or a mere guess; for what we seek to know is *how* the law governing the expansion of $\pi$ determines whether or not the sequence of sevens occurs, as all that we have is this law and the *finite* expansions which it determines. Unlike Brouwer, Wittgenstein does not seek to reject the *tertium non datur* but to analyse what sense it has in such contexts as the growing expansion of $\pi$. Wittgenstein differs from Brouwer also in his view of non-constructive existence proofs in mathematics. A non-constructive existence proof (*Remarks*, IV, 46) does not of course tell you as much, does not give the same information as, a constructive proof, but we can understand it to the extent that we can make use of it. Some of the reviews of the *Remarks* claim Wittgenstein's position to be even more strictly finitist than Brouwer's, but this is clearly not a justifiable claim. Brouwer sought to *rewrite* mathematics but Wittgenstein seeks to understand mathematics as it is. Thus in *Remarks*, IV, 52 he states his position with the utmost clarity, as follows :

> The philosopher must twist and turn about so as to pass by the mathematical problems, and not run up against one – which would have to be solved before he could go further.
>
> His labour in philosophy is as it were an idleness in mathematics. It is not that a new building has to be erected, or that a new bridge has to be built, but that the geography, *as it is now*, has to be judged. We certainly see bits of the concepts,

but we do not clearly see the declivities by which one passes into others.

That is why it is of no use in the philosophy of mathematics to recast proofs in new forms. Although there is a strong temptation here. Even 500 years ago a philosophy of mathematics was possible, a philosophy of what mathematics was then.

Wittgenstein comes closest to Brouwer in his analysis of the notion of a non-denumerable class. He finds in Cantor's diagonal process a *method* for determining a decimal different from each of a given sequence of decimals, and in fact Cantor's first use of the diagonal process was precisely of this kind. Since all *algebraic* real numbers may be enumerated in a simple sequence, the diagonal method establishes the existence of a *transcendental* real number, a real number which differs from all algebraic real numbers and is therefore *not* algebraic. This is the practical use of the method. But there is also a 'perverse' use of the method in which it is applied to show the existence of a non-denumerable class. Let us suppose, the familiar argument runs, that the *totality* of real numbers has been enumerated in a sequence; then the diagonal method produces a real number which is not in the sequence, and so the sequence does not contain all real numbers, contrary to our initial hypothesis. The supposition that an enumerating sequence for all real numbers *exists* has been refuted, and so there is no such sequence. But have we also achieved more than this? Does the proof, that no enumerating sequence exists, at the same time *create* a non-denumerable set? In the second appendix to the first part of the *Remarks* Wittgenstein draws the opposite conclusion, that there is no system of real numbers, no super-system, no set of irrational numbers of higher-order infinity. He arrives at this conclusion by observing that all that mathematics provides us with are *examples* of real numbers and no provision is made for the concept of the *totality* of real numbers. Real numbers can be produced without end, and every sequence of real numbers determines a new real number, but there is nothing over and above this process of generation. Later in the *Remarks* when considering Dedekind's method of cuts we meet

275

the same idea again; there are just those cuts which are defined by specific real numbers, and these are so diverse (2, $e$, $\pi$, for instance) that no general concept of real numbers emerges.

In an axiomatic theory of sets which contains the power set axiom, the axiom which *supplies* the set of all subsets of a set, the diagonal method serves to prove that the power set of a denumerable set is non-denumerable; but of course the *existence* of the power set is provided by the power set axiom, not the diagonal process. Yet even in an axiomatic theory of sets non-denumerability is only relative, as Skolem showed. For a fundamental theorem of mathematical logic assures us that every consistent set of sentences has a denumerable model, so that, in particular, if axiomatic set theory is consistent the theory has a denumerable model; and in the model the set of all subsets of a set has *denumerably* many members, despite the fact that it is a *theorem* of the theory that this set is non-denumerable. Skolem explains the paradox as showing that any axiomatic set theory is necessarily incomplete, the power set of a denumerable set being non-denumerable *within* the theory only because the theory lacks the function which enumerates the set.

The problem of the occurrence of three consecutive sevens is not of course a good illustration of the type of question raised by the rope in Wittgenstein's lecture, for mathematics has not yet found the analogue of the device for testing an infinite string. A much better illustration is provided by the problem of the infinitude of prime numbers. Suppose we ask whether there is a greatest prime number. We examine the natural numbers in turn and find various primes, but can we ever know whether there is a greatest prime or not? No matter how many numbers we test for primality if we do not happen to find a prime greater than some prime $p$ we cannot say whether there is a greater prime than $p$ or not; so long as we have no other procedure but to test the numbers one by one the question whether there is a greatest prime is a pseudo-question, for it is unanswerable. Only by the creation of a new procedure (the invention of a new piece of mathematics) does the question acquire a sense. As is well known, Euclid found such a procedure, a procedure of remarkable elegance and simplicity. Ignoring unit factors, it is clear that the *smallest* factor of any number is necessarily prime, and it is equally clear that none of the numbers from 2 to $n$ is a factor of the number which exceeds by unity the product of the first $n$ numbers. Thus the least factor of this number is both prime and greater than $n$, and since $n$ is arbitrary it follows that there is no greatest prime number.

The most interesting situation arises when it can actually be shown that there is *no* device to deal with the infinite case. This situation has attracted a great deal of interest in the past thirty-five years, and a number of problems have been shown to be incapable of resolution, the most recent being the tenth problem of the series of problems which Hilbert proposed at the turn of the century. Hilbert's tenth problem was to find a procedure which would tell us whether any arbitrarily chosen polynomial equation (in two or more unknowns) has a solution in integers or not. Of course given a polynomial we can test each set of values of the variables in turn to see whether or not it is a root, but lacking any other procedure it would be impossible to say whether a particular equation has a root or not, since however many sets of integers we tested without finding a root there would remain the possibilities that we might chance to find a root, or that no root exists. Early this year a young Russian mathematician Yu. Matjesevič succeeded in showing that no uniform procedure exists for deciding whether a polynomial equation (in more than one unknown) has a root or not.

A proof of impossibility is a characteristic trait of Western mathematics. Several famous problems in Greek mathematics like the ruler and compass trisection of an angle, squaring the circle, deriving the parallel postulate, have all been shown to be impossible in the past century-and-a-half. Wittgenstein was deeply interested in such proofs of impossibility; within the framework of ruler and compass constructions how can you *try* to show that a construction is impossible? Only in an entirely different setting can the problem be properly posed and solved. It makes no sense, Wittgenstein argued, to talk of the non-existence of a construction, in the context of constructions. The mathematical proof of non-existence gives the problem a meaning which it previously lacked, by creating a new language in which the question can be asked and answered. In the *Remarks* Wittgenstein raises the further question of the relation of the impossibility proof to the would-be trisector. 'Can the proof of impossibility *compel* the trisector to give up his search? I suppose it compels him only in so far as he understands the proof of impossibility; his giving up the search is a measure of his understanding of the proof', and his failure to give up the search either indicates an inability to understand the proof (which of course involves ideas quite different from ruler and compass constructions) or a recognition that what he was looking for was different from what had been shown to be impossible. Many trisectors in fact discover highly ingenious approximate trisections and the same thing is true of circle squarers to a lesser degree. Fermat's problem – to show that, if $n > 2$, the equation $x^n + y^n = z^n$ has no solution in positive integers – has fascinated mathematicians, professional and amateur alike, and here the impossibility proof has yet to be discovered. Wittgenstein of course held that it was a pseudo-problem, and that despite its temptingly simple-sounding formulation, the question still makes no sense. The mathematics in which the question can be asked and answered has yet to be discovered. Certainly it is true that the only substantial progress ever made with the problem, E. Kummer's solution for all regular prime values of $n$, involved the creation of the entirely new concept of an ideal. It was perhaps, paradoxical though it sounds, a measure of Gauss's great insight into mathematics that, as far as we know, the problem did not receive any attention from him. Many an amateur has vainly devoted his life to the problem, for unlike the angle trisectors their efforts have produced nothing of value comparable with the approximate trisections some trisectors achieved. It has recently become fashionable to say that the great scientists are those who ask the questions which they can answer – science as the art of the soluble – and this of course is only another way of stating Wittgenstein's dictum that (in mathematics) it is the solution which gives a sense to the problem.

Gödel's discovery in 1931 of the incompleteness of Arithmetic was the crowning achievement in impossibility proofs. Gödel showed that there is an arithmetical property $G(x)$ such that, if arithmetic is consistent, each particular number 0, 1, 2, . . . has the property G yet neither the universal sentence $(\forall x)G(x)$ nor its contrary $(\exists x) \neg G(x)$ is provable in Russell's *Principia Mathematica*. I do not think Wittgenstein heard of Gödel's discovery before 1935; on hearing about it his immediate reaction, with I think truly remarkable insight, was to observe that it showed that the formalization of arithmetic with mathematical induction and the substitution of numerals for variables fails to capture the concept of natural number, and the variables must admit values which are not natural numbers. For if, in a system $\mathscr{A}$, all the sentences $G(n)$ with $n$ a natural number are provable, but the universal sentence $(\forall n)G(n)$ is not, then there must be an interpretation of $\mathscr{A}$ in which $n$ takes values other than natural numbers for which $G(n)$ is not true (in fact in 1934, Th. Skolem had shown that this was the case, independently of Gödel's work). In his discussion of Gödel's undecidable sentence in the *Remarks*, Wittgenstein does not mention this aspect of Gödel's discovery but concentrates upon the meaning of *true* when one says that Gödel discovered a true but unprovable sentence. Wittgenstein takes the line that *true* here means provable in some other system, so that Gödel's sentence is regarded as provable in some system $\mathscr{A}$, say, but not in another system $\mathscr{B}$. His position is quite simply that the only sense in which a mathematical proposition can be said to be true is that there is some system (not necessarily completely formalized) in which it is provable, that in mathematics *true* means *provable*. This of course is bound up with Wittgenstein's overall view of the nature of mathematics, which we shall consider shortly, but let us return to Gödel's sentence. I think that Wittgenstein was misled by the use of the word *true* in this connexion. There are two possible interpretations of the word *true* in connexion with Gödel's sentence. We may simply appeal to the *tertium non datur* to assert that *one* of $(\forall x)G(x)$, $(\exists x) \neg G(x)$ is true, and since neither of these sentences is provable (in Gödel's version of *Principia Mathematica*) one of the sentences is both true and unprovable (without committing ourselves to saying which one is true). Alternatively we may choose to say that the universal sentence $(\forall x)G(x)$ is true because each of its instances $G(0)$, $G(1)$, $G(2)$, . . . is provable (and so true). This would be in accordance with the *standard* interpretation of a universal sentence. The philosophical problem of truth in mathematics is not, I think, raised by the Gödel sentence. In fact I think the *philosophical* significance of Gödel's result has been misunderstood. Any proof of the independence of one axiom $\mathscr{A}$, say, from a set of axioms $\mathscr{S}$, establishes $\mathscr{A}$ as undecidable in $\mathscr{S}$, and many examples of proofs of independence were known before Gödel's discovery – for instance the proof of the independence of the parallel axiom in Euclidean geometry. Of course what was new in Gödel's work was the discovery of a *method* for producing undecidable sentences in any rich enough formalization of arithmetic, which showed that no (recursive) set of axioms for arithmetic was complete.

Wittgenstein's analysis of mathematical induction was in my opinion one of his profoundest contributions to the philosophy of mathematics. There is no reference to this work in the *Remarks*, but the more recently published *Philosophische Grammatik* (written between 1932 and 1934) contains a detailed discussion. As in the Cambridge lectures he considers a proof by induction of the associative law,

$$(1) \qquad (a+b)+c = a+(b+c),$$

with addition defined by the recursion $a+0 = a$, $a+(b+1) = (a+b)+1$. The traditional proof of (1) by induction runs as follows. For the value 0 of $c$ both sides of (1) are equal to $(a+b)$, in consequence of the definition $a+0 = a$. Suppose now that (1) holds for some value C of $c$. Then

$$(a+b)+(C+1) = \{(a+b)+C\}+1, \text{ from the definition,}$$
$$= \{a+(b+C)\}+1, \text{ by the inductive hypothesis,}$$
$$= a+\{(b+C)+1\}$$
$$= a+(b+C+1),$$

which shows that if (1) holds for the value C of $c$ then it holds also for the value C+1 of $c$, whence since it holds for the value 0 of $c$, it holds for all values of $c$. In his lectures Wittgenstein analysed this proof in the following way. He started by criticizing the argument as it stands by asking what it means to *suppose* that (1) holds for some value C of *c*. If we are going to deal in suppositions, why not simply suppose that (1) holds for any *c*. Following Skolem, he then rewrites the proof as follows :

$$(a+b)+(c+1) = S((a+b)+c)$$
$$a+(b+(c+1)) = a+((b+c)+1) = S(a+(b+c))$$

(where I have written S for the successor function),
and observes that $(a+b)+(c+1)$ is the same function S of $(a+b)+c$ that $a+(b+(c+1))$ is of $a+(b+c)$. Since $(a+b)+0 = a+(b+0)$ it follows that we may obtain both $(a+b)+c$, and $a+(b+c)$ by applying the same function S to $a+b$ the same number of times, so that $(a+b)+c$, $a+(b+c)$ are equal. To put the argument in a more general form, Wittgenstein is seeking to replace induction by the rule of inference,

$$f(0) = g(0), f(Sx) = \phi(f(x)), g(Sx) = \phi(g(x)) \vdash f(x) = g(x).$$

This is none other than a rule affirming the *uniqueness* of the function defined by the recursive definition,

$$f(0) = a, f(Sx) = \phi(f(x)).$$

In place of induction we have the far more intuitively acceptable notion of the uniqueness of the function defined by recursion. Of course it is by no means obvious from a single example that every use of induction in arithmetic can be presented in this way, but in my development of arithmetic in an axiom-free equation calculus I showed that this was indeed the case. In fact it suffices to affirm the uniqueness of just a few special recursions, namely

$$f(Sx) = f(x) \vdash f(x) = f(0)$$
$$f(Sx) = Sf(x) \vdash f(x) = f(0)+x$$
$$f(Sx) = Pf(x) \vdash f(x) = f(0) \dot{-} x$$

(where P is the predecessor function).

Wittgenstein's criticism of mathematical induction, it must be conceded, is more a criticism of the language in which the method was traditionally presented than of the method itself. The inference from $P(x)$ to $P(Sx)$, for some property P, does not involve a knowledge that P holds for some number $x$. Rather we are seeking to infer $P(Sx)$ in a system which has been enriched by the axiom $P(x)$, no substitution being made in $x$ in the derivation of $P(Sx)$. The position is different in the equation calculus where the omission of induction as a postulate is justified, not by any criticism of induction, but because induction is *provable* in the calculus. It is interesting to note in passing that (in some fragments of arithmetic) the *axiom* of induction,

$$[P(0) \ \& \ (\mathbf{V}x)\{P(x) \rightarrow P(Sx)\}] \rightarrow (\mathbf{V}x)P(x)$$

and the rule of inference,

$$(P(0), \ P(x) \rightarrow P(Sx) \vdash P(Sx)$$

are not equivalent.

In the realist-formalist controversy in the philosophy of mathematics Wittgenstein's *Remarks* offers a solution that is crystal clear and satisfyingly uncompromising. The true propositions of mathematics are true because they are provable in a calculus; they are deductions from axioms by formal rules and are true in virtue of valid applications of the rules of inference and owe nothing to the world outside mathematics. A mathematical calculus is a calculus for the *transformation* of signs. But mathematics is not a mere game, because the natural numbers *have a use* outside mathematics, and this use of numbers in ordinary language is what gives mathematics its meaning. It is essential, he says in the *Remarks*, that numbers should also be used in *mufti*. The equation $2+2 = 4$ is a derivable consequence of the definition of addition in the sign calculus of mathematics; if the world changed so that it ceased to be the case that whenever we placed two apples on a shelf on which two already stood then only three apples remained instead of four, then the rule $2+2 = 4$, *qua rula* would in no way lose its mathematical validity, but it would *lose its application* in the world. We should no longer have a *use* for it outside mathematics and it would therefore be deprived of meaning. Mathematics finds not its verification but its application in the world as it is. It is a consequence of the rule $2+2 = 4$ that the sentences:

I have two pennies in each hand
I have four pennies in my hands

have the *same meaning*, but nothing in mathematics can tell us whether they are true or false, for their truth or falsehood is a matter of fact, not a mathematical convention.

Of course it is no accident that mathematics has applications in the real world; rules like $2+2 = 4$ were originally expressions of observed fact, that two objects and two objects make four objects, and only subsequently acquired their status as transformation rules of a calculus. The calculus was designed with its application in mind but like a theory in physics, only parts of mathematics are directly applicable to the world. What gives mathematics as a whole its sense is the relationships between the parts; it is because the proof of a proposition joins that proposition to the rest of mathematics, and shows where it belongs, that Wittgenstein's dictum is correct that if you want to know what a mathematical proposition means you must look at its proof.

In the *Philosophische Grammatik* he formulates the relationship between mathematics and its application in the following way. 'The connection of sentences of everyday life about lines and planes with geometry, is not that both speak of similar things, or that geometry deals with idealizations of everyday objects, but is the connection between these sentences and their grammar. The geometrical line does not stand in relation to the boundary between two colours as something finer to something coarser but as possibility to actuality' (p. 319 ff).

Wittgenstein's position is as entirely opposed to the neo-realism that is so fashionable today as it was opposed to Hilbert's formalism. Neo-realism stems from Gödel's view of the nature of mathematics, which sees the mathematician as a discoverer exploring a world of mathematics as the physicist explores the real world. I do not know of any defence of this position which is more than an individual expression of conviction that what the mathematician 'finds' is so natural and inevitable that it must have been there before, or have been preordained. Wittgenstein is equally convinced that 'the mathematician is an inventor, not a discoverer' (*Remarks*, I, 167), that 'a mathematical proposition is the determination of a concept following upon a discovery' (*Remarks*, III, 47), and that 'the mathematician creates essence' (*Remarks*, I, 32). This of course is bound up with Wittgenstein's well maintained distinction between calculation and experiment, and between internal and external properties. It is an internal property of the class {*a*, *b*, *c*} that it has three members and an external property of my door that is green; a door remains the same door, change its colour how you will, but it makes no sense to talk of changing the number of the class {*a*, *b*, *c*}. Mathematical propositions express internal properties, empirical propositions external properties. The neo-realist does not really want to say that mathematical propositions are empirical but he would like to explain logical necessity as a sort of physical necessity – it is so in mathematics, not because we made it so, but because it had to be so.

In the first lecture of Wittgenstein's which I heard in 1931, to which I have already referred, he said that you can invent a machine that will not work but you cannot invent a game that will not work. This sums up the difference between physical and logical possibility in a nutshell. A rocket may be designed with the utmost care, every calculation checked and rechecked, and yet you cannot tell whether it will take off or not until it is fired. The design itself cannot tell you if it will work. If it does not work then you explain the failure by saying perhaps that certain laws of physics do not apply at such high temperatures, or that the chemistry of the fuel was different from what had been expected. But if you invent a game, you invent the rules of the game; the rules may be inconsistent, but if this is so it shows itself in the rules (and there is nothing that needs to be put to the test of experience). A game may be logically impossible, an invention physically impossible.

The distinction between calculation and experiment is a subtle one. If you multiply $23 \times 27$ and obtain 621, is this an experiment? You can check the result by repeating the multiplication, or by obtaining the result in another way, for instance by adding 27 repeatedly for 23 times. Do the rules of arithmetic not compel the answer to be 621? We can lay the proof that $23 \times 27 = 621$ out before us and check every step to ensure that it is correct. We can, in this particular instance, find a short proof which we can take in at a glance, namely

$$(2 \times 10 + 3) (2 \times 10 + 7) = 2 \times 2 \times 100 + 2 \times 10 \times (3+7) + 21 = 2 \times 3 \times 100 + 21 = 621,$$

and the temptation to look at the calculations as an experiment is removed. Suppose however we say that if we perform a very big calculation we can never be sure that we do not make a mistake, however many times we repeat the calculation, just as Shanks made a mistake in his calculation of the digits of $\pi$. But then, is there any other way of obtaining the result, than by performing the calculation? and if we are not prepared to accept calculation as the way of obtaining the result then we have deprived the search for a result of all meaning.

The distinction between physical and logical possibility is I think at the bottom of Zeno's paradox. Certainly we know that Achilles catches the tortoise; are we then forced to conclude that it is logically possible to carry out an *infinite* number of steps? If we draw a line from one end to the other of the unit interval $(0, 1)$, do we at the same time draw a line from 0 to $\frac{1}{2}$, from $\frac{1}{2}$ to $\frac{3}{4}$, from $\frac{3}{4}$ to $\frac{7}{8}$ and so on indefinitely. In thinking this must be so, are we not confusing the physical possibility of drawing these lines with the logical possibility of naming points in the interval $(0, 1)$? We can name as many points as we please, and we can draw as many segments as we please, but it makes no sense to talk of drawing *all* the segments, because no end to the task is specified – after each segment there remains another. But when we say there are *infinitely* many points in $(0, 1)$ we do not mean we can name them all, only that we can give a rule for naming them.

Some years after the lecture in 1931 I reminded Wittgenstein of what he had said about inventing a game that will not work.

Of course I can invent a game that will not work, he retorted. Try playing draughts with ten-ton pieces.

## REFERENCES

Ludwig Wittgenstein: *Remarks on the Foundations of Mathematics.* Ed. by G. H. von Wright, R. Rhees and G. E. M. Anscombe, translated by G. E. M. Anscombe (Oxford, 1956).
Ludwig Wittgenstein: *Philosophische Grammatik.* Ed. by R. Rhees (Oxford, 1970).

# MATHEMATICAL GENERALITY

## ALICE AMBROSE

'Induction is the process of discovering general laws by the observation and combination of particular instances. It is used in all sciences, even in mathematics. . . . We may observe, by chance, that

$$1+8+27+64 = 100$$

and, recognizing the cubes and the square, we may give to the fact we observed the more interesting form :

$$1^3+2^3+3^3+4^3 = 10^2.$$

. . . Does it often happen that such a sum of successive cubes is a square? . . . In asking this we are like the naturalist who, impressed by a curious plant or a curious geological formation, conceives of a general question. Our general question is concerned with the successive cubes

$$1^3+2^3+3^3+4^3+ \ldots +n^3.$$

We are led to it by the 'particular instance' $n = 4$. . . . The special cases $n = 2, 3$ are still simpler, the case $n = 5$ is the next one. . . . Arranging neatly all these cases, as a geologist would arrange his specimens of a certain ore, we obtain the following table :

$$
\begin{aligned}
1 &= 1 &&= 1^2 \\
1+8 &= 9 &&= 3^2 \\
1+8+27 &= 36 &&= 6^2 \\
1+8+27+64 &= 100 &&= 10^2 \\
1+8+27+64+125 &= 225 &&= 15^2.
\end{aligned}
$$

287

It is hard to believe that all these sums of consecutive cubes are squares by mere chance. . . . In a similar case, the naturalist would have little doubt that the general law suggested by the special cases heretofore observed is correct. Here the following theorem is strongly suggested by the induction :

The sum of the first $n$ cubes is a square.

. . . In mathematics as in the physical sciences we may use observation and induction to discover general laws. . . . Many mathematical results were found by induction first and proved later. Mathematics presented with rigor is a systematic deductive science but mathematics in the making is an experimental inductive science."[1]

This excerpt presents an illustration of the analogies mathematicians find between mathematical and empirical investigations. It makes the number theory appear 'as the natural history of the domain of numbers',[2] and it seems entirely natural that it should do so. Proceeding 'by induction from numerical examples',[3] a mathematician will frequently describe his examination of special cases as confirming a conjecture, or supporting a generalization, and go on to predict that subsequent 'empirical evidence'[4] for it will bear it out. Propositions which have been 'reached and stated as probably true by induction'[5] may, or may not, be doubted, depending on the extent and nature of the evidence; the discovery of an exception to a generalization will confirm the doubt that the generalization holds for the totality of elements in the domain. Wittgenstein has claimed that such accounts of the mathematician's work, which could equally well describe the work of the natural scientist in his laboratory, are misleading; and often he counters them with descriptions which seem quite unnatural. For

[1] G. Polya, *How to Solve It* (Princeton University Press, 1945), pp. 103–6.

[2] L. Wittgenstein, *Remarks on the Foundations of Mathematics* (Macmillan Co., New York, 1956), p. 117.

[3] G. H. Hardy's description of Ramanujan, *Proc. London Mathematical Society* (2), XIX (1921), p. lviii.

[4] Phrase taken from R. Courant and H. Robbins, *What is Mathematics?* (Oxford University Press, London, 1941), p. 30.

[5] P. E. B. Jourdain, *The Nature of Mathematics* (Edinburgh, 1912).

example, despite its being a proper use of language to say that certain books deal with conic sections or with ideal numbers, and to say that this is the subject mater of geometry or number theory, we find Wittgenstein asserting that arithmetical propositions say nothing about numbers and geometrical propositions nothing about cubes.[6] Such an assertion seems either to be false or else to have some point which is not immediately evident. What construction is to be placed on his claim that many instances of the natural use of language are misleading? It is of course obvious that such language does not lead mathematicians astray in the pursuit of their subject. It is also obvious that Wittgenstein's comments are directed to pronouncements which the mathematician *as philosopher* makes. These pronouncements, and their opposites as well, he held to be the outcome of tempting ways of describing what the mathematician does when he attempts to prove some mathematical proposition he thinks to be true.

One of the well-known things Wittgenstein said about philosophical views was that they are products of linguistic confusion, 'misunderstandings concerning the use of words, [which are] caused, among other things, by certain analogies between the forms of expression in different regions of language'.[7] We have a tendency to assimilate to each other expressions which have different functions in language; we try to talk of very different things by means of the same schema.[8] Ordinary language plays into this tendency; witness the differences concealed by 'having a pain', 'having an idea', 'having a dollar', 'having a friend'. In this paper my concern is with analogies highlighted, and differences minimized, by descriptions of what is done in mathematics which are modelled after descriptions of work in the experimental sciences. Wittgenstein represents himself as 'try[ing] to counteract the misleading effect of certain analogies'.[9] Sometimes his own pronouncements appear to be as much pieces of philosophy – as much subject to intractable debate – as the views he supposes these analogies to lead to. If his statements are what they appear

[6] My lecture notes, 1933–4, taken preceding dictation of *The Blue Book*.
[7] *Philosophical Investigations* (Basil Blackwell, Oxford, 1953), p. 43.
[8] Lecture notes, 1939.
[9] *The Blue Book* (Basil Blackwell, Oxford, 1958), p. 28.

on the surface to be, then like the traditional philosopher he is countering one philosophical position with another, and we must take him to suppose these analogies mislead the mathematician into *false* positions of which he should be disabused.

This is one possible construction to be placed on the claim that analogies between the forms of expression in different regions of language are misleading. But there is another interpretation, an iconoclastic one, which may be what prompted him to raise the question, 'Where does our investigation get its importance from, since it seems only to destroy everything interesting, that is, all that is great and important?'[10] According to this interpretation, showing an anology to be misleading is the same thing as showing that it leads to a philosophical view, where the 'view' is merely the semblance of a true-or-false statement and in fact has no truth-value. Wittgenstein said there is a confusion pervading all philosophy, that of looking at the rejection of a form of symbolism as though a proposition had been rejected as false.[11] The traditional philosopher, then, is charged with misconceiving what he is doing – what it is his argumentation supports. Accordingly a mathematician's pronouncement on 'the objectivity and reality of mathematical facts' is characterized as 'something for philosophical treatment – . . . like the treatment of an illness'.[12] Wittgenstein's intention, then, is to cure or prevent the illness. The cure consists, not in solving the philosophical problem which is its cause, but in dissolving it, making it 'completely disappear'.[13]

It seems to me more plausible that one should be misled into a wrong idea about the nature of a position than that one should be misled into a false position – given the history of philosophical fashions, where what was once false now parades as true, and sooner or later falls out of fashion again and is rejected as false. In philosophy, it would seem, truth-value is determined by fashion. In the present paper I shall try to illustrate the thesis that linguistic analogies mislead philosophers into the wrong idea

---

[10] *Philosophical Investigations*, p. 48.
[11] *The Yellow Book*. Notes taken by Alice Ambrose and Margaret Masterman in the intervals between dictation of *The Blue Book*.
[12] *Philosophical Investigations*, p. 91.
[13] ibid., p. 51.

that the truth of a position is under debate. The problems under consideration will centre on the character of mathematical generalizations and their relations to singular propositions which instantiate them and to exceptions which refute them. What we are inclined to say about them, i.e. what Wittgenstein calls the 'raw material' of philosophy,[14] takes the form of descriptions analogous to accounts in natural science. The descriptions stress the analogies and consequently mute the differences. Often it is only a short step from these descriptions to a philosophical position. What I shall try to show is that analogies are used to justify a new use of language[15] – not to support a truth – that 'what [the philosophers] wants is . . . a new notation'.[16] The hold the analogies have on our minds is to be broken by emphasizing the differences. This was one of Wittgenstein's methods, and I shall be in his debt in a number of instances for specific ways of counteracting the analogies.

It will be useful to begin with certain assertions which clearly parallel assertions made about natural science : that generalizations are propositions about a totality of elements; that true existential propositions that contradict them state a truth about some individual within the domain of elements; that singular propositions which suggest a generalization we believe to be true are themselves discovered by observation; and that a proof of the generalization at the same time demonstrates what holds for each such special case. One's first reaction to these assertions is that they are unobjectionable, that their similarity to statements in the experimental sciences are open for all to see, and that no harm results from pointing it out. The fact that differences are slurred over does not gainsay the similarities.

However, what a little reflection shows is that minimizing a difference is related to a philosophical view as a preconscious thought is related to its conscious expression. The analogous descriptions just cited all conspire to make a certain philo-

[14] ibid., p. 91.
[15] See 'Wittgenstein on Universals', *Essays in Analysis* (George Allen and Unwin Ltd., London, 1966), where I develop this thesis for a relevant problem.
[16] *The Blue Book*, p. 57.

sophical position seem as natural as the descriptions themselves, namely, the Platonist position that there is a domain of objects which one needs but observe and explore in order to come to truths about them. Except for these objects, what could guarantee the truth of existence-propositions and singular propositions? In fact this question presents a consideration which makes the Platonist view appear as a wholly reasonable answer. Mathematical conjectures, attempts to prove generalizations suggested by observed special cases, the discovery of exceptions which upset generalizations, proofs by mathematical induction starting from cases – all may be described as being about objects which merely differ from the objects of empirical science in being abstract or ideal rather than concrete.

Then why not accept the description? What objection is there to taking the analogies between mathematical and inductive generalizations at face value and accepting the philosophical position to which they lead? What reason is there for supposing the analogies *mis*lead? There is a short and obvious answer to this question. This is that the existence of counterviews which also make claims to truth present a permanent stalemate. While Platonist philosophers maintain that the truths of mathematics assuredly hold for a sphere of objects existing independently of the mind and of which the mind is directly aware, other philosophers find it 'strange that such a notion could ever have existed';[17] and there is no coming to a decision between these positions when taken to be what they appear to be : true or false. It would seem that there is no explaining one philosopher's claim that he is aware of abstract objects when he understands mathematical terms and the counterclaim of another philosopher that when he understands number expressions, say, he is aware of no such objects.

Analogies between mathematical and inductive generalizations tempt one to the Platonist view, but there are considerations, so far not mentioned, which tempt one to deny it and to adopt a counterview. These considerations call attention to the *differences* between the two types of generalization. A conventional philoso-

---

[17] Edward Kasner and James Newman, *Mathematics and the Imagination* (Simon and Schuster, New York, 1940), p. 359.

pher takes these differences to bear on the truth or falsity of a position. At times Wittgenstein seems to do likewise, although a quite different use of them can be made. Whatever the use, it is important to see what these differences are. Wittgenstein is reported to have remarked, 'We are much more inclined to say "All these things, though looking different, are really the same" than we are to say "All these things, though looking the same, are really different".'[18] He also remarked that facts to which he draws attention are such as 'we know quite as well as he, but which we have forgotten or at least are not immediately attending to'. Obvious facts of difference will be our starting point.

First, a true mathematical generalization has what Kant called 'strict universality', which is to say that it is not logically possible for there to be an exception to it. This means that its subject and predicate are connected by 'inner necessity', or what comes to the same thing, that the generalization can be restated as an entailment. For example, 'For any polygon of $n+2$ sides, the sum of its angles is $n \times 180°$' can be restated as: '*being a polygon of $n+2$ sides* entails *having angles which sum up to* $n \times 180°$'. This feature of universally quantified propositions of mathematics is the wellspring of all other differences: if true, they are *a priori* true; it is logically out of the question for them to have a different truth-value. Owing to their necessity, constructions which serve as proofs of geometrical propositions are not experiments, despite the fact that any construction is a particular temporal activity. The interesting thing is that straight edge, pencil, and paper can be dispensed with. Mere *description*, for example, of the division of a line by straight edge and compass is sufficient to prove the generalization 'a straight line can be divided into any number of equal parts by straight edge and compass'. The actual construction need not be carried out. But description of an experiment is by no means sufficient for establishing the expected result. Experimentation on whatever is the subject of the generalization has to be carried out. Were a Euclidean construction an experiment, 'it could not prove the result for other cases'.[19]

[18] Lectures, 1939.
[19] *Philosophische Bemerkungen* (Basil Blackwell, Oxford, 1964), p. 152. My own translations throughout.

Empirical generalizations and mathematical generalizations, despite looking alike because both have the form 'All $f$'s *are* $g$'s, differ radically in their relation to singular propositions of the form $fx.gx$ and $fx \sim gx$, i.e. to what we call instances and exceptions. The difference is that the instances do not confirm in the sense of 'bearing out' a hypothesis, for an entailment holds regardless of instances. Instances give no support. Nor is it conceivable that anything of the form $fx. \quad gx$ should upset it. Wittgenstein remarked that it is 'a misfortune that our language denotes such fundamentally different things by the words "question", "problem", "investigation", "discovery". And similarly for the words "conclusion", "proposition", "proof".'[20] The same also applies to the quantifier 'all'. Its use in 'All cats are independent' is altogether different from its use in 'All cats are feline'. An empirical generalization can have any number of supporting instances, however great, without removing the *possibility* of a falsifying instance. And this possibility is not removed by the truth of the generalization. With an entailment neither of the two possibilities, of confirmation and falsification, is open to it. For if it is inconceivable for a proposition to have an exception, then instances play no role in supporting it. Where instances cannot in principle falsify they also cannot in principle confirm its truth. If every instance *must*, logically, support the generalization, then 'supporting instance' means nothing more than 'instance', and the claim that every instance is a supporting instance is quite empty. The question then arises whether a generalization of the form 'All $f$'s are $g$'s can properly be said to be *about f's*.

Mathematical beliefs present another difference, however much 'the clothing of our language'[21] makes them look like ordinary beliefs. We do properly say that we believe no odd numbers are perfect on that Fermat believed that for $n > 4$, numbers of the form $2^{2^n}+1$ are prime. In the first case we believe in default of knowing. And in this respect 'believe' seems to have the same correlated contrast term 'know' which it has in the usual, empirical contexts. However, in empirical contexts it is logically possible

[20] ibid., p. 190.
[21] *Philosophical Investigations*, p. 224.

both to believe and to know the same proposition. But suppose that 'no odd numbers are perfect', like 'for all $n > 4$, $2^{2n}+1$ is prime' is false. Falsity is here self-inconsistency. The marvel then is how belief is possible about what is unthinkable. We are reminded of Cardinal Newman's explanation of how those who are ignorant of the Bible because they cannot read may nevertheless be saved: they can believe that what the Bible says is true without knowing *what* it says. What is it that people believed when they tried to trisect the angle by straight edge and compass? And what would it be to succeed? 'It used to be said that God could create anything, except what was contrary to the laws of logic',[22] and presumably He could conceive of every task except what was logically impossible. If there is an oddity about the idea of believing what is unthinkable, there is likewise an oddity about the idea of believing what is thinkable, where what is thought of is true necessarily, e.g. $25 \times 25 = 625$. 'Can someone *believe* that $25 \times 25 = 625$?', Wittgenstein asks. 'What does it mean to believe that? How does it show up that he believes it?'[23] Again, usually what one believes one can wish to be the case, even though one's belief is discovered to be false. How different is 'the grammar of belief' in the usual circumstances and in mathematics comes to light when one considers 'whether it makes sense to say: "I wish twice two were five!"'[24] or 'I wish there were an even prime greater than 2'. Not only this, there is some sort of impropriety in saying one wishes for what cannot conceivably fail to be the case, e.g. that one wishes that the sum of the first six consecutive cubes should be a square.

A further interesting difference is that various tenses can be used in the expression of what is believed in mathematics without in any way altering the sense. One can express the same belief, for example, about the division of 1 by 3, by saying either that 3 will recur or that 3 does recur. Except where '3 will recur' is used to predict the digit in a person's calculations, 'will recur'

[22] *Tractatus Logico-Philosophicus*, 3.031, translated by C. K. Ogden (Harcourt Brace, New York, 1922).
[23] *Zettel*, translated by G. E. M. Anscombe, (Basil Blackwell, Oxford, 1967), p. 73. Slight alteration in translation.
[24] ibid., p. 121.

is not temporal. In fact it can be replaced by the tenseless logical 'must'. By contrast, to believe 'He will write "3" ' is very different from believing 'He is writing "3" ', and clearly neither statement is identical with one in which the logical 'must' replaces the tensed verb. Consequently a mathematical prediction differs characteristically from the prediction of an event which could fail to take place. Once an entailment is established, prediction that it holds for other cases than those considered is like predicting that the fifth day will follow the fourth.[25] Of what is predicted in mathematics it is an impropriety of language to say 'Experience indicates that this will be the case' (e.g. that 3 will recur, or that for the next value of $n$, say $n = 2$, the polygon having $n+2$ sides will have angles whose sum is $360°$).

Having cited differences which seriously raise the question, How can one talk of believing a mathematical proposition, whether a false one or a true one?', it has to be admitted that the answer is that one can. We say we conjecture, as many people have, about the distribution of primes, that we notice a regularity, such as Polya describes, and go on to prove that what one has observed must be so, that we make predictions and hazard that something is very likely true. What is common talk cannot be dismissed out of hand. At the same time it is paradoxical. There seems to be something wrong about predicting what can have only one possible truth-value; it is like predicting that it will either rain or not rain. (And if that truth-value is falsity, *what* has one predicted? Do the words 'Ten years from now a donkey will be born which is not an animal' make a prediction?) There seems something wrong about talk of likelihoods when the probability of the proposition in question must be 0 or must be 1 and cannot sensibly be said to have any intermediate values between 0 and 1. And yet such talk is commonplace.

The following description of *reductio ad absurdum* proof, from Polya, is a good example of language which bears its meaning on its face, yet at the same time is paradoxical. Suppose 'we wish to prove that it is impossible to fulfil a certain condition,

---

[25] Wittgenstein's example, taken from a manuscript entitled 'Grundlagen der Mathematik'.

that is, that the situation in which all parts of the condition are simultaneously satisfied can never arise. But, if we have proved nothing yet, we have to face the possibility that the situation could arise . . . although such a situation appears extremely unlikely'.[26] If by assuming $p$ one proves $\sim p$, *what* did one assume? And is there a 'possibility that the situation [assumed in $p$] could arise'? Yet nothing is more common than *reductio ad absurdum* proofs which begin: 'Suppose $p$'. Again, it seems correct to describe a particular mathematical truth as having been suggested by observation of several instances of it, and later demonstrated. Undoubtedly it was first discovered by measurements of particular right triangles that the length of the hypotenuse was the square root of the sum of the squares of the other two sides. At any rate the measurements must have been taken as a warrant for the generalization, just as data about observed cases are taken as inductive grounds for an empirical proposition. But the Pythagorean theorem is demonstrable, whereas what is empirical, i.e. what has two possible truth-values, is not demonstrable, i.e. is not at the same time confined, in principle, to one truth-value.[27]

I wish now to develop one paradoxical consequence of Polya's account of a mathematician's procedure in more detail. Consonant with his account of the 'inductive' procedure preceding a demonstration, he develops a calculus of 'plausibilities' analogous in some ways to the calculus of probability, where plausibility is equated with degree of belief. Inasmuch as no numerical value can be attached to plausibility, with the exception of 0 and 1 (corresponding, resp., to knowledge of a proposition's refutation and proof), he contents himself with an algebra which expresses changes in degrees of belief in a proposition during an investigation rather than attempting to assign an 'absolute' degree of belief to it at the outset.[28] It is unnecessary to go into the detail of this algebra. Suffice it for our purpose to look at his conclusions: 'The plausibility of a theorem can only increase when a

[26] *How to Solve It*, p. 152.

[27] cf. *Philosophische Bemerkungen*, p. 145. 'A generality cannot be at the same time empirical and demonstrable.'

[28] 'Heuristic Reasoning and the Theory of Probability', *American Mathematical Monthly*, vol. 48, p. 457.

consequence of the theorem is confirmed', and 'The plausibility of a theorem can only decrease when a hypothesis of which the given theorem is a consequence is refuted'.[29] The plausibility of a proposition may in the course of an investigation change to 0, if a consequence of it is found to be false, and to 1, if it, or a hypothesis from which it follows, is proved. These limiting values to which the plausibilities tend are of special importance in seeing what is paradoxical about this account despite there being something 'right' about it.

Since empirical investigation is the model here, it is instructive to compare the mathematical case with the case of an empirical proposition which lends itself to being made more and more plausible by the examination of cases. Rendering an empirical proposition certain is a continuation of the procedure which renders it plausible to a degree. Enough confirming instances are amassed to make its denial absurd, because investigation of further cases seems absurd. (How often must one test whether litmus paper turns red in acid in order to be justified in declaring that this is certain?) But no matter how *factually* absurd its denial becomes, the logical possibility of its being true remains. *No* number of confirming instances eliminates the logical possibility of a disconfirming instance coming up. It is this logical possibility which positivists used to support their philosophical claim that all propositions other than tautologies and so-called basic propositions are nothing more than probable hypotheses. No finite number of favourable cases, they held, could count as *conclusively* verifying an empirical generalization; nothing short of an infinite number will do. I shall not discuss the use they made, in coming to their philosophical theory, of the fact that empirical generalizations can in principle always be disconfirmed.[30] What is important here is the fact itself and its relation to our use of the words 'plausible' and 'probable'. These words are so used that a proposition can only be said to be more or less plausible or probable

[29] ibid., p. 464.

[30] See M. Lazerowitz' 'Strong and Weak Verification II' *The Structure of Metaphysics*, where the thesis is developed that what passes as a theory puts forward an academic reform of language which stresses the difference between entailment-propositions and empirical generalizations.

when the same thing can be said of its negation. Experience can render an empirical proposition more and more plausible by fresh confirming instances, or less and less plausible by discovery of the falsity of hypotheses from which it follows. But these same facts also render its negative less and less plausible, or more and more plausible, respectively. Even when an empirical proposition is true and its plausibility goes over to certainty, one must allow the logical possibility of its negation being true or at least of being made plausible.

This is not the case with regard to a mathematical proposition. A mathematical proposition which is made more and more plausible 'inductively' and then *proved* is at the moment of proof shown to be *a priori*. When the value 1 attaches to a mathematical proposition, its negative cannot, in principle, have any of the remaining degrees of plausibility, except 0, which like 1 denotes what is logically necessary, not what is psychologically certain. ' "Mathematical certainty" is not a psychological concept.'[31] So Polya's account has the consequence that a proposition can be rendered plausible when it is such that by its very nature its denial cannot be rendered plausible. Given the use of 'plausible' which is the model for his account, a paradox can be elicited. This is that the proposition which fresh trials supposedly make more and more plausible is such as to be incapable of being plausible. Demonstrating that it is true or giving a *reductio ad absurdum* proof of its falsity shows that neither it nor its negative can be plausible. What we shall call Polya's Paradox is that his account describes a proposition being made plausible which by its very nature is such that the concept *plausible* does not apply to it.

The source of the paradox lies in treating an entailment-proposition as though it could be confirmed by instances. An *a priori* true proposition has no confirmation any more than it has a refutation. And this is what seems right about Wittgenstein's statement, in lectures of 1933–4, that arithmetical propositions are not about numbers nor geometrical propositions about cubes. Yet on second thoughts this statement of his, understood

[31] *Philosophical Investigations,* p. 224.

as making a factual claim, seems plainly to be false. And Wittgenstein allows as much. In his 1939 lectures he is reported as saying 'If asked "Which propositions of Euclid are about triangles?" I have no objection to saying the propositions on p. 30 are about triangles, those on p. 40 are about circles, etc. I don't say it's *wrong* to say that mathematical propositions are about numbers.' So his earlier statement, which suggests there remains nothing for them to be about, if not about numbers or figures, would seem to fall under the paradox to which Moore called attention in his celebrated 'Defence of Common Sense': 'the strange thing that philosophers should have been able to hold sincerely, as part of their philosophical creed, propositions inconsistent with what they themselves *knew* to be true'.[32] Wittgenstein of course knew that there are mathematical propositions which are about numbers (regardless of how misleading he thought it is to say this). In a non philosophical situation he would be as surprised as anyone else by someone's saying they are not. Unlike a person who tells us that mineralogy is not about plants, but who can go on to tell us what it is about, a person who says that number theory is not about numbers cannot go on to explain what its subject matter is. If he knows the meaning of the term 'number theory' he knows it is about numbers. Analogously, Polya knew it is true that statements of arithmetic and number theory are *a priori*, that however great the appearance of their being inductively confirmable, they are not like 'All crows are black'.

Mill said of 'the Science of Number' that 'its first principles are generalizations from experience',[33] 'experimental truths',[34] 'known by early and constant experience . . .; they are proved by showing to our eyes and our fingers that any given number of objects, ten balls for example, may by separation and rearrangement exhibit to our senses all the different sets of numbers the sum of which is equal to ten.'[35] He cites with approbation Herschel's statement that 'A truth, necessary and universal, relative to any object of our knowledge, must verify itself in every instance

[32] *Philosophical Papers* (George Allen and Unwin, London, 1959), p. 41.
[33] *A System of Logic* (Harper, New York, 1856), pp. 167–8.
[34] ibid., p. 164.
[35] ibid., p. 167.

where that object is before our contemplation.'[36] Now Polya puts forward no such theory about the nature of necessary propositions; but his account of the procedure by which a mathematician 'augments or diminishes his confidence in a theorem which is still only a conjecture'[37] treats a generalization as Mill would have done on the basis of his theory. He did this while knowing, in fact remarking, the essential difference between 'heuristic reasoning', which does not prove a proposition, and 'rigorous demonstration', which does.

When Wittgenstein said that arithmetical propositions say nothing about numbers and geometrical propositions nothing about cubes, he immediately went on to say that geometry 'gives the grammar of the word "cube" as arithmetic gives the grammar of "number" ', and also that 'geometry constitutes the meaning of the word "cube" '.[38] Taken together these statements suggest that Wittgenstein held a traditional philosophical view, conventionalism, about the nature of mathematical propositions, and in general, about necessary propositions. Moore reports that in his lectures of 1930–3 Wittgenstein appeared to hold that '$p$ is impossible' meant the same as 'the sentence "$p$" has no sense',[39] and that 'red is a primary colour' says something about the word 'red'.[40] Now claims of this sort are as obviously false as the claim that arithmetic says nothing about numbers. Any statement reporting the usage of a word in a given language is empirical, and therefore cannot be identical with a necessary proposition. Since this is obvious it may be taken for granted that Wittgenstein was aware of it. And if he nevertheless took a conventionalist position, then as M. Lazerowitz points out in his essay in this volume, the paradox Moore called attention to applies to him : that he sincerely held that necessary propositions are verbal, while knowing that they are necessary and therefore not verbal.

It is natural to assume that mathematical propositions are 'about' something – if not about numbers and geometrical figures,

[36] ibid., p. 163.
[37] op. cit., *American Mathematical Monthly*, vol. 48, p. 450.
[38] Notes of lectures, 1933–4.
[39] *Philosophical Papers*, pp. 275–6.
[40] ibid., p. 291.

then about symbols. Mill's conclusion was that 'Since . . . neither in nature, nor in the human mind, do there exist any objects exactly corresponding to the definitions of geometry, while yet that science cannot be supposed to be conversant with non-entities; nothing remains but to consider geometry as conversant with such lines, angles, and figures as really exist.'[41] This conclusion, however, leaves it a puzzle as to why the inaccuracy of drawn figures makes no difference to the truth of a theorem. This consideration is cited not for critical purposes but to indicate its similarity to a counterposition Mill thought to be false, the conventionalist position that mathematical propositions are about 'mere symbols'.[42] Both positions are examples of the 'regulative' formula Lazerowitz discusses in detail in his essay, viz. that a literally meaningful statement must be *about something*. This is the formula which Wittgenstein later began to see as a 'grammatical obsession' – grammatical because when we say a reality must correspond to a meaningful statement, instead of asserting a fact we are merely exhibiting a prejudice in favour of certain grammatical forms.[43] However much we may pretend to have arrived at a fact of ontology, what we are doing is highlighting the name-object pattern that exists in ordinary language. The phrase we are wedded to in this context is 'is about something'. The question, 'What are geometrical propositions about?' sounds like the question, 'What are propositions of mineralogy about?'; and the answer tells us an analogous thing, that it is about 'such figures as really exist', or about 'ideal figures', or about 'words'. The denial is in the same case. Both question and answers are construed in accordance with one model: 'What is "Cats are independent" about?', Answer: 'Cats'. A remark of Wittgenstein's, as reported in lectures of 1939, is suggestive of what he had in mind when he spoke of trying to counteract the misleading effect of certain analogies: 'Being about' means two entirely different things, and to say mathematical propositions are about numbers 'may lead to an enormous confusion'. The

[41] *A System of Logic*, p. 149.
[42] ibid., pp. 164–7.
[43] My notes of lectures, 1934–5.

confusion he was very likely referring to was the Platonic theory that numbers, as contrasted with groups of things exemplifying a number, 'are to be reckoned among the things that are',[44] and that geometry is about 'the absolute square and the absolute diameter',[45] to which the drawn figures are related as the less accurate to the ideal. Plato describes abstract objects as constituting the domain suitable to the mind's contemplation, and it is this picture which Wittgenstein considers an impediment to a proper understanding of mathematical language. His therapeutic advice to look at the use of words is directed to 'removing the bias, which forces us to think that the facts *must* conform to certain pictures embedded in our language'.[46]

Evidently what he was objecting to here was analogous treatment of mathematical and experiential propositions in disregard of differences. The question, 'What are mathematical propositions about?', has, as he observes regarding a philosophical step taken in another connexion, already 'commit[ted] us to a particular way of looking at the matter. (The decisive movement in the conjuring trick has been made, and it was the very one that we thought quite innocent.)'[47] What is crucially important here, to prevent being taken in by the question, is getting clear on the nature of *a priori* necessity. Wittgenstein's use of metaphor, e.g. when he speaks of the different 'grammars' of necessary and empirical propositions, is suggestive, but it is also an obstacle to obtaining a clear view. What I wish to show here is that the two paradoxes, the one implied by Polya's account of the 'inductive' procedure for arriving at generalizations about numbers and the one that comes out of Wittgenstein's denial that the generalizations are about numbers, will disappear once the nature of necessary propositions is made explicit. What is correct and what is misleading about the claims each makes will become clear on seeing which features of *a priori* necessity are responsible for the paradox.

Necessary propositions have two faces, one of which is in

[44] *Sophist*, Sec. 238, Jowett translation.
[45] *Republic*, Book VI, Sec. 511.
[46] *The Blue Book*, p. 43.
[47] *Philosophical Investigations*, p. 103.

eclipse when the other is in the focus of attention. And each face has a different, and opposing thing to say. The face they present to most people is that of asserting a fact, and this they do in virtue of the form of speech in which they are cast. The two propositions, 'Red is a primary colour' and 'Red is a colour in many flags', wear the same linguistic dress, the fact-claiming, or fact-reporting, indicative mood. But the first is bound up with the fact that recourse to the dictionary definition of the phrase 'primary colour' occurring in the expression of it, is all that is required to establish its truth. Now, it is merely a convention, a quite arbitrary matter, that 'primary colour' is used in English to cover red, blue, yellow, and green, and only these (alternatively, that the word 'red' is the name of one of the four primary colours). That it does so is an empirical fact: the phrase might be used otherwise, and if it were, the statement that it is so used would be false. The fact that 'Red is a primary colour' expresses an *a priori* truth thus rests on what is arbitrary, viz. English usage. This is not to say that the fact that it expresses a necessary truth is an arbitrary matter. Given the conventions (which *are* arbitrary) that 'red' is the name of a primary colour and that 'primary colour' means what it does, the meaning of the sentence is determined by the meanings these words have and by the grammatical rules governing their combination. As this is put in the *Tractatus*: 'In our notations there is indeed something arbitrary, but *this* is not arbitrary: that *if* we have determined something arbitrarily, something else must be the case.'[48] That a sentence denotes something necessarily true is thus not arbitrary (unless the sentence is treated as a linguistic unit and arbitrarily *given* a meaning in the way a word is); but it *is* nevertheless an empirical fact. Similarly, it is an empirical fact that the sentence ' "Primary colour" applies, as a matter of usage, to the colour red' (or "red" is the name of one of the primary colours expresses a contingent proposition. What is definitely not either arbitrary or empirical is the fact that the *proposition* that red is a primary colour is necessary. *Being red* entails *being a primary colour*. In commenting on 'the colour system' Wittgenstein remarks: 'Then there is

[48] 3.342.

something arbitrary about this system? Yes and no. It is akin both to what is arbitrary and to what is non-arbitrary'.[49] What is arbitrary is the verbal fact about the usage of the terms 'red' and 'primary colour' which makes it true that the sentence 'Red is a primary colour' expresses a necessary proposition. This round-about connexion of the necessary proposition with a verbal fact of course does not make it true to say that the necessary proposition is identical with any proposition *about the terms* 'red' and 'primary colour'. The proposition, ' "Primary colour" applies as a matter of usage, to the colour red', is about the phrase 'primary colour'; but since it is an empirical truth, the necessary proposition cannot be identified with it.

Seeing that the use of words is not the subject matter of *a priori* propositions makes it more tempting to fall back on what the similarity between mathematical and empirical generalizations suggests, namely, that 'All *f*'s are *g*'s is about the totality of *f*'s. To focus on the fact-stating aspect which 'All *f*'s are *g*'s presents is to ignore the verbal aspect which is so plainly visible to the conventionalist. The appeal, and at the same time the paradox, of Polya's description is the result of emphasizing this verbal similarity. On the other hand, what is right about his account of the 'inductive' testing of a conjectured theorem rests on the connexion of the theorem with a verbal fact. Since a mathematical proposition – or any logically necessary proposition – is not the same as a proposition about terminology, it needs to be made more explicit what this connexion is.

For this purpose it will be useful to compare the inductive generalization 'Lions are carnivores' (1) with 'Lions are felines' (2), and both of these with the verbal statements 'The word "carnivore" applies to whatever "lion" applies to' (3), and 'The word "feline" applies to whatever "lion" applies to' (4). (3) and (4), in being about words, clearly are not about the same subject matter as are statements which do not mention words. (1), (3), and (4) are all contingent propositions. To see how (2) and (4) are related, and that (1) and (3) are not so related, it will be useful to look at facts about the sentences which express them. This

[49] *Zettel*, p. 66e.

will have the advantage of allowing us to compare a set of *empirical* facts, namely, that sentence '(2)' expresses a necessarily true proposition and that sentences '(1)', '(3)', and '(4)' all express true empirical propositions, albeit of different kinds. It is important to repeat that it is a mere matter of fact that a sentence in a given language expresses something necessary (or as the case may be, contingent). A sentence which expresses a given proposition expresses it as a matter of empirical fact; it could be the case that it expressed a different proposition or no proposition at all.

Now what must be known in order to know the fact that '(2)' expresses what is necessarily true, and that the other three sentences express what is in fact true? The answer to this question will set out the relation between *proposition* (2) and a verbal fact without committing us to conventionalism, i.e. to identifying (2) and (4). To know the empirical fact that '(2)' says what is true is also to know the empirical fact that '(4)' says what is true; and conversely. In other words, knowing that '(2)' expresses a true proposition, namely, that lions are felines, requires no more than knowing the use of words, here 'lion' and 'feline'. The case is quite different with sentences '(1)' and '(3)'. To know that '(1)' says what is true one needs to know an extra-linguistic fact, a fact only to be learned by observation of the things the word 'lion' refers to. No amount of knowledge of usage will give us this information. And to know that '(3)' says what is true, i.e. to know the verbal fact that 'carnivore' does apply to what 'lion' applies to, one has to know the *nonverbal* fact expressed by '(1)', namely a fact about lions. Now if knowing that '(2)' expresses a necessarily true proposition comes to knowing that '(4)' expresses a factually true verbal proposition, no knowledge of lions being required, then one cannot say that the sentence 'Lions are felines' makes an assertion about lions. The fact that it expresses a necessity is the same fact which verifies that ' "Feline" applies to whatever "lion" applies to' expresses a truth about English usage.[50] And this is a fact about the use of the nouns

---

[50] This account of the relation between a necessary proposition and a verbal fact is in essentials given in various places by M. Lazerowitz. See especially *The Structure of Metaphysics*, pp. 266–71, *Studies in Metaphilosophy*, pp. 46–56, as well as his essay in this volume.

occurring in the sentences, not about what they are used to refer to.

But the following should be especially noted. Although the fact that 'Lions are felines' expresses a true *a priori* proposition is equivalent to the fact that ' "Feline" applies to whatever "lion" applies to' expresses a true verbal proposition, the first sentence does not *state* what it is, i.e. the verbal fact, that we must know in order to know that what it says (the proposition it expresses) is true. What it asserts is the nonverbal proposition that lions are felines. One must take care not to mix the verbal and nonverbal idioms – not to confuse 'the proposition that lions are felines is necessary' with 'the sentence "Lions are felines" expresses what is necessarily true', and go on to equate, as do conventionalists, the proposition that lions necessarily are felines with the proposition that 'feline' applies to what 'lion' applies to.

Wittgenstein's remark about the propositions of logic applies to any necessary proposition, namely, that their 'correct explanation must give them a peculiar position among all propositions'.[51] One peculiarity has been noted, that one can know that sentences for them express something true without having any factual knowledge about things, in our example, knowledge about lions. Nor does a sentence for a necessary proposition ('Lions are felines') refer to a word (the word 'lion'). The verbal sentence, ' "Feline" applies to what "lion" applies to', has words as its subject of discourse, whereas we are left with no subject matter for 'Lions are felines'. Similarly, a sentence denoting mathematical generalizations of the form 'All *f*'s are *g*'s will not be about f's.

Let us now return to Wittgenstein's statement that arithmetical propositions are not about numbers. They are also not about numerals. Presumably any necessary proposition falls under his characterization of tautologies, namely, that they say nothing. This sounds extremely paradoxical since it suggests that sentences such as '$2+2 = 4$' are meaningless. The claim that they say nothing while nevertheless being intelligible presents a puzzle. Were a person to say that mineralogy is not about plants but

[51] *Tractatus*, 6.112.

then go on to say it is not about minerals either, we should say he did not know the meaning of 'mineralogy'. Obviously Wittgenstein cannot be charged with not knowing what 'arithmetic' means, nor can he be supposed to have looked into arithmetic and seen that it was not about numbers, the way someone might look into a room and see that certain persons were not there. What then can he be saying? Inasmuch as it is proper English to say arithmetic is about numbers, is his statement, to use Moore's word, a 'howler'?

One possible construction to be placed on it is that it is a philosophical view, and a false one. This may be the case, inasmuch as Wittgenstein had one foot in the past and one in the future. But note what this interpretation involves when coupled with his claim that philosophical propositions are not empirical. The assertion that no proposition of arithmetic is about numbers is then restatable as an entailment: *being arithmetical* entails *not being about numbers*. The associated verbal statement is that 'being about numbers' applies to nothing that 'arithmetical' applies to. And this statement about the use of the words 'arithmetical' and 'numbers' is obviously false. Since Wittgenstein did not have a wrong idea about how these words are used, so that his statement cannot be construed as being a misdescription of the use of terms, only one interpretation remains plausible. This is that he was changing usage but concealing the verbal thing that he was doing by couching his pronouncement in the ontological idiom.[52] The idiom suggests that the existence of numbers is being denied – that it is being denied that there is something which arithmetic is about. Since the existence of arithmetic is admitted, the verbal statement associated with his claim comes to rejecting number talk. 'Being about *numbers*' will fail to apply to anything arithmetical. By contrast, the phrase 'being about numerals' is not suppressed, although it is not introduced in a concealed way by his taking the conventionalist position that arithmetical propositions are about numerals. What he says often bears the mark of a conventionalist position, but he also at other

[52] See developments of a similar thesis in connexion with other philosophical views in M. Lazerowitz' *Philosophy and Illusion*.

times is more cautious, as when he says, 'Mathematical propositions are *preparations* for the use of language, almost as definitions are',[53] but he does not say they are definitions, or about symbols. At times he makes cautionary remarks to put us on our guard against adopting a conventionalist view: 'If you say "2+2 = 4" is about the *mark* "4", be careful'.[54] He states explicitly that 'the number 4' and 'the mark "4" ' are not interchangeable expressions.

The question is why, if he is unwilling to say that '2+2 = 4' is about symbols, he is willing to assert the equally objectionable proposition that it is not about numbers. There can be no doubt that he had a *point* in mind, that he intended a special kind of work for his paradoxical assertion. This can be grasped if we recall the therapeutic advice reported from his lectures.[55] 'Don't ask for the meaning of a word, ask for its use'. We can in the present connexion use a related therapeutic formula, 'Don't speak of the meaning of a word, speak of its use'. Talk about numbers is talk about the meanings of number-words. The metaphysically inclined philosopher proceeds from this point into Platonic metaphysics via the tacit reasoning: the meaning of a number-word is something, not nothing, and hence is an entity in its own right. Wittgenstein's statement is to be understood as a special kind of counter to the tendency to speak of meanings as abstract entities. 'The question . . . "What is the number one?" produces in us a mental cramp. We feel we can't point to anything in reply . . . and yet ought to point to something. (We are up against one of the great sources of philosophical bewilderment: a substantive makes us look for a thing that corresponds to it.)'[56] When the metaphysician says the geometer reasons 'not about the figures that he draws, but the absolute square and the absolute diameter' and that 'numbers are to be reckoned among the things that are' he is *inventing* a subject matter, in name if not in fact, to correspond to substantive terms which do not have a use to refer to

---

[53] Lectures, 1939.
[54] Lecture notes, 1934–5.
[55] By John Wisdom, Moral Science Club paper.
[56] *The Blue Book*, p. 1. The reading originally dictated: 'we try to find a substance for a substantive'.

things one can point to. When he 'perceives that a substantive is not used as what in general we should call the name of an object . . . he can't help saying . . . that it is the name of an ethereal object'.[57] It is this sort of object he supposes himself to be referring to when in the guise of a commonsense statement he makes the pronouncement, pregnant with metaphysics, that arithmetic is about numbers.

This pronouncement has the advantage, and the disadvantage[58] of being in accord with ordinary language; whereas Wittgenstein's denial that arithmetical propositions are about numbers has a verbal correlate which goes against ordinary language, viz. that 'being about numbers' does not apply to anything 'arithmetical' applies to, or alternatively, that 'being arithmetical and about numbers' has no use. The point of saying what he does, together with its shocking verbal correlate, has its explanation in the linguistic illness for which it is a corrective. In respect of purpose, it is of a piece with what appears to be his conventionalism, and hence it is useful to look at his characterizing necessary propositions as rules of grammar in conjunction with the statement that arithmetical propositions are not about numbers. By first construing both as traditional philosophical positions we can get an insight into the use Wittgenstein put them to by applying to them his own description of a confusion which he considered pervasive in philosophy : looking at the rejection of a form of symbolism as though we were rejecting a proposition as false.[59] A complementary confusion, we might add, is looking at the *introduction* of a special new way of speaking as though we were advancing a proposition as true.

This latter characterization seems to apply to the statement that necessary propositions are rules of grammar, and as a special case, that arithmetic gives the grammar of 'number'. The form of speech employed suggests that a theory is being elaborated about their nature. It is clear that the effect is to introduce a stretched use of the phrase 'rule of grammar'. (Similarly, conven-

---

[57] ibid., p. 47.
[58] A disadvantage because the language conceals that a piece of metaphysics is being advanced.
[59] *The Yellow Book.*

tionalists who express their position by the words 'necessary propositions are verbal' stretch the use of the word 'verbal'.) To extend 'rule of grammar' to cover propositions which make no mention of words is to introduce a linguistic innovation. It is an innovation which serves to bring to the fore a connexion with a verbal fact which sentences for necessary propositions conceal, and which serves for Wittgenstein a further and more important purpose. Disregarding for the moment this further purpose, it is well to take note of Wittgenstein's account of what underlies a philosophical position, and which certainly underlies conventionalism:

> Our ordinary language, which of all possible notations is the one which pervades all our life, holds our mind rigidly in one position, as it were, and in this position sometimes it feels cramped, having a desire for other positions as well. Thus we sometimes wish for a notation which stresses a difference more strongly, makes it more obvious, than ordinary language does, or one which in a particular case uses more closely similar forms of expression than our ordinary language.[60]

Conventionalism as a philosophical position stresses, in the non-verbal form of speech, a difference between necessarily true and contingently true propositions, which was brought out earlier by considering the difference between knowing that the sentence 'Lions are felines' expresses something true and knowing that the sentence 'Lions are carnivores' expresses something true. In another way conventionalism stresses a similarity, namely, that 'The sentence "Lions are felines" expresses a necessary proposition' and 'The sentence " 'Feline' applies to what 'lion' applies to" express a true empirical proposition' have the same verification.

What makes Wittgenstein's conventionalism different from that of the philosopher is the use he makes of his characterization of necessary propositions as rules of grammar. By exaggerating the verbal aspect of sentences denoting necessary propositions he provides an antidote to Platonic metaphysics. As is known, G. H.

---

[60] *The Blue Book*, p. 59.

Hardy considered that his function as a mathematician was to 'discover or *observe* . . . mathematical reality . . . which lies outside us',[61] the reality consisting of invariant relations between entities of a subtle kind. The purpose of Wittgenstein's conventionalism was to avoid the idea that necessary propositions, if not about concrete objects, must be about abstract ones, whose entailment relations they assert. Calling them rules of grammar, which Wittgenstein knew did not use the term in the conventional way, was a piece of therapy in several respects. For one thing, a rule of grammar, being arbitrary, cannot be justified by pointing to objects which verify it. Consider the 'rule of grammar', 'There are four primary colours'. On this he comments that one is not tempted to justify it by saying, 'But there really are four primary colours'. For '. . . saying that the rules of grammar are arbitrary is directed against the possibility of this justification, which is constructed on the model of justifying a proposition by pointing to what verifies it.'[62] For another thing, calling necessary propositions rules of grammar turns attention to their *use*, namely, to govern the use of language. While recognizing that $25 \times 24 = 600$ is not a rule for handling signs, he points out that 'it would stand in the relation of a rule to a *proposition* using this equation'.[63] For example, if one said one had in the period of a year made twenty-four deposits of £25 each and in the end had a total of £650, the equation would serve as a rule to preclude the statement as an inconsistency. Emphasis on this function diverts attention away from the question of what the equation is about, a question which results from 'the decisive movement in the conjuring trick' already having been made: acceptance of the formula that a meaningful sentence *must* be about something.

The point of the statement that arithmetical propositions are not about numbers is similar. If taken as asserting an *a priori* truth about what is not the case, it may be understood as presenting in a concealed way a change in an ordinary form of

[61] *A Mathematician's Apology* (Cambridge, 1941), pp. 63–4.
[62] *Zettel*, p. 61e.
[63] Lecture notes, 1934–5.

speech, the change consisting in suppression of talk about numbers. So interpreted it is an example of the *rejection* of a form of symbolism 'as though a proposition were being rejected as false'. This is to look upon it as being a philosophical position, presented as a counter to Platonism. But it need not be so construed. It is plausible that, just as his conventionalism is understandable as a therapeutic technique for avoiding Platonism, so his statement about arithmetic can be understood as being another way of avoiding the same metaphysical view. On the verbal level it is directed against taking numerals as names of objects. In line with the advice, 'Don't speak of the meaning of a word, speak of its use', he turned attention to the use of number-words and away from talk about numbers, with the aim of stressing the difference between nouns like 'lion' which denote things one can point to, and numerals which do not. He expresses his perception of the difference in the form of a philosophical theory. This presents a puzzle, just as did his conventionalistic claim for Moore,[64] that to say '2 is a number' is to say ' "2" has a use'. The latter is on a par with the previously cited claim which Moore discussed in his paper, that '*p* is impossible' comes to ' "*p*" has no sense'. These statements become less puzzling if we look at them as having a special point. We should now clarify the advantage of speaking of the use of an expression rather than speaking of its meaning. As is well known, Wittgenstein compared language with a box of tools. The tools have a use, but their uses are not additional objects in the tool box, nor are they transcendent objects housed in a non-material tool box. The phrase 'use of a word', since it denotes a function, does not tempt one to look for an object corresponding to it as does 'meaning of a word'. There is no temptation to think that the phrase 'use of a word' names an object. The therapy hidden in the statement that arithmetic is not about numbers is summed up in what he said, presumably to the metaphysical mathematician: 'On mathematics: "Your concept is wrong. However, I cannot illumine the matter by fighting against your words, but only by trying to turn your attention away from certain expressions, illustrations, images,

---

[64] Expressed in a discussion I had with him.

and *towards* the *employment* of the words." [65] The explanation of Wittgenstein's paradoxical statements thus lies in their aim, the avoidance of a metaphysical position. He stretches the term 'grammatical rule', or rejects a common form of speech, in order to break the hold of a linguistic obsession.

The explanation of Polya's Paradox is quite different, although understanding it likewise hangs on our getting clear about the nature of *a priori* propositions. Supposing that they have a subject matter – abstract entities – may be at the root of Polya's treatment of them after the model of empirical generalizations. But it is the failure to see the two faces of *a priori* propositions in clear separation from each other which is responsible for the paradox. As a first step towards resolving the paradox, let us take note of the fact that it makes sense to speculate on whether a given *sentence* expresses a necessary proposition, for this is to speculate on an empirical matter. Whether the sentence states a necessary proposition can be made more or less plausible, or can be made implausible. What is paradoxical is the idea that a necessary *proposition* might be made plausible, say, by citing confirming cases, when it is inconceivable that its negation be plausible inasmuch as there are no conceivable exceptions to it.

The fact that a mathematical generalization can be stated as an entailment is the important difference between it and an inductive generalization. And it is this difference which makes it paradoxical to speak of a mathematical generalization being supported by instances, the more instances the greater its plausibility. Yet however paradoxical, it may sound equally paradoxical to say that one cannot be in doubt about a mathematical proposition if in fact it is necessary, and that one cannot believe it is true if in fact it is not. Nevertheless, as the following illustration shows, to hold that one *can* believe that a proposition is true when it is not, leads to a quite unacceptable consequence. Suppose one believes that all numbers $n$ of the form $n^2 - n + 41$ are prime, and by trying out 0, 1, 2, 3, . . ., 19, which we shall call cases $C_1$, $C_2$, $C_3$, . . ., $C_{20}$, we find, as we say, that the generalization holds. Note the character of the supporting cases.

[65] Zettel, p. 82e.

The statement about each that it is prime is a necessary proposition, e.g. 41 is prime ($n = 0, 1$), 43 is prime ($n = 2$), 47 is prime ($n=3$), 53 is prime ($n=4$). . . . Are we in a position to say, as Euler did in connexion with a theorem he was attempting to prove, 'Each of us can convince himself of its truth by the actual calculation of the cases $C_1$, $C_2$, $C_3$, . . . as far as he may wish; . . . it seems impossible that the law which has been discovered to hold for 20 terms, for example, would not be observed in the terms that follow.'[66]

If we reply that we are ready to believe that the law will continue to hold in subsequent cases, then we must be able to cope with the following considerations. To believe on the basis of examined cases that the generalization is true is to believe that the cases tend to show an entailment to hold and that it is possible for it to be true. Suppose now that one tries out the value $n = 41$ in the function $n^2-n+41$ *is prime*. The result is '$41^2$ is prime', a contradiction. And what this result shows is that the proposition 'for all $n$, $n^2-n+41$ is prime' is an *a priori* impossibility. This being the case, *that* proposition could not have been the one before one's mind, the one which was thought to be true when values were found that satisfied the function. We cannot say that a proposition was thought to be *a priori* true and that *it* turned out to be otherwise. The truth-value of a proposition of number theory is internal to it. It would not be *that* proposition without having that truth-value. Hence it cannot be said that the necessary singular proposition of the form $fn.\sim gn$ ($n = 41$) which refutes the generalization shows that its actual truth-value is different from the *possible* truth-value indicated by the necessary singulars of the form $fn.gn$. Its possible and actual truth-values are identical. And the fact that the singular proposition, 'for $n = 41$, $n^2-n+41$ is not prime' is necessary is equivalent to the fact that 'all numbers $n$ of the form $n^2-n+41$ are prime' is logically impossible, i.e. it shows that there is no entailment. As Wittgenstein puts it, 'The special case refutes the general proposition from within, not in an

[66] From a schematic abstract given by G. Polya, *American Mathematical Monthly*, vol. 48, p. 454.

315

external manner . . . not as the existence of a one-eyed man refutes "All men have two eyes".[67] To refute a proposition 'in an external manner' is to produce a counterinstance whose negation is conceivable. 'This man has one eye' *could* be false, and therefore the generalization *could* be true. Also, 'This man has two eyes' could be false, and therefore the generalization could be false. This is the sort of situation where instances can support a generalization, that is, make it probable that it has one of two possible truth-values. But if an exception is inconceivable, then instances do not make probable exclusion of a possibility since there is no possibility to exclude. Counting two sheep together with three more and finding there are five does not support the proposition that $2 + 3 = 5$ since it does not reduce the likelihood that there are exceptions. Were an exception possible, the proposition would not be *a priori*.

Despite these considerations, it is a commonplace that mathematicians do 'make conjectures', 'believe to be true' what they are attempting to prove, and are sometimes 'convinced' by a few special cases. Hence there must be some way of accounting for the propriety of such language. We all understand the following comment from Descartes: 'In order to show by enumeration that the area of a circle is greater than that of any other figure of the same perimeter, we do not need to make a general investigation of all the possible figures, but it suffices to prove it for a few particular figures whence we can conclude the same thing, by induction, for all the other figures.'[68] The propriety of this account, and of Euler's and Polya's accounts, will appear, and the paradox will be explained, if, so to speak, we ask for a change of venire. It is the propositional idiom, the coupling of plausibility talk with *propositions*, which is at the root of the paradox. By moving from talk of propositions to talk of verbal expressions the paradox will be dissolved, which is another way of saying it will be understood. The following simple comparison is instructive. Consider the *proposition* expressed by the sentence '57 is factor-

[67] *Philosophische Bemerkungen*, p. 214.
[68] *Oeuvres*, edited by Adam and Tannery, vol. 10 (1908), p. 390. Translation as given by G. Polya, op. cit., p. 456.

able', and suppose I say I believe it to be false. Then it cannot be the proposition that 57 is factorable that I believe to be false, for no proposition which is or could be false can be that proposition. However, and this is important to note, there is no paradox whatever in saying one believes that the sentence '57 is factorable' *says* what is false or that '57' denotes a prime number, for this is merely to have a false empirical belief.

We recall that the fact that a sentence of the form 'All $f$'s are $g$'s' expresses something *a priori* true is equivalent to the fact that the sentence ' "$g$" applies to what "$f$" applies to' expresses an empirical truth about language. Let us call ' "$g$" applies, in point of usage, to what "$f$" applies to' the verbal counterpart of the necessary proposition 'All $f$'s are $g$'s,' or alternatively, ' "$f$ but not $g$" has no use'. The necessary existential proposition of the form $(\exists x)fx.gx$ has correspondingly, as its verbal counterpart, that some sentence resulting from substitution on $fx.gx$ expresses a necessary truth. And the singular necessary proposition of the form $fa.ga$ which instantiates the generalization will have as its verbal counterpart, ' "$f$" and "$g$" apply jointly to $a$ in virtue of the rules governing their use'. We are now in a position to put what Polya wants to say without paradox. Suppose we find a number of cases $a$, $b$, $c$ to which '$f$' and '$g$' apply in virtue of the rules governing these terms. For example, suppose that the rules for the use of 'being of the form $n^2-n+41$' and 'prime' dictate their conjunctive application to 41 ($n = 1$), or alternatively, that '41 but not prime' has no use. (This is the verbal counterpart of the specific *a priori* necessity, *41 is prime*.) Finding a number of cases to which these expressions apply makes it plausible that the rules governing them will continue to dictate their application. That is, they will make it plausible that the sentence of the form 'All $f$'s are $g$'s' expresses a necessary truth. With regard to the example at hand, the rules governing the expressions 'being of the form $n^2-n+41$' and 'prime' dictate that 'being of the form $n^2-n+41$ and not prime' has a use and hence that it is false that it has no use, i.e. they show that 'All numbers of the form $n^2-n+41$ are prime' does not express a necessity.

A mathematician who turns to examination of cases does so in default of having a demonstration. If he finds singular propositions instantiating the generalization, he may, like Euler, hazard the guess that the law holds for all other instances – that 'it seems impossible' that it should not. This is an ontologically formulated way of asserting something to which such talk is appropriate, namely, statements about terminology. Plausibility talk is appropriate to the verbal counterparts of entailment-propositions, for these are empirical. It is an empirical matter whether or not certain combinations of terms have a use in mathematical language, that is, whether the sentences in which the combination occurs expresses something true in virtue of linguistic rules. The great difference between establishing that a sentence of the form 'All *f*s are *g*s' expresses a law of nature and establishing that it expresses a mathematical law is that in the first case one turns to confirming fact and in the second one engages in something similar to a calculation – a calculation in accordance with the rules for using appropriately related words, which is terminated by the sentence expressing the result. The use of the word 'law' in the two phrases 'law of nature' and 'mathematical law' provides concealment of this difference ('holds our mind rigidly in one position'). In consequence we speak of being convinced of the truth of both sorts of propositions, of their being plausible, etc. 'Conjecture', 'belief', 'plausibility' are appropriately used in connexion with empirical propositions. And since it is an empirical matter whether the sentence we believe to express a necessary truth does so, there are no paradoxical consequences involved in a person's speculating on this. But when it is believed that a *proposition* that has only one possible truth-value is very likely true (or false), then the two faces of necessary propositions have been fused. Paradox arises from describing their nonverbal face in a way that is proper only to their verbal face. That there is something right about what Polya says rests on the fact that his talk is entirely appropriate to the verbal correlate which an *a priori* proposition has. And that (in non-philosophical contexts) we do not engage in cumbersome talk about sentences rather than about propositions, creates no difficulty.

# APPENDIX

# LIST OF BOOKS MENTIONED IN THE TEXT

Aaron, R. I. *The Theory of Universals*, Clarendon Press, Oxford, 1952.

Ambrose, A. *Essays in Analysis*, Allen & Unwin, London, 1966; Humanities Press, New York, 1966.

Aristotle *Categories and De Interpretatione*, Tr. Ackrill, Oxford, 1963.

Austin, J. L. *Philosophical Papers*, Oxford U.P., London, 1961.

Ayer, A. J. *The Problem of Knowledge*, Macmillan, London, 1956; Penguin, Baltimore, Maryland, 1956.

—— *Thinking and Meaning*, H. K. Lewis, London, 1947.

Berkeley, G. *Works*, Ed. Jessop and Luce, Nelson, London, 1948–57; University of Texas Press, Austin, Tex., 1953.

Black, M. *A Companion to Wittgenstein's Tractatus*, Cambridge U.P., Cambridge, 1964; Cornell U.P., Ithaca, N.Y., 1964.

Courant, R. and Robbins, H. *What Is Mathematics?*, Oxford U.P., London-New York, 1941.

Edwards, P. (Ed.) *Encyclopaedia of Philosophy*, Collier-Macmillan, London-New York, 1967.

Fann, K. T. *Ludwig Wittgenstein: The Man and His Philosophy*, Delta Book, Dell Pub. Co., New York, 1967.

Flew, A. G. N. *Logic and Language*, Blackwell, Oxford, 1953; Philosophical Library, New York, 1953.

Freud, S. *An Autobiographical Study*, Tr. J. Strachey, Hogarth, London, 1963; Norton, New York, 1963.

—— *Complete Introductory Lectures on Psychoanalysis*, Tr. & Ed. J. Strachey, Allen & Unwin, London, 1971; U.S. title : *A General Introduction to Psychoanalysis*, Tr. J. Riviere, Liveright, New York, 1935.

—— *Inhibition, Symptom and Anxiety*, Ed. & Tr. Strachey, Hogarth, London, 1961.

Hobbes, T. *Elements of Philosophy*, Ed. Molesworth, London, 1839. *Leviathan*, Ed., Oakshot, Oxford U.P., London, 1909.

Hume, D. *A Treatise of Human Nature*, Ed. L. A. Selby-Biggs, Oxford U.P., London, 1967.

319

Jones, E. *The Life and Work of Sigmund Freud*, Penguin, Harmondsworth, 1967; Doubleday, Garden City, N.Y., 1963.

Küng, H. *The New Catholic Encyclopaedia*, McGraw-Hill, New York, 1967.

Lazerowitz, M. *Studies in Metaphilosophy*, Routledge, London, 1964; The Humanities Press, New York, 1958.

—— *The Structure of Metaphysics*, Routledge, London, 1955; U.S. Dist. The Humanities Press.

—— *Philosophy and Illusion*, Allen & Unwin, London, 1968; U.S. Dist. The Humanities Press.

Locke, J. *Essay Concerning Human Understanding*, Collier-Macmillan, London, 1965.

Mace, C. A. *British Philosophy in the Mid-Century, A Cambridge Symposium*, Allen & Unwin, London, 1966.

MacIntyre, A. C. *The Unconscious*, Routledge, London, 1958; Humanities Press, New York, 1958.

McKeon, R. *Selections from Medieval Philosophers*, Scribners, New York, 1856.

Malcolm, N. *Ludwig Wittgenstein: A Memoir*, Oxford U.P., London, 1962, New York, 1958.

Mill, J. S. *A System of Logic*, Longmans, London; Harper, New York, 1856.

—— *An Examination of Sir William Hamilton's Philosophy*, 1865.

Moody, E. A. *The Logic of William of Ockham*, Sheed & Ward, London-New York, 1935.

Moore, G. E. *Philosophical Papers*, Allen & Unwin, London, 1959; Macmillan, New York, 1959.

—— *Ethics*, Oxford U.P., 1912.

—— *Principia Ethica*, Cambridge U.P., 1903.

Pap, A. *Elements of Analytic Philosophy*, New York, 1949.

Pitcher, G. (Ed.) *Wittgenstein: The Philosophical Investigations*, Macmillan, London, 1968; Doubleday, Garden City, N.Y., 1966.

Plato *Plato's Republic*, Ed. I. A. Richards, Cambridge U.P., Cambridge, 1966.

Polya, A. *How To Solve It*, Oxford U.P., London, 1945; Princeton U.P., Princeton, 1945.

Price, H. H. *Thinking and Experience*, Hutchinson's University Library, 1953.

Quine, W. V. *From a Logical Point of View*, Harvard U.P., 1961.

Russell, B. *An Inquiry into Meaning and Truth*, Allen & Unwin, London, 1940; Penguin Books, Baltimore, 1962.

—— *Introduction to Mathematical Philosophy*, Allen & Unwin, London, 1919; Macmillan, New York, 1919.

—— *The Problems of Philosophy*, Oxford U.P., London-New York, 1967.

Ryle, G. *The Concept of Mind*, Hutchinson, London, 1960; Barnes & Noble, New York, 1960.

Schlick, Moritz. *Gesammelte Aufsätze*, Vienna, 1938.

Stace, W. T. *The Theory of Knowledge and Existence*, Clarendon Press, Oxford, 1932.

Watkins, J. W. N. *Hobbes' System of Ideas*, Hutchinson, London, 1965.

Wisdom, J. *Problems of Mind and Matter*, Cambridge U. P., Cambridge, 1963.

Wittgenstein, L. *The Blue and Brown Books*, Ed. G. E. M. Anscombe, Blackwell, Oxford, 1958; Harper & Row, New York, 1965.

—— *Lectures and Conversations on Aesthetics, Psychology, Religious Belief*, Ed. C. Barrett, Blackwell, Oxford, 1968; University of California Press, Berkeley, Ca, 1966.

—— *Notebooks 1914–16* (in German and English), Ed. G. E. M. Anscombe, Blackwell, Oxford, 1961; Harper, New York, 1961.

——*Philosophische Grammatik*, Ed. R. Rhees, Suhrkamp, Frankfurt am Main, 1969; Basil Blackwell, Oxford, 1969.

—— *Philosophical Investigations* (in German and English), Blackwell, Oxford, 1953; Macmillan, New York, 1953.

—— *Philosophische Bemerkungen*, Ed. R. Rees, Blackwell, Oxford, 1964.

—— *Remarks on the Foundations of Mathematics*, Tr. G. E. M. Anscombe, Blackwell, Oxford, 1965; Macmillan, New York, 1956.

—— *Tractatus Logico-Philosophicus*, Tr. C. K. Ogden, Routledge, London, 1922; Harcourt Brace, New York, 1922.

—— *Tractatus Logico-Philosophicus*, Tr. Pears and McGuinness, Routledge, London, 1961; Humanities Press, New York, 1961.

—— *Zettel* (in German and English) Blackwell, Oxford, 1967; University of California Press, Berkeley, Ca, 1967.

Woozley, A. *Theory of Knowledge*, Hutchinson, London, 1966; Barnes & Noble, New York, 1966.

# INDEX

Aaron, R. I., 159–60, 162n., 169–71
Abelard, Peter, 155–7
Ackrill, J., 155n.
Alexander, S., 272
Ambrose, Alice, 16n., 147n., 236n., 249n., 290n., 291n.
Anscombe, G. E. M., 39n., 40–1, 45n., 140n., 181n., 295n.
Aristotle, 104, 140, 153–5, 166–7n., 176–7
Augustine, St., 120–1, 141n., 225
Austin, J. L., 160–1, 166, 176
Ayer, A. J., 162n., 163, 169n., 173, 179n., 255–6

Babbitt, M., 124n.
Bamborough, R., 172–4, 176
Barrett, C., 74, 77n., 78n., 79n., 81n., 82n., 85n., 87n., 89n., 90n.
Berkeley, George, 154n.
Black, M., 225n.
Blanshard, B., 270n.
Bouwsma, O. K., 188
Bradley, F. H., 267
Britton, K., 226n.
Brouwer, L. E. J., 271–5
Butler, Joseph, 261

Cantor, Georg, 275
Courant, R., 288n.
Coxeter, H. M. S., 16n.

Dedekind, R., 275–6
Descartes, René, 45, 140, 316

Donagan, A., 152n., 161n., 163, 177, 183, 184n.
Duncan-Jones, A. E., 162n.

Edwards, P., 154n.
Engelmann, Paul, 94
Epicurus, 83
Euclid, 276
Euler, Leonard, 315–8

Fann, K. T., 226n.
Fermat, Pierre de, 278, 294
Feuer, L., 73n.
Flew, A. G. N., 152n.
Frege, Gottlob, 141n., 227–8, 231, 271–2
Freud, Sigmund, 74ff., 264–5

Gauss, Carl Friedrich, 278
Gödel, Kurt, 278–80, 283
Goodstein, R. L., 16n.

Hallie, P. P., 150–1n.
Hamilton, Sir William, 152
Hampshire, S., 39n.
Hardy, G. H., 288n., 311–2
Herschel, Sir John, 300–1
Hilbert, David, 277, 283
Hobbes, Thomas, 154–7, 167
Hospers, J., 73n.
Hume, David, 41–3, 47–9, 154n., 167, 231

James, William, 141n., 232
Jourdain, P. E. B., 288n.
Jung, Carl, 87

Kant, Immanuel, 140, 237, 240–1, 264n., 293
Kassner, E., 292n.
Kripke, S., 138n.
Kummer, E., 278
Küng, G., 154n.

Langford, C. H., 21
Lazerowitz, M., 18n., 21, 73, 147n., 252n., 269n., 293n., 301, 302, 306n., 308n.
Leibniz, Gottfried Wilhelm, 115, 154, 242–3
Lewis, C. I., 238
Littlewood, J. E., 15
Lloyd, A. C., 161n., 168n., 169n.
Locke, John, 62, 63n., 65, 67, 70, 167, 244

Mace, C. A., 147n.
MacIntyre, A. C., 73
Malcolm, N., 21, 74, 94, 230n.
Masterman, M., 16, 18, 236n., 290n.
Matjesevič, Y., 277
McGuinness, B., 266n.
McKeon, R., 155n.
Mill, John Stuart, 152, 154, 181n., 300–2
Moody, E. A., 158n.
Moore, G. E., 13–17, 74, 77n., 78n., 92, 97, 106–8, 141n., 148, 152, 153n., 162n., 175n., 180, 188–9, 234, 247–54, 269, 272, 300–1, 313

Newman, James, 292n.
Newman, John Henry, Cardinal, 295

Ockham, William of, 158n.
O'Connor, D. J., 164–5, 172, 178–9
Ogden, C. K., 266n., 295n.
Orwell, George, 48n.

Pap, A., 162n.
Paul, G. A., 21
Pears, D., 162–3, 266n.
Pitcher, G., 173n.
Plato, 87, 93–4, 140, 141, 160, 162n., 176, 292, 303, 313
Plotinus, 158n.
Polya, G., 287–8, 296–301, 303, 305, 314–8
Price, H. H., 162n., 165–6, 168

Quine, W. V., 161n.
Quinton, A., 175n.

Ramanujan, 288n.
Ramsey, F. P., 228
Rhees, R., 95n., 181n., 286n.
Richman, R. K., 175–6
Robbins, H., 288n.
Rorty, R., 139n.
Russell, Bertrand, 42, 43n., 57–61, 141n., 152, 162n., 168–9, 177, 183–4, 227–8, 231, 272, 279
Ryle, G., 73

Schlick, M., 44, 57, 66–71
Shanks, W., 273, 285
Skinner, F., 16n., 22, 23, 24, 25
Skolem, Thoralf, 276, 279, 281
Sraffa, P., 228

Stace, W. T., 37, 54–5, 63
Storer, T., 42–3n.
Strawson, P. F., 173
Stroud, B., 123n.

Thomson, Judith Jarvis, 39n.

von Wright, G. H., 95n., 181n., 226n.

Waismann, F., 95n.
Watkins, J. W. N., 156–7
Whitehead, A. N., 227
Wisdom, J. O., 73n.
Wisdom, John, 17, 21, 162n., 265, 309n.
Woozley, A. D., 154, 165–9, 172n.

Zeno, 285